PENGUIN BOOKS

NEHRU & BOSE

Rudrangshu Mukherjee is vice chancellor and professor of history at Ashoka University. Earlier, he taught at Calcutta University; he has held visiting appointments at Princeton University, Manchester University and the University of California, Santa Cruz. He was the editor of the editorial pages of the *Telegraph*, Calcutta, and continues in that role as a consultant. He is the author and editor of several books which include *Awadh in Revolt, 1857–58: A Study of Popular Resistance* and *Spectre of Violence: The 1857 Kanpur Massacres*, as well as *The Penguin Gandhi Reader*.

NEHRU & BOSE
Parallel Lives

RUDRANGSHU MUKHERJEE

PENGUIN BOOKS

An imprint of Penguin Random House

PENGUIN BOOKS

USA | Canada | UK | Ireland | Australia
New Zealand | India | South Africa | China | Singapore

Penguin Books is part of the Penguin Random House group of companies
whose addresses can be found at global.penguinrandomhouse.com

Published by Penguin Random House India Pvt. Ltd
4th Floor, Capital Tower 1, MG Road,
Gurugram 122 002, Haryana, India

Penguin
Random House
India

First published in Viking by Penguin Books India 2014
Published in Penguin Books 2015

ISBN 9780143425656

Typeset in Sabon by R. Ajith Kumar, New Delhi
Printed at Manipal Technologies Limited, India

www.penguin.co.in

MIX
Paper | Supporting
responsible forestry
FSC® C043100

This is a legitimate digitally printed version of the book and therefore might not
have certain extra finishing on the cover.

Contents

Contents

Introduction

Born in Calcutta five years after India's independence, I was brought up in the shadow of Jawaharlal Nehru and Subhas Chandra Bose. One was the first prime minister of India, and during my childhood the most important public figure in the country. The other was the most revered icon in Bengal's political pantheon. In public discourse and in informal conversations the two figures were often seen as rivals, and many Bengalis were convinced that Subhas, by far the greater man as many Bengalis believed, was deliberately eclipsed in national politics by Jawaharlal who always acted at the behest of Gandhi. But it was Subhas, his admirers averred, who ultimately brought freedom to India. As a child and as an adolescent, I was taught to disregard these views that glorified Subhas at the expense of Jawaharlal and Gandhi. I use the word 'taught' advisedly since this was an important component of the non-formal history lessons that my father imparted to me. My father—the most important intellectual influence on my life till I went to college—was not an admirer of Subhas. He recognized the latter's patriotism but saw him as being misguided because he had sought an alliance with Hitler and the Axis powers in the 1940s. My father had pronounced anti-fascist and anti-Stalinist views and saw himself as an unabashed Nehruvian. Jawaharlal, according to him, had the right ideas and attitudes. My 'history lessons' at home were thus slanted in favour of Jawaharlal; Subhas was rather neglected.

As a student of history in college and in university, this indifference towards Subhas was fortified by the manner in which the Indian national movement was taught. He was not seen as belonging to the mainstream. By this time, my own understanding of fascism and European history of the 1930s and 1940s had also evolved and this had strengthened the anti-fascist and anti-totalitarian sentiments embedded in my mind by my father. Inevitably, this understanding did not enhance my appreciation of Subhas. On the contrary, they confirmed the opinion that his attempt to free India with Japanese help was erroneous and short-sighted. To be honest, my growing discomfiture about Subhas's role in the Indian national movement was aggravated by the attitude of his followers: their worshipfulness, their refusal to accept his marriage and that he had a daughter, and, above all, their bizarre conviction that Subhas was still alive, hiding in a cave in the Himalayas or in Siberian exile from where he would soon emerge to deliver India from the woeful state into which it had fallen under Jawaharlal and the Congress. My rational self could see that Subhas should not be visited by the odd views and credulity of his followers but I will be dishonest if I do not confess that the views of his followers did colour my own assessment of Subhas.

This, then, was not an easy book for me to write. I was conscious all the time that in the process of reading the historical documentation and writing, I was struggling against the grain of some of my own prejudices, assumptions and intellectual baggage. This was true not only for Subhas but also for Jawaharlal. My views about the latter had been formed not only by my father's affinity and admiration for the man but also by those of Sarvepalli Gopal, my teacher, later a friend, and, of course, the biographer of Jawaharlal. It was Gopal who convinced me through the innumerable conversations that we had that it was important to think critically about Jawaharlal since that was what he wanted posterity to do. By the time I was nearing middle age my views on Nehru had become more nuanced and complex than they had been when I was in my teens or even in my early twenties. This book in many ways is my coming to terms with these two remarkable individuals whose presence I could not escape because of when and where I was born.

This book is also an exploration of a friendship that did not quite blossom. It withered only to have a brief afterlife. It is remarkable how closely, on parallel lines, the lives of Jawaharlal and Subhas moved: less than ten years separated them chronologically; both were born to relative affluence; both went to Cambridge; both gave up what could have been lucrative careers and joined the Indian national movement under the leadership of Gandhi; both were aware of what was happening in Europe and in Asia, and their exposure to these developments radicalized their own ideas; both saw themselves as men of the left and were attracted to socialism. Given this background, it was not surprising that they were drawn to each other. For a few years in the 1930s, they were close enough to be called friends—sharing views, reading similar books, and championing the same causes within the national movement. But by the late 1930s, the growing political distance between the two men was obvious. Their disagreements grew from their differing understanding of the course of the national movement, their attitudes towards Gandhi, their views on fascism and from the very different mental landscapes they inhabited. By the early 1940s, the friendship and the affection were things of the past. But after Subhas's sudden and untimely death, Jawaharlal could not forget the bonds they had shared and he revised his views about Subhas and the Indian National Army. Subhas, alas, was not there to experience this afterglow which is obvious from what Jawaharlal had to say and write immediately after Subhas's death.

The Jawaharlal–Subhas relationship was not smooth but it was a poignant one. This relationship, however, has not received the attention it deserves from historians. The perception of this lack made me think about reconstructing their friendship and its unravelling. The focus of the book is their relationship and there is no attempt to tell the full story of their rich lives. The book is expressly not a biography of the two men.

The backdrop to the relationship was, of course, the national movement. It shaped the thoughts and the deeds of the two men from the early 1920s to the years just preceding Independence. This was a period of tumult as Gandhi transformed and galvanized the Congress by bringing it closer to the masses who responded to his call first of non-cooperation and then of civil disobedience. Both Jawaharlal and Subhas experienced and participated in this excitement and placed the goal of complete independence from British rule firmly on the agenda of the Indian national movement. Their emphasis on this goal was important since in the late 1920s and the 1930s, the British, to maintain their dominance in India, were making constitutional concessions to seek the collaboration of influential sections of the Indian population. Neither Jawaharlal and Subhas were quite taken in by such gestures and remained unswerving in their commitment to *purna swaraj*. This often made the two of them battle against those within the Congress who were lured by the prospect of holding office in the provincial governments. They did not always win in this struggle and their responses to the failure were very different: it made one of them more assertive, and the other more resigned and introspective.

There were other sources of disappointment. Gandhi's withdrawal of both the non-cooperation and the civil disobedience movements exasperated the two radical young men. They were bewildered by his emphasis, at this critical phase of the national movement, on social uplift and spinning. They yearned to go forth into battle to confront British rule while Gandhi throughout the 1930s was reluctant to call a mass movement on the grounds that neither the Congress nor the people were prepared for it. Those close to Gandhi within the Congress worked, often as backroom politicians, to keep off young leaders who could challenge their and Gandhi's control over the Congress. Both Jawaharlal and Subhas were at different times victims of these machinations. Again, they reacted differently to such manoeuvres. Jawaharlal yielded, Subhas rebelled. These differing reactions were determined by their contrasting attitudes to Gandhi and his role in India's freedom movement. Both admired and respected Gandhi but Subhas was reluctant to surrender completely to Gandhi's influence and control. Jawaharlal was critical of Gandhi but dependent on him. Gandhi, in his turn, saw Jawaharlal as his chosen heir, and Subhas more as a somewhat rebellious and prodigal son. The friendship of Jawaharlal and Subhas could not escape all these influences—they made and unmade their relationship.

The book looks at these factors and also at the contrasting personalities and intellectual orientations of the two men. They were friends but never soulmates and confidants. Their friendship was moulded less by personal affinities and affections and more by politics. It fell apart because of politics. It was not a relationship that could transcend and override political differences. Yet, as far as one can tell from the existing documentation, there was no sense of rivalry between the two of them. This book tries to tell this complicated story of two men caught in turbulent times, testing their convictions sometimes against each other but always for India and its freedom.

1

Growing Up

The two protagonists of this book were born within eight years of each other: Jawaharlal Nehru on 14 November 1889 and Subhas Chandra Bose on 23 January 1897. Neither spent their childhood in any of the emerging colonial cities of Calcutta, Bombay and Madras. Jawaharlal lived his early years in Allahabad in what was then the United Provinces, and Bose lived his in Cuttack in Orissa. Both were born into relative affluence since their fathers, Motilal Nehru and Janakinath Bose, were successful lawyers—the former in Allahabad and the latter in Cuttack. Janakinath certainly did not enjoy the opulence of Motilal but Subhas lacked for nothing when he was growing up although he did not have the luxury of a tennis court and a swimming pool that Jawaharlal had in the house that his father had bought and refashioned.

Jawaharlal, an only child for the first eleven years of his life, was doted upon by all around him—mother, father (in spite of the occasional scoldings) and the servants. Subhas had a happy childhood but he was one of nine children; there is no evidence that he was pampered.[1] In both families there was a premium on education, especially the best education the English could offer. For

---

[1] The obvious sources for information about the childhood of the two men are the autobiographies they wrote. See Jawaharlal Nehru, *An Autobiography* (London, 1936, repr. 1939), and Subhas Chandra Bose, *An Indian Pilgrim*, in *Netaji: Collected Works*, (ed.) Sisir Bose, vol. 1 (Calcutta, 1980).

the first fifteen years of his life, Jawaharlal was educated at home: first by two English governesses and then by F.T. Brooks, a young Irish-French theosophist who had been recommended by Annie Besant. Subhas, on the other hand, was sent to school at the age of five: the Protestant European School run by Baptists. Subhas spent seven years there. Only 'towards the end', he was to write later, 'did I have a vague feeling of unhappiness, of maladaptation to my environment'.[2] One reason for this was the fact that the school was meant for European and Anglo-Indian boys and girls. Indians formed a minority of 15 per cent of the students. No Indian language was taught but Latin declensions were. After seven years, Subhas was moved to Ravenshaw Collegiate School, an institution that had mostly Bengali and Oriya teachers and students.

If Subhas had not been trained to read and write Bengali until he was twelve, Jawaharlal's private Sanskrit teacher, a renowned Sanskrit scholar called Ganganatha Jha, tried in vain to teach Jawaharlal the classical Indian language. But, from Brooks, Jawaharlal had imbibed a love for reading and English literature: '[T]he Lewis Carroll books were great favourites, and *The Jungle Books* and *Kim*. I was fascinated by Gustave Dore's illustrations to *Don Quixote*, and Fridtjof Nansen's *Farthest North* opened out a new realm of adventure to me. I remember reading many of the novels of Scott, Dickens and Thackeray, H.G. Wells's romances, Mark Twain and Sherlock Holmes stories. I was thrilled by *The Prisoner of Zenda*, and Jerome K. Jerome's *Three Men in a Boat* was for me the last word in humour. Another book stands out still in my memory—it was Du Maurier's *Trilby*, also *Peter Ibbetson*.'[3] This was standard fare for anyone going through the steps of an anglophone education in Jawaharlal's generation and even later. He also developed a love for poetry and this 'to some extent endured and survived the many other changes to which I have been subject'.[4] Brooks initiated in

[2] *An Indian Pilgrim*, p. 26.

[3] *An Autobiography*, p. 14.

[4] Ibid. This explains why late in life as a busy prime minister he copied out and kept on his table the famous lines of Robert Frost: 'The woods are lovely, dark and deep,

Jawaharlal an interest in science; from Brooks, in his early teens, he also acquired a fascination for theosophy, and sought his father's permission to join Besant's Theosophical Society. Motilal laughingly gave the permission and Jawaharlal was initiated into the Society by Besant herself. But theosophy was a passing fad; it disappeared as soon as Brooks stopped tutoring the boy. Spirituality—'I began to think, consciously and deliberately, of religion and other worlds,'[5] he was to write—was not part of young Jawaharlal's serious concerns.

This was in sharp contrast to Subhas's adolescent years. Subhas saw his arrival in Ravenshaw Collegiate School as a moment of liberation. He gained in self-confidence and made friends. He also found in the headmaster, Beni Madhav Das, someone he could look up to and 'adore'.[6] He was inspired by his exemplar—even after Das had ceased to be the headmaster of the school—'to love nature and be inspired by her, not merely aesthetically but ethically as well'. This led young Subhas to nature-worship—'I would choose a beauty spot on the river-bank or on a hill or in a lonely meadow in the midst of an enchanting sunset-glow, and practice contemplation.'[7] During this period lasting for five or six years, identified by Subhas as 'one of the stormiest periods in my psychical life', he not only suffered mental anguish but also his attention shifted from his studies in school. He became aware of his sexuality and this he considered 'unnatural and immoral'.[8] What he was looking for was 'a central principle, which I could use as a peg to hang my whole life on, and firm resolve to have no other distractions in life'.[9] His search and his angst seemed to end with the discovery of the writings of Vivekananda, the Bengali Hindu monk who had inspired many Indians with his address to the Parliament of Religions in Chicago in 1893 and had

---

/ But I have promises to keep, / And miles to go before I sleep, / And miles to go before I sleep.' S. Gopal, *Jawaharlal Nehru: A Biography*, 3 vols (London, 1975 to 1984), vol. 3, p. 267.

[5] *An Autobiography*, p. 15.

[6] *An Indian Pilgrim*, p. 32.

[7] Ibid., pp. 34–35.

[8] Ibid., p. 36.

[9] Ibid.

established, before his untimely death in 1902 at the age of thirty-nine, the monastery of Belur Math near Calcutta. Reading these writings, young Subhas discovered the central tenet of Vivekananda's teachings to be the following—*atmano mokshartham jagaddhityaya* (for your own salvation and for the service of humanity). Subhas was only fifteen when he made this discovery—it was perhaps his epiphany, and as a result, in his own words, 'everything was turned upside down'.[10] It was inevitable that Subhas would move from Vivekananda to the latter's guru and mentor Ramakrishna Paramahamsa from whose sayings and simple lifestyle he imbibed the spirit of *tyaga* (sacrifice). There was something else that the young convert took away from Vivekananda's message. He was drawn to his commitment to service for the motherland, especially by Vivekananda's cry, 'Say brothers at the top of your voice—the naked Indian, the illiterate Indian, the Brahman Indian, the Pariah Indian is my brother.' This, for Subhas, was not only an appeal for equality but also of faith in oneself—a form of national self-assertion.

Subhas's interest in Ramakrishna and Vivekananda did not stop at reading their works. He gathered together a group of students to discuss their lives and writings and sayings. He felt his soul had been inflamed and he wanted to take the necessary steps to achieve his own salvation through service to humanity. From blind obedience to his parents he moved to complete devotion to the Divine Mother. This created problems at home and Subhas 'began to feel more at home when away from home'.[11] He was drawn to yoga and to sadhus. Recalling this phase of his life, he wrote, 'I remember that I became very liberal with beggars, fakirs and sadhus, and whenever any of them appeared before our house, I helped them with whatever came within my reach. I derived a peculiar satisfaction from the act of giving.'[12] Realization soon dawned that this was not enough, that the 'service of humanity which included service of one's country' was paramount. By the time he was sixteen, Subhas had had his first

---

[10] Ibid., p. 38.

[11] Ibid., p. 40.

[12] Ibid., p. 44.

experience of 'what may be glorified with the appellation of village reconstruction work'.[13] He went with his friends to a village to teach in the primary school there and they were made to feel welcome and their activities encouraged. But in another village, they were treated with suspicion and considered enemies: '[I]t did not take us long to understand that whenever well-dressed men had come into the village they must have done so as tax-collectors or in some similar capacity, and had behaved in such a manner as to create this gulf between the villagers and ourselves.'[14] Subhas Bose's discovery of India had begun.

When Subhas was marking out the first steps of his spiritual quest as an adolescent of fifteen, Jawaharlal had finished his schooling at Harrow and his undergraduate degree from Trinity College, Cambridge. While Subhas in remote Cuttack was acquainting himself with the writings of Vivekananda, Jawaharlal, in the words of his biographer, was 'caught up in the whirl of London life'.[15] Jawaharlal was at Harrow for two years from 1905. There was nothing remarkable about his stay there though he remained a loyal Harrovian: in prison in the 1930s he drew up lists of poets and politicians who had been to Harrow, and stuck pictures of his old school in his diary.[16] He was not an outstanding student, though the headmaster in the school report of October 1906 did note that the boy 'has brains'.[17] Outside the school curriculum, British politics interested him as did the early growth of aviation. News from India, when it trickled through, agitated him. He heard about Lala Lajpat Rai's and Ajit Singh's deportation, about Swadeshi and boycott in Bengal and about the activities of Tilak.[18] For good work in school, he got one of G.M. Trevelyan's books on Garibaldi as

---

[13] Ibid., p. 44.

[14] Ibid., p. 45.

[15] Gopal, *Jawaharlal Nehru*, vol. 1, p. 26.

[16] Gopal, ibid., vol. 1, p. 20.

[17] Ibid., p. 19.

[18] *An Autobiography*, p. 18. The Swadeshi movement was sparked off by the decision of Lord Curzon, in 1905, to partition Bengal. Tilak advocated a boycott and was opposed to the mendicancy of moderate Congress leaders.

a prize. He obtained the other two volumes, and the deeds of the Italian hero inspired him: 'visions of similar deeds in India came before me, of a gallant fight for freedom'.[19] He left Harrow of his own volition as he found the school too restricting for the ideas that he was beginning to harbour. He 'wanted to go to the wider sphere of the university'.[20] He chose to go to Trinity College, Cambridge, in Michaelmas term of 1907, having cleared the admission test in the spring of that year.

Jawaharlal's Cambridge career was as undistinguished as his time in Harrow. He took a tripos in the natural sciences. He made an effort to involve himself in many aspects of Cambridge life. He joined the Magpie and Stump, the college debating society, but spoke only once. For this failure to speak with greater regularity, he had to pay a fine as per the rules of the society. He joined the Trinity Boat Club and was moderately successful as a cox. He played tennis and rode regularly.[21] He frequented the Majlis but there too he hardly spoke. He ascribed this to his shyness and diffidence.[22] In Cambridge, he fashioned his life as an aesthete and a dilettante, inspired by Walter Pater and Oscar Wilde. In his autobiography, he described his attitude at this point of his life as 'a vague kind of cyrenaicism—a long Greek name to the desire for a soft life and pleasant experiences'.[23] He admitted that he 'was superficial and did not go deep down into anything'. He went down from Cambridge in 1910 with a second-class honours degree and was called to the bar from the Inner Temple. His parents did not want him to take the Indian Civil Service examination as becoming a member of the heaven-born service would entail taking a transferable job. They wanted their son to be near them after his long absence from home.[24]

The only remarkable incident during Jawaharlal's time in England

[19] Ibid., p. 19.

[20] Ibid.

[21] Gopal, *Jawaharlal Nehru*, vol. 1, pp. 22–25.

[22] *An Autobiography*, p. 21.

[23] Ibid., p. 20.

[24] Ibid., p. 24.

took place soon after he had come down from the university. While on holiday in Norway, he and a friend went to wash themselves in a stream that was a roaring torrent. Jawaharlal slipped and fell into the freezing water and was rendered numb without any control over his limbs. He was swept away and had to be dragged out by his friend. The rescue was timely as two to three hundred yards ahead, the mountain stream went down a precipice, forming a waterfall.[25]

Jawaharlal was to write, a trifle harshly perhaps, that when he returned to India, he 'was a bit of a prig'.[26] He described his days in Cambridge as being without disturbance 'moving slowly on like the sluggish Cam'.[27] Yet, what disturbed him 'sometimes was the political struggle in India'—news of Tilak's activities and conviction, and of Aurobindo Ghose. He identified himself, sitting in England, with the Extremists within the Congress.[28] On this issue, the obedient son differed with his father. He accused Motilal of being 'immoderately moderate'; he stoutly defended Bipin Chandra Pal when his father contemptuously described him as 'the great bathroom hero of Barisal'.[29] Thus Jawaharlal was not totally unaware of the political developments in India. What is true, however, is that there was nothing in his childhood and youth that foretold the turn his life would take in the future. It is this that warrants his biographer's description of this period of his life as the 'unformative years'.[30]

But were the years really 'unformative'? From his growing-up years, Jawaharlal took away a love for reading and a love for poetry. These stayed with him throughout his life. In Harrow and Trinity from a distance he became aware of the political movements in

---

[25] Ibid., pp. 25–26.

[26] Ibid., p. 26.

[27] Ibid., p. 19.

[28] Ibid., p. 21.

[29] Gopal, *Jawaharlal Nehru*, vol. 1, pp. 22–23; however, Jawaharlal was embarrassed when Pal spoke in Cambridge in terms of a narrow Hindu attitude, described India as God's chosen and acted like a demagogue in the presence of a small audience.

[30] These two words are the chapter heading of the first chapter of volume one of Gopal's biography. The first chapter describes Jawaharlal's childhood and years in Harrow and Cambridge.

India: here were the first stirrings of what was to become a calling in adult life. From his school and university days he developed certain attitudes to life and to education. He wrote to his father in October 1911, 'I am an ardent believer in a child—or for the matter of that a grown-up person—being endowed with a lot of imagination, and can conceive of no greater evil than for a person to be totally devoid of it. Of course too much imagination is bad for one, but I had rather suffer from that than from the other extreme.'[31] In April 1912, reflecting on his education, he wrote, 'To my mind education does not consist of passing examinations or knowing English or mathematics. It is a mental state and if this is not present it matters little how many examinations a person has passed.'[32] These were attitudes that were to stay with him. Equally importantly, he came back from England with certain values that he considered English and with a certain attachment to things English and to Britain. These were sustaining influences through his life and they exerted not a little influence on the decisions he took and the policies he adopted.[33] In spite of these enduring continuities, the transformation of a self-confessed prig into a much-loved public figure and future prime minister was entirely unexpected and uncharted.

Jawaharlal's student days were without any major incidents. Subhas's were exactly the opposite. For one thing he was a very good student. In the matriculation examination in March 1913, he came second in Calcutta University which in those days conducted the examination. This determined Subhas's next step. He moved from Cuttack to Calcutta and joined Presidency College which in those days, according to Subhas, had distinct groups of students. There were the studious and the rich; there was another group committed to secret revolutionary activities; and finally, students who 'considered themselves to be the spiritual heirs of Ramakrishna and Vivekananda'.[34] Given the interests that Subhas had already

---

[31] Quoted in Gopal, *Jawaharlal Nehru*, vol. 1, p. 27.

[32] Ibid., p. 28.

[33] Ibid., p. 28, makes this point.

[34] *An Indian Pilgrim*, p. 57.

developed in Cuttack, it was to the last group that he gravitated. It was a period of intellectual growth. The members of the group he associated with were all voracious readers; new books on philosophy, history and nationalism were read with enthusiasm and new ideas were discussed and circulated. But politically, the group was hostile to terrorist activity and conspiracy. The emphasis was on spirituality. In the winter of 1913, the group held a camp in Santipur, upriver from Calcutta, where the young men lived like monks, wearing saffron robes. The camp was raided by the police, fortunately without any serious consequences.[35]

This period of Subhas's life was marked by a kind of intellectual restlessness. He went to Murshidabad to learn about the pre-British history of Bengal. In 1914, he travelled to Santiniketan to see Rabindranath Tagore who had been awarded the Nobel Prize the year before. He went to attend a meeting in the Town Hall in Calcutta on Gandhi's satyagraha movement in South Africa. The meeting was addressed by Surendranath Banerjee whose style of public speaking left an imprint on Subhas's mind. There were visits to pilgrimage centres and to sadhus, a search for a guru. The strongest influence during this period was that of Aurobindo Ghose to whom Subhas was attracted not because of the 'mysticism surrounding [his] name' but because of his writings, especially in the journal *Arya* that Aurobindo edited. It was Aurobindo's philosophy that drew Subhas who was tormented by Sankara's doctrine of maya—'[it] was like a thorn in my flesh. I could not accommodate my life to it nor could I easily get rid of it. I required another philosophy to take its place.'[36] The teachings of Ramakrishna and Vivekananda had impressed him but had not 'succeeded in liberating me from the cobwebs of Maya'. The writings of Aurobindo helped in the process of emancipation by working out 'a reconciliation between Spirit and Matter, between God and Creation, on the metaphysical side and supplemented it with a synthesis of the methods of attaining the truth—a synthesis of Yoga as he called it.' What moved him also

---

[35] Ibid., pp. 60–61.
[36] Ibid., p. 63.

was Aurobindo's passion and devotion to the motherland: by words such as 'I should like to see some of you becoming great; great not for your own sake, but to make India great, so that she may stand with head erect amongst the free nations of the world. Those of you who are poor and obscure—I should like to see your poverty and obscurity devoted to the service of the motherland. Work that she might prosper, suffer that she might rejoice.'[37] The spiritual quest of the young Subhas was becoming interwoven in his mind with a growing commitment to his country and to its subservient status. This patriotism was nurtured also by his awareness of racial discrimination against Indians under British rule.[38]

There is one aspect of this period of growing up that should be noted here even though it means breaking somewhat the chronological framework of the narrative. When Subhas was no longer a student of Presidency College (for reasons to be discussed shortly), in the middle of 1917, he joined India's Territorial Army, a university unit in the India Defence Force. The training, which Subhas joined with great enthusiasm, began in the Calcutta maidan under officers and instructors from the Lincoln's Regiment stationed in Fort William. The soldiers were in mufti, some even wore dhotis; but this changed when after two months the trainees had to get into military uniform, pitch their tents and do their drill with rifles. There was even musketry practice in the rifle range outside Calcutta. Subhas did not fail to note the changed circumstances of his life: 'What a change it was,' he wrote in his autobiography, 'from sitting at the feet of anchorites to obtain knowledge about God, to standing with a rifle on my shoulder taking orders from a British army officer.'[39] Subhas took to the pleasures of soldiering and wrote a vivid account of his training in his memoirs. He confessed that he had developed a strong bond of loyalty towards the commanding officer, Captain Gray. His position as a soldier gave him an air of self-importance and self-confidence. As soldiers, Subhas and his

---

[37] Ibid., p. 64.

[38] Ibid., pp. 72–73.

[39] Ibid., p. 91.

peers in the force had rights that were denied to other Indians. In his words, 'To us as Indians, Fort William was out of bounds, but as soldiers we had right of entry there, and as a matter of fact the first day we marched into Fort William to bring our rifles, we experienced a queer feeling of satisfaction, as if we were taking possession of something to which we had an inherent right but of which we had been unjustly deprived. The route marches in the city and elsewhere we enjoyed, probably because it gave us a sense of importance. We could snap our fingers at the police and other agents of the Government by whom we were in the habit of being harassed or terrorized.'[40] Being a soldier gave Subhas a sense of power which he rather enjoyed. It also enabled him, however superficially, to turn the tables on those who represented the oppressive arms of the government. The irony was, of course, that he could do this only by donning a uniform supplied by the government. This early exposure to things military had obvious bearing on developments in Subhas's later life.

History tells us that Subhas was pursued by controversy from his youth. His first brush with controversy occurred while he was still a student at Presidency. On 10 January 1916, he heard that a professor of history in the college, E.F. Oaten, had 'manhandled' some students of his batch. As the class representative, Subhas went to the principal, Henry R. James, with the demand that Oaten apologize to the students concerned. Oaten claimed that he had been disturbed by the noise some students had been making outside his classroom and had only 'taken them by the arm'; this, the principal said, could not be interpreted as either an insult or as manhandling. In any case, Oaten was a member of the government's educational service and therefore the principal was in no position to get Oaten to apologize to the students. The students decided to call a strike in the college the next day. The strike was successful. This was something unprecedented not only in Presidency but in any college in the city. It was, the authorities rightly believed, bound to encourage defiance and insubordination among the students. Oaten appeared to calm

---

[40] Ibid., p. 92.

things down by meeting the student representatives and settling the issue. This placatory gesture became meaningless when the next day he ordered ten out of the twelve students in his history class to leave the class for having taken part in the strike.

On 15 February, the college was agog with the news that Oaten had again 'manhandled' a student—of first-year chemistry. This time the students took a different kind of action. They got hold of the professor at the bottom of the college staircase and gave him a severe beating. Oaten later said that he did not suffer any serious injury but Subhas recalled in his autobiography that Oaten had been 'beaten black and blue'.[41] Oaten was not even sure that Subhas had been part of the group that had thrashed him. An orderly reported that he had seen Subhas and another student leave the scene of the incident. The assault became a cause célèbre and led to the government closing down the college sine die. The principal was suspended but before this order could take effect, he suspended Subhas after telling him that he 'was the most troublesome man in the college'. Subhas sought the permission of the university to continue his studies in another college but this was not granted. This meant he had been rusticated from the University of Calcutta.

Before the Committee of Enquiry presided over by Ashutosh Mukherji, the legendary vice chancellor of Calcutta University, Subhas refused to name any of the students involved even though in his autobiography he admitted that he was an 'eyewitness'. The committee asked him a direct question—did he consider the action of the students to be justified? Subhas's reply was that the action was not justified but 'the students had acted under great provocation'. He then told the committee about the misdeeds of the Britons in Presidency College over the last few years. In the committee's report, Subhas was the only student who was named. His fate was thus sealed.[42]

---

[41] Ibid., p. 77. My account of the Oaten incident is totally dependent on the very balanced reconstruction of it in Sugata Bose, *His Majesty's Opponent: Subhas Chandra Bose and India's Struggle Against Empire* (Harvard and Delhi, 2011), pp. 28–31.

[42] *An Indian Pilgrim*, pp. 78–79.

The question that remains—and perhaps will remain forever—concerns Subhas's *direct* involvement in the assault on Oaten. There are two pieces of evidence cited by his most recent biographer that are relevant. In 1921, in a letter to his brother Sarat, his confidant, Subhas wrote that he should have taken responsibility for the attack in a more forthright way instead of simply refusing to name the students who had been involved. More significantly, later in life when his young nephews raised the incident with him and prodded him, 'he simply smiled and did not give a direct answer'.[43]

The upshot of all this was that Subhas's education was interrupted. He left Calcutta to go back to Cuttack. Back in Cuttack, where there were no words of recrimination from his family, Subhas marked time by immersing himself in social work. This also exposed him to the many kinds of prejudices that existed at that time in Indian society. After one year, he came back to Calcutta to try his luck with the Calcutta University authorities, especially with Ashutosh Mukherji, 'the virtual dictator of the University'.[44] While waiting for the university to give its verdict, Subhas tried to get himself recruited to the 49th Bengalees but failed because of his defective eyesight. This was another instance of Subhas's early fascination for things military. The authorities of Calcutta University relented, and Subhas joined Scottish Church College to study philosophy. He did well in his BA examinations—standing second in the university and securing a first class. But he felt he had not fulfilled his own expectations.[45] At this point an unexpected door opened up before Subhas. His father in consultation with his brother Sarat decided to send Subhas to England to study for the ICS examination.

Subhas arrived in England in late October 1919 and managed to secure admission into Fitzwilliam Hall in Cambridge even though Michaelmas term had already begun. He enrolled for the Moral

---

[43] Sugata Bose, *His Majesty's Opponent*, p. 28. Bose also records (p. 31) that much later there was a reconciliation between Subhas and Oaten, and the latter wrote a poem on Subhas referring to the incident in Presidency College.

[44] *An Indian Pilgrim*, p. 88.

[45] Ibid., p. 93.

and Mental Sciences Tripos. He also began preparations for the ICS examination. This involved the study of eight or nine different subjects. Subhas worked hard and was amply rewarded. In the ICS examination, he was placed fourth in the order of merit. This was no mean achievement for someone who had had barely six to seven months to prepare for the examination. But the success came with a heavy price tag—a crisis of conscience. It was immediately obvious to him that it was impossible for him to join the service without making 'a clean sweep of my past life', by giving 'the go-by to all my dreams and aspirations'.[46] There was the lure of a comfortable life that the ICS presented; he also had to think of his parents who had so many expectations of him. He struggled with the dilemma for seven months and bared his heart to Sarat in a series of letters. He was aware that joining the ICS would bring him worldly comforts but all 'these acquisitions [would be] made at the expense of my soul'. He believed 'it is hypocrisy to maintain that the highest ideals of one's life are compatible with subordination to the conditions of service which an ICS man has got to accept.'[47] He did not deny that refusing to join the service would entail a life of struggle but he averred that 'life loses half its interest if there is no struggle'. He wanted to dedicate his life to the service of the country and this was not possible from within the chains of the service—'[N]ational and spiritual aspirations,' he wrote to Sarat, 'are not compatible with obedience to Civil Service conditions.'[48] It was the example of Aurobindo Ghose rather than that of R.C. Dutt—the civil servant who became famous for his two-volume account and critique of the Indian economy under the British Raj—that beckoned to him.[49] He found the idea of serving an alien bureaucracy thoroughly repugnant.

Subhas wrote to his parents to seek their permission to take 'the vow of poverty and service'. He had before him, he wrote, the

---

[46] Ibid., p. 106.

[47] Ibid., p. 108.

[48] *An Indian Pilgrim*, pp. 108–9.

[49] 'The path of Arabindo Ghosh [sic] is to me more noble, more inspiring, more lofty, more unselfish though more thorny than the path of Ramesh [sic] Dutt.' Ibid., p. 111.

example of C.R. Das, who had at a mature age given up everything.[50] He had written to Das who had replied to say that sincere workers committed to the motherland were scarce. Subhas was convinced that there was enough work for him back in India. All this was underpinned by the conviction that '[w]e have got to make a nation and a nation can be made only by the uncompromising idealism of Hampden and Cromwell'.[51] The time was ripe in India for every Indian to wash his or her 'hands clean of any connection with the British government . . . The best way to end a government is to withdraw from it. I say this not because it was Tolstoy's doctrine nor because Gandhi preaches it—but because I have come to believe in it.'[52] Thus, not persuaded by any 'philosophy of expediency' nor by his father's strong disapproval, Subhas sent in his resignation on 22 April 1921. 'The die is cast,' he wrote to Sarat the day after.[53]

Subhas returned to India in July 1921 in a mood that was radically different from the one that had informed Nehru's return nine years earlier. One reason for this was, of course, the fact that the political context in India had undergone a transformation between 1912 and 1921. The two years signified more than an interchange of the last two numerals. There were, however, more profound differences of attitude between the two individuals. Nehru went out to Harrow, his first and only school, as a rich man's son whose father was keen to westernize him. He came back to India by way of Cambridge and the Inner Temple without achieving anything outstanding and with no firm decisions about his future. He could afford this luxury of indecision because of the cushion of his father's wealth and affection. He had developed some intellectual interests and had become aware of political developments in India. But these interests and the awareness were not deep enough to influence his life or to bring about any changes within him. He had not encountered any serious challenges either to his conscience or to his consciousness.

---

[50] Ibid.

[51] Ibid., p. 115.

[52] Ibid.

[53] Ibid.

He seemed happy, if not smug—note his own use of the word 'prig' to describe himself—about where life's current was taking him. He did not foresee, when he came back from England, any eddies or cataracts in the near future.

Subhas's growing-up experiences were on a different trajectory. By the time he left Cuttack to go to Presidency College in Calcutta, he had already made up his mind about the direction his life was to take. Recalling this period, he wrote in his autobiography, '[W]hen I left school, I had . . . made certain definite decisions for myself—I was not going to follow the beaten track, come what may; I was going to lead a life conducive to my spiritual welfare and the uplift of humanity: . . . I was not going in for a worldly career.'[54] The Oaten episode, apart from imparting to him a lesson in courage, honour and self-respect, also gave him a 'foretaste of leadership . . . and of the martyrdom it involves'. He came to realize, 'I had established a precedent for myself from which I could not easily depart in future.'[55]

The crucial decision in Cambridge after clearing the ICS examination seemed to be a case of a resignation foretold. What is more difficult to explain is why Subhas agreed in the first place to proceed to Cambridge to sit for the ICS examination. Was it only to please his father who had high expectations from a son who was an outstanding student in the University of Calcutta? Before he left for Britain, Subhas told a professor, 'My father wants me to throw away the ten thousand rupees.'[56] This statement was made as a desperate response to a senior academic who was trying to dissuade Subhas to take the ICS; the professor felt Subhas did not stand a chance. But did the statement contain a hint of something else? Was there within Subhas already an ambivalence towards joining the ICS? He knew he had to prove himself to his father and to himself; he did this by being very successful in the examination, standing fourth. Having made his point, he followed the dictates of his conscience. Parental and social expectations did not prevail over his conscience and his

[54] Ibid., p. 51.

[55] Ibid., p. 80.

[56] Ibid., p. 95.

sense of duty. The decision to respond to the calling of service to the motherland was the culmination of the first phase of Subhas's development as a nationalist.[57]

Because Subhas had chosen his path early in life—much earlier than Nehru did—some contradictions were already evident. Nehru's life, since he had taken no major decisions, appeared smooth and seamless. So, what were the contradictions in Subhas's life as evident in the growing-up years? It is important to note these contradictions in Subhas's life especially as they acquire some salience in the context of some of his future choices. When he was writing to his brother about not joining the ICS, Subhas had written the telling line, 'Every Government servant whether he be a petty chaprasi or a provincial governor only helps to contribute to the stability of the British Government in India.'[58]

Yet Subhas had made three attempts in his youth to don the British military uniform. First, on his return from Cuttack to resume his studies in Calcutta, he tried to get recruited to the 49th Bengalis; second, as a student of Scottish Church College, he had joined India's Territorial Army and, as we noted, had rather enjoyed the experience; and in Cambridge, he, with some other Indian students, had applied for enlistment in the University Officers' Training Corps. When their applications were denied, Subhas, on behalf of the students, took up the matter with the secretary of state for India, the Earl of Lytton. Subhas told him that the students were more interested in the training than in joining the army. It is odd that it did not occur to Subhas, who was already a convert to the cause of nationalism, that the army in British India, in its various fronts and units, was the principal instrument of British dominance in India, the imprimatur of British rule. To join it or one of its fronts could also been seen as much a cooperation or collaboration as joining the steel frame of the ICS. What drew Subhas, as he told the secretary of state, was the prospect of training (he had enjoyed the training with the Territorial

---

[57] See Ranajit Guha, 'Nationalism and the Trials of Becoming' in Ranajit Guha, *The Small Voice of History: Collected Essays* (Delhi, 2009), pp. 520–33.

[58] *An Indian Pilgrim*, p. 115.

Army on the Calcutta maidan). This attraction to military discipline and training was to manifest itself in the choices he made in the early 1940s. In many different ways thus—in the commitment to nationalism and service to India and the attraction to army life and training—the template of Subhas's life had been constructed in the course of his growing-up years.

'The die is cast,' Subhas had written before he left England. On arriving in India on 16 July 1921, he rushed to see Gandhi. His slightly senior contemporary Jawaharlal, when he returned to India, had not cast his dice on the board of life. He remained his father's son: nationalism had not begun to determine his process of becoming.

2

Baptism in Politics

Jawaharlal came back to India when he was twenty-three years old, Subhas when he was twenty-five. In terms of political culture and activity, the India they came back to was not the same. When Jawaharlal returned, as he himself noted in his autobiography, India was politically 'very dull'.[1] He tried to involve himself in Congress activity, especially to escape from what his biographer calls the 'vacuous, parasitic life of upper middle class Indian society in Allahabad'.[2] He visited the Bankipore Congress as a delegate over Christmas 1912 and found it 'very much an English-knowing upper class affair where morning coats and well-pressed trousers were greatly in evidence. Essentially it was a social gathering with no political excitement or tension.'[3]

But this was about to change. In December 1915, Tilak and his group were allowed to re-enter the Congress but his attempts to set up a proper working committee geared towards making the Congress a political party were foiled. Consequently, Tilak took the step of establishing the Home Rule League for agitational work; he was joined in this by Annie Besant. It was to the Home Rule Leagues that Jawaharlal was drawn, especially to the one started by Besant whom he had known from his childhood. Political matters

---

[1] *An Autobiography*, p. 27.

[2] Gopal, *Jawaharlal Nehru*, vol. 1, p. 29.

[3] *An Autobiography*, p. 27.

became a little more exciting for him. The government added to the excitement and, in fact, provided a fillip to the movement when, in a fit of panic, it passed an order that interned Besant at a hill station. According to Jawaharlal, 'it vitalized the Home Rule Movement all over the country' but he added the movement 'did not touch the masses'.[4]

His first meeting with Gandhi was around the time of the Lucknow Congress in the winter of 1916. Gandhi had returned to India the previous year and was in the process of establishing himself in Indian politics. He appeared 'distant and different and unpolitical' to young Jawaharlal. Such sentiments turned to enthusiasm at the news of Gandhi's campaign for the peasants against the indigo planters in Champaran. Jawaharlal was also inspired by some speeches of Sarojini Naidu in Allahabad and also by Roger Casement's 'wonderful speech' at his trial for treason in 1916. The latter 'seemed to point out exactly how a member of a subject nation should feel'. Looking back at his own political views during the war years, Jawaharlal wrote, 'It was all nationalism and patriotism and I was a pure nationalist, my vague socialist ideas of college days having sunk into the background.'[5] His mind had thus become drawn to a cause, though the call to active politics was yet to come.

The 1919 Rowlatt Act and its aftermath—the satyagraha, violence and disturbances followed by police action in various towns of India and the massacre at Jallianwala Bagh—galvanized Jawaharlal into action. He became part of the Congress inquiry team to look into the violence. Jawaharlal was deputed to accompany Chittaranjan Das to look into what had happened in Amritsar. He made detailed notes of what he had seen at Jallianwala Bagh.[6] On the basis of the inquiry and his observations, he wrote to *The Bombay Chronicle* on 6 October 1919: 'The evidence of respectable citizens of Amritsar shows that people were made to crawl not on their hands and knees

[4] Ibid., p. 31.

[5] Ibid., p. 35.

[6] See 'Notes on the Occurrences in the Punjab' in *Selected Works of Jawaharlal Nehru*, (ed.) S. Gopal (Delhi, 1972; repr. 1974), vol. 1, pp. 130–140.

but on their bellies after the manner of snakes and worms.'[7]

It was in the course of the satyagraha call that Jawaharlal for the first time gave in to Gandhi's wishes in spite of his own sentiments and desires. When he had first read about the proposed satyagraha, Jawaharlal was 'afire with enthusiasm and wanted to join the Satyagraha Sabha immediately' without even considering the consequences of law-breaking and jail-going. But his father was against all this; he considered jail-going to be useless, and hated the idea of his only son going to jail. Father and son were in deep conflict, especially as the son's heart was set on joining the satyagraha even if it caused suffering to his father. At this point, Gandhi came to Allahabad at Motilal's request and the two of them had long talks. Gandhi then advised Jawaharlal 'not to precipitate matters or to do anything which might upset father'. Jawaharlal was not happy at this but he did not protest.[8]

Reflecting on his own political activities and attitudes during this period of his life, Jawaharlal was candid enough to write, 'My politics had been those of my class, the bourgeoisie . . . I was totally ignorant of labour conditions in factories or fields.' He knew of the existence of poverty and misery but had no direct exposure to them.[9] His experience and his consciousness broke away from these elite fetters in a dramatic and unexpected manner. In June 1920, 300 to 500 peasants led by an itinerant preacher calling himself Baba Ramachandra came to Allahabad all the way from the interior of Pratapgarh and Jaunpur. Their purpose was to draw the attention of the prominent politicians of Allahabad to their plight. They may have even come to see Gandhi.[10] It was from this encounter that Jawaharlal first learnt of the wretched conditions of the peasantry

---

[7] Ibid., p. 149.

[8] This incident is recounted in *An Autobiography*, pp. 41–42.

[9] Ibid., pp. 48–9.

[10] Nehru, in *An Autobiography* (p. 51), writes that they came to see prominent politicians, and he, on learning that they were squatting on one of the ghats of the Jamuna, went to meet them; but Gopal (*Jawaharlal Nehru*, vol. 1, p. 46) writes that they came in the hope of meeting Gandhi. They failed to find Gandhi and met Jawaharlal instead.

in Awadh and of the power and dominance of the taluqdars of that region. The peasants wanted Jawaharlal to come back to the villages with them, to see for himself, to make inquiries and to protect them from the wrath of the taluqdars. They would not take no for an answer. Nehru promised a visit a couple of days later, and when he went, he visited villages far away from the railway and even pukka roads. What he saw was a revelation to him.[11] This was Jawaharlal's first encounter with the rural world and rural people of India.

What Jawaharlal witnessed was a 'whole countryside afire with enthusiasm and full of a strange excitement'. He was amazed how 'enormous gatherings would take place at the briefest notice by word of mouth. One village would communicate with another and the second with the third, and so on and presently whole villages would empty out, and all over the fields there would be men and women and children on the march to the meeting place. Or, more swiftly still, the cry Sita Ram—Sita Ra-a-a-a-m—would fill the air, and travel far in all directions and be echoed back from other villages, and then people would come streaming out or even running as fast as they could. They were in miserable rags, men and women, but their faces were full of excitement and their eyes glistened and seemed to expect strange happenings which would, as if by a miracle, put an end to their long misery.'[12] What Jawaharlal saw and so vividly described was a classic case of peasant mobilization.[13]

The mobilization of the protest of the peasants in Awadh that Jawaharlal saw had underlying causes that went back to the wooing of the taluqdars as 'natural leaders' by British policymakers.[14]

---

[11] *An Autobiography*, p. 51.

[12] Ibid., p. 52.

[13] For an analysis of the general characteristics of peasant mobilization, see Ranajit Guha, *Elementary Aspects of Peasant Insurgency in Colonial India* (Delhi, 1983), especially chapter 4. The peasant movement that Jawaharlal saw is described in detail in Majid Siddiqi, *Agrarian Unrest in North India: The United Provinces (1918–22)*, (Delhi, 1978); another account, differing only in analytical nuances, is Gyanendra Pandey, 'Peasant Revolt and Indian Nationalism: The Peasant Movement in Awadh, 1919–1922' in *Subaltern Studies I: Writings on South Asian History and Society*, (ed.) R. Guha, (Delhi, 1982), pp. 143–97.

[14] See P.J. Musgrave, 'Landlords and Lords of the Land: Estate Management and

On these men the British bestowed special status. The origins of the taluqdars varied; they could be local rajas, officials, revenue collectors who had acquired an independent and powerful position over land and land revenue before the British annexation in 1856, or a handful of persons who for their loyalty during the revolt of 1857 had been given landed estates that had been confiscated from notorious rebel taluqdars. Three-fifths of the cultivated area of Awadh was settled with the taluqdars in the post-pacification arrangements. There are many descriptions available about the position of privilege that the taluqdars enjoyed and their role in the countryside of Awadh, but for the purposes of this book it is perhaps apt to quote the one written by Jawaharlal: 'The taluqdars and the big zamindars, the lords of the land, the "natural leaders of the people" as they are proud of calling themselves, had been the spoilt children of the British Government, but that Government had succeeded, by the special education and upbringing it provided or failed to provide for them, in reducing them, as a class, to a state of complete intellectual impotence. They did nothing at all for their tenantry, such as landlords in other countries have to some little extent often done, and became complete parasites on the land and the people. Their chief activity lay in endeavouring to placate the local officials, without whose favour they could not exist for long, and demanding ceaselessly a protection of their special interests and privileges.'[15]

Since the first land-revenue settlements favouring the taluqdars, the majority of the peasants of Awadh had been reduced to tenants-at-will or to landless labourers, having lost their customary rights that had no official record. The pressure was particularly severe on the Kurmis and Muraos, cultivating castes who formed a considerable part of the tenantry and numbered around one million in Awadh. The rise in their rents, in the district of Rae Bareli, for

---

Social Control in UP, 1860–1920', *Modern Asian Studies*, (July 1972), vol. 6, no. 3; T.R. Metcalf, *The Aftermath of Revolt: India 1857–1870* (Princeton, 1964), and *Land, Landlords and the British Raj: Northern India in the Nineteenth Century* (California, 1979).

[15] *An Autobiography*, p. 58.

example, varied from 30 to 80 per cent (rising to 100 per cent in a couple of cases) even though prices had risen gradually.[16] Apart from rent enhancements, there were the levies that the taluqdars arbitrarily imposed on their tenants: noting these, Jawaharlal wrote, 'a marriage in the family, cost of the son's education in foreign countries, a party to the Governor or other high official, a purchase of a car or an elephant' all called for special exactions which had special names like *motrauna* (tax for purchase of motor) or *hathauna* (tax for purchase of elephant) and so on.[17] In Pratapgarh, some peasants told the deputy commissioner in 1920 of the *murdafaroshikanun* (law for the sale of corpse) by which they meant the law that allowed immediate enhancement of rent on, or sale of, the land of a dead tenant. They added with a dash of black humour that a new kind of Mahabrahmin (the lowest among the Brahmins because they subsist on funeral gifts) had come into existence. This creature prayed for an epidemic so that he could collect vast amount of murdafaroshi fees. The new Mahabrahmin, the peasants said, was the landlord, and added, '[B]efore the ashes are cold on the pyre this Mahabrahmin has to be satisfied.'[18]

To make things worse for the smallholding peasants, the cost of living and pressure of population on land increased steadily from the late nineteenth century. One result of this was growing indebtedness. This left the peasants with no other option save depending on their valuable crops, viz. wheat and rice, to pay their interest dues and other exactions; thus the area under rice and wheat cultivation increased. For their own subsistence, the bulk of the rural folk depended on maize, barley, jowar and bajra. There was thus a demand for these inferior grains at a time when the area over which they were cultivated was shrinking. This led to the prices of these grains rising even more sharply than those of wheat and rice in the first two decades of the twentieth century.[19]

[16] See Gyanendra Pandey, 'Peasant Revolt and Nationalism', pp. 145–46.

[17] *An Autobiography*, p. 54.

[18] Pandey, 'Peasant Revolt and Nationalism', p. 147.

[19] Majid Siddiqi, *Agrarian Unrest in North India*, chapter 2.

All these factors lay behind the revolt of the Awadh peasantry that Jawaharlal witnessed after the First World War. Protests began around 1919 with kisan sabhas being formed in Pratapgarh. By the middle of 1920, the movement had found a leader in Baba Ramachandra, a Maharashtrian who had served as an indentured labourer in Fiji, had become a sadhu and then had started propagating Hindu scriptures in places such as Pratapgarh, Sultanpur and Jaunpur. He took on the task of organizing kisan sabhas and enabled the peasants to develop a sense of solidarity. It was Baba Ramachandra who had led the peasant delegation to Allahabad and had persuaded Jawaharlal to come and see the rural world of Awadh for himself. This movement, before Jawaharlal's awareness of it, had acquired a considerable support base. In Pratapgarh district alone, there were 585 panchayats, and in Rure, the village in Pratapgarh where the first kisan sabha had been set up, 100,000 peasants were said to have registered with the association.[20] The movement, Jawaharlal noted, was completely ignored in the cities with no newspaper mentioning a line about it.[21]

This neglect was no longer possible when large-scale peasant demonstrations at Fursatganj and Munshiganj bazaars in Rae Bareli district were fired upon by the police on 6 and 7 January 1921. Violence had been in the air for some time and there were reports from Rae Bareli of shops being looted and of the burning of crops that had been grown in the *sir* (personal) lands of the zamindar. It was on 5 January that some peasant leaders came to see Jawaharlal to request him to visit Rae Bareli. His initial reluctance—he had just returned from the Congress session in Nagpur—was overcome by reports that the situation was indeed serious. He took the night train and arrived in Rae Bareli on the afternoon of 7 January. He learnt that some peasant leaders had been arrested a few days back and imprisoned in the local jail. A large number of peasants had then marched to Rae Bareli to stage a mass demonstration. They had been emboldened to do this because in the autumn of the previous year

---

[20] Pandey, 'Peasant Revolt and Nationalism', p. 148.

[21] *An Autobiography*, p. 55.

when some peasant leaders had been arrested in Pratapgarh, peasant demonstrators had filled the court compound on the day of the trial. The magistrate had held the trial in camera the next day and the accused were discharged. The peasants saw this as a great triumph. In January 1921 in Rae Bareli, seeing the gathering of peasants, the authorities feared a replay of the Pratapgarh incident. The main body of the peasant protesters had been stopped just outside Rae Bareli on the banks of the Sai River. There was also a large police and military presence. Jawaharlal rushed to the spot in spite of the district authorities' request to him to leave Rae Bareli. As he neared the river, he heard sounds of firing and was stopped at the bridge by the military. He was surrounded by frightened peasants and he held a meeting with about 2000 peasants present. He tried to calm them but was aware of the 'unusual situation with firing going on on their brethren within a stone's throw . . . and the military in evidence everywhere'. Many peasants died in the police firing.[22]

This direct exposure to peasant action and police atrocities moved Jawaharlal. A few days later he wrote, recalling the experience, 'I do not know how they felt but I know what my feelings were. For a moment my blood was up, non-violence was almost forgotten— but for a moment only. The thought of the great leader, who by God's goodness has been sent to lead us to victory, came to me, and I saw the kisans seated and standing near me, less excited, more peaceful than I was—and the moment of weakness passed. I spoke to them in all humility on non-violence—I, who needed the lesson more than they did—and they heeded me and peacefully dispersed. On the other side of the river, however, men lay dead and dying. It was a similar crowd with a similar object. Yet they poured their hearts' blood before they would disperse.'[23] Over the next few days, Jawaharlal travelled across the area visiting the wounded and seeing the conditions for himself.[24] Peasant violence was soon to spread over the districts of Rae Bareli, Faizabad and Sultanpur—with the looting

[22] This account is from *An Autobiography*, p. 60.

[23] Nehru, 'The Rae Bareli Tragedy' in *Selected Works*, vol. 1, p. 212.

[24] See 'Statement in Pratap Case' in ibid., pp. 217–25.

of bazaars, attacks on landlords and encounters with the police. The gravity of the situation made the governor of the United Provinces observe in March 1921: 'You have seen in three districts in southern Oudh [Awadh] the beginnings of something like revolution.'[25]

It was among these peasants who were up in protest against oppression that Jawaharlal found himself in 1920–21. He wandered among them, listening to their grievances and speaking to them in groups or in large meetings. It was not only his first exposure to rural India but also the beginning of his involvement in serious politics, a kind of politics that was different from attending the annual winter sessions of the Indian National Congress. Jawaharlal took away some lessons from this experience. '[I]t lifted the veil,' he wrote, 'and disclosed a fundamental aspect of the Indian problem to which nationalists had paid hardly any attention.'[26] It also revealed to him the wretched condition of the peasants, and this left an indelible picture on his mind: 'ever since then [his first visits to the villages of Pratapgarh] my mental picture of India always contains this naked, hungry mass'.[27] A new picture of India emerged before him: 'naked, starving, crushed, and utterly miserable'.[28]

His 'wanderings among the kisans' also aided his personal evolution as a political and mass leader. Before his visits to the villages, he had hardly ever spoken at a public gathering; the prospect had frightened him. But, '[t]hese peasants took away the shyness from me and taught me to speak in public . . . how could I be shy of these poor unsophisticated people?' He, however, did not speak to them as an orator, he 'spoke to them man to man, and told them what I had in my mind and in my heart'.[29] These reflections came more than a decade after the experience. His immediate reaction is worth quoting: 'I have had the privilege of working for them, of

---

[25] Quoted in Pandey, 'Peasant Revolt and Nationalism', p. 143.

[26] *An Autobiography*, p. 63.

[27] Ibid., p. 57.

[28] Ibid., p. 52.

[29] Ibid. The words 'wanderings among the kisans' are Nehru's; he used them as the title of the chapter in his autobiography that describes this phase of his life.

mixing with them, of living in their mud-huts and partaking in all reverence of their lowly fare. And I, who for long believed in the doctrine of the sword, have been converted by the kisans to the doctrine of non-violence. I have come to believe that non-violence is ingrained in them and is part of their very nature . . . It is not the masses but we, nurtured in an atmosphere of the West, who talk glibly of the inefficiency of peaceful methods. The masses know the power of *Ahimsa*.'[30]

This passage occurs in an article that appeared in *The Independent* (a newspaper established by Motilal Nehru) on 22 January 1921, i.e. two weeks after Jawaharlal had been in Rae Bareli following the police firing on 6 January. There is an admission in this passage that the conversion to the doctrine of ahimsa came not from his encounters with Gandhi but from his direct exposure to and involvement with the lives of the peasants of Awadh. This immediate and unqualified admission of the process of conversion to non-violence got erased in the later reflections and recollections of Jawaharlal. On the memory of how critical the influence of the peasants had been on his political development fell the shadow of Gandhi.

It was inevitable, given the timing of the peasant rebellion in Awadh, that it would come to be linked to the Non-Cooperation Movement that Gandhi began from January 1921. In that very month, when he visited UP, Gandhi issued a series of instructions to the peasants of the area, adding that attainment of swaraj would be impossible unless these instructions were strictly observed. The instructions were:

1. We may not hurt anybody. We may not use our sticks against anybody. We may not use abusive language or exercise any other undue pressure.
2. We may not loot shops.
3. We should influence our opponents by kindness, not by using physical force nor stopping their water supply nor

---

[30] Nehru, 'The Rae Bareli Tragedy' in *Selected Works*, vol. 1, p. 211.

the services of the barber and the washerman.

4. We may not withhold taxes from government or rent from the landlord.

5. Should there be any grievances against zamindars they should be reported to Pandit Motilal Nehru and his advice followed.

6. It should be borne in mind that we want to turn zamindars into friends.

7. We are not at the present moment offering civil disobedience; we should, therefore, carry out all government orders.

8. We may not stop railway trains nor forcibly enter them without tickets.

9. In the event of any of our leaders being arrested, we may not prevent his arrest nor create any disturbance. We shall not lose our cause by the government arresting our leaders, we shall certainly lose it if we become mad and do violence.

10. We must abolish intoxicating drinks, drugs and other evil habits.

11. We must treat all women as mothers and sisters and respect and protect them.

12. We must promote unity between Hindus and Muslims.

13. As amongst Hindus we may not regard anyone as inferior or untouchable. There should be the spirit of equality and brotherhood among all. We should regard all the inhabitants of India as brothers and sisters.

14. We may not indulge in gambling.

15. We may not steal.

16. We may not tell an untruth on any account whatsoever. We should be truthful in all our dealings.

17. We should introduce the spinning wheel in every home and—male and female—should devote their spare time to spinning. Boys and girls should also be taught and encouraged to spin for four hours daily.

18. We should avoid the use of all foreign cloth and wear

cloth woven by the weavers from yarn spun by ourselves.

19. We should not resort to law courts but should have all disputes settled by private arbitration. The most important thing to remember is to curb anger, never to do violence and even to suffer violence done to us.[31]

Through these instructions, Gandhi and the Congress were attempting to establish control over a powerful movement that had begun outside the fold of the Congress and Gandhian leadership.[32] The instructions show the usual Gandhian emphasis on the importance of being non-violent during the course of protest. But as Gyanendra Pandey points out, some of the instructions had a bearing on some incidents that occurred in the districts of southern Awadh when Jawaharlal had been among the peasants. For example, the instruction that prevented looting: Rae Bareli, Faizabad and Sultanpur had all witnessed looting of bazaars by peasants and the burning of crops belonging to landlords. Instruction number 9 was made in the context of the gathering at Rae Bareli in early January 1921—a gathering to which Jawaharlal was an eyewitness—after some peasant leaders had been arrested and kept in the Rae Bareli jail. There was a violent aftermath to this assembly as already narrated. Gandhi obviously wanted to prevent the occurrence of such violent incidents which often followed when peasants gathered to protest against what they saw as police high-handedness. But in so doing, he was stopping one of the principal modalities of peasant protest and of peasant organization and solidarity. He did not want the peasants to do anything that did not have his approval. The instructions were thus directed to regulate peasant activism.[33]

For all his admiration for the peasants of southern Awadh, their

---

[31] *Gandhi*, vol. 19 (Ahmedabad, 1966), pp. 419–20; also see Pandey, 'Peasant Revolt and Nationalism', p. 153.

[32] For the propensity of Gandhi to discipline and control mass movements, see Ranajit Guha, 'Discipline and Mobilize' in *Subaltern Studies VII: Writings on South Asian History and Society,* (Delhi, 1992), (ed.) Partha Chatterjee and Gyanendra Pandey, pp. 69–121.

[33] This paragraph is based on Pandey, 'Peasant Revolt and Nationalism', pp. 154–56.

courage and their fortitude, Jawaharlal was aware of the potential of violence inherent in the protests. Looking back, he wrote, 'Agrarian upheavals are notoriously violent, leading to *jacqueries*, and the peasants of part of Oudh in those days were desperate and at white heat. A spark would have lighted a flame. Yet they remained amazingly peaceful.' The credit for the peace belonged to the Congress, according to Jawaharlal, 'for the new creed of non-violence was stressed wherever the Congress worker went. This may not have been fully appreciated or understood but it did prevent the peasantry from taking to violence.'[34] As one of the leading Congress workers who went out into the countryside of Awadh to be among the peasants, Jawaharlal spoke to them again and again to remain calm and to maintain peace. He spoke also to temper the peasants' hatred of zamindars; on one occasion, a couple of years after 1921, he preached kisan–zamindar unity.[35] The socialism of his college days had indeed faded from his mind; what prevailed over his consciousness was the vision of 'the great leader, who, by God's goodness has been sent to lead us to victory'.[36]

Jawaharlal may not have been aware then or since that the attempts of the Congress to remove or reduce violence from the peasant movements was actually welcomed by the government of the time. The Administration Report of the United Provinces, 1920–21, noted, 'Serious as these [kisan] disturbances have been, they would undoubtedly have been far more serious, had not the leaders considered that the time had not yet come for pushing things to extremes.'[37] Jawaharlal was seen by the government as an unwitting collaborator in the maintenance of law and order.

In his autobiography, Jawaharlal put forward the view that '[t]he Indian *kisans* have little staying power, little energy to resist for long'. He was amazed that the peasants in Awadh had resisted for so long. But they began to worry. He reasoned that this tiredness was

---

[34] *An Autobiography*, p. 59.

[35] Speech at Tanda, 5 March 1923: cited in Gopal, *Jawaharlal Nehru*, vol. 1, p. 54.

[36] 'The Rae Bareli Tragedy' in Nehru, *Selected Works*, vol. 1, p. 212.

[37] Cited in Gopal, *Jawaharlal Nehru*, vol. 1, p. 55.

the outcome of the conditions in which the peasants were forced to live and 'the determined attack of the government on the movement'. It did not strike him that the restraining influence of the Gandhian instructions may have taken away from the movement's momentum. When the movement revived in the form of the Eka Movement, Jawaharlal was nowhere on the scene. The Non-Cooperation Movement and the national stage had claimed him. In early July, giving testimony before the court on the events in Pratapgarh and Rae Bareli, he had announced, 'I want every resident of India to join the non-cooperation movement.' Unknown to him, far away in his old university another young man had also been similarly inspired.

Such was Subhas's eagerness to join the national struggle that was on in India in 1921 that on 16 July, the very afternoon that he arrived in Bombay from London, he went to see Gandhi at Mani Bhawan where the latter usually stayed in Bombay. Many years later, he vividly recalled the scene. He entered a room covered in Indian carpets; at the centre of the room, facing the door, Gandhi sat surrounded by his closest followers. Subhas was somewhat embarrassed to find that he was the only person in the room in western dress; all the others were dressed in home-made khadi. Subhas apologized for his attire. Gandhi with his characteristic hearty smile put him at ease. The main purpose of Subhas's visit was to 'get from the leader of the campaign . . . a clear conception of his plan of action . . . I wanted to understand the Mahatma's mind and purpose.'

As the conversation proceeded, Subhas showered Gandhi with questions which the latter answered patiently. In Subhas's mind there were three issues on which he wanted elucidation. First, he wanted to know how the different aspects of the movement were going to culminate in the non-payment of taxes, the last stage of the campaign. Second, how were non-payment of taxes and civil disobedience going to force the British to leave and leave the Indians free? And third, how could Gandhi promise swaraj within one year? Gandhi's answer to the first question completely satisfied Subhas but he was not convinced by Gandhi's answers to the other two questions. He was unable to understand what Gandhi's real expectations were.[38] It appeared to him that for Gandhi, swaraj within one year was a question of faith. Gandhi's answers left Subhas 'depressed and disappointed'. Gandhi had failed to cast a spell on him.[39]

Subhas's initial response to Gandhi was thus in sharp contrast to Nehru's. The latter had found Gandhi to be distant but this feeling swiftly turned to starry-eyed reverence. For Nehru, Gandhi was like a gift of divine providence, while for Subhas, Gandhi was a human being who equivocated. Subhas wanted a leader he could steadfastly, if not blindly, follow. But he had met a leader who, in Subhas's youthful perception, lacked clarity of vision. These initial responses would inform the two men's attitudes to Gandhi later on in their lives.

On Gandhi's advice, Subhas travelled to Calcutta to work with C.R. Das with whom he had corresponded from Cambridge. Back in Calcutta, Subhas began to live with his brother, Sarat, and threw himself into Congress work. If he had been disappointed after meeting Gandhi, he was inspired after meeting C.R. Das. He felt that Das was 'a man who knew what he was about—who could give all that he had and who could demand from others all they could give'. In Das he had found a leader.[40] Subhas was given the responsibility for the publicity of the Bengal Provincial Congress Committee and was appointed principal of the National College that had just been started. He began writing for the nationalist cause. This was a period of great turmoil in Bengal and in all other parts of India.

At the end of July 1921, the All India Congress Committee met in Bombay and decided to step up the Non-Cooperation Movement that had begun in January, by concentrating on the boycott of foreign cloth and burning it in public bonfires; it also decided it would boycott the visit of the Prince of Wales, which was scheduled for November. Gandhi gave a call for flooding the prisons with

---

[38] Subhas Chandra Bose, *The Indian Struggle, 1920–42* in *Netaji: Collected Works*, (ed,) Sisir K. Bose and Sugata Bose, vol. 2, pp. 58–59.

[39] Ibid., p. 59.

[40] Ibid., p. 60.

volunteers. The more radical step of non-payment of taxes was again deferred although the movement had clearly moved from the intelligentsia to the masses. The Prince of Wales, when he arrived in Bombay on 17 November 1921, was greeted by a countrywide hartal. Calcutta on that day was totally paralysed: at the head of this boycott was Subhas, who directed the Congress volunteers in the city. The government retaliated by declaring all national volunteer organizations to be illegal.

The Congress decided to challenge this ban. But Das opted against a head-on confrontation with the government. He wanted to make a 'modest beginning' by sending out volunteers in batches of five to sell khadi cloth. The volunteers would be in mufti. If the government took action against such groups, the public would be convinced that the government was acting in an arbitrary and unjustified manner and thus they would rally under the Congress flag. This was Das's calculation. He further suggested that his wife, Basanti Devi, be among the first group of volunteers. The government reacted in exactly the manner that Das had thought it would. It arrested Basanti Devi, and as the news of her arrest spread in Calcutta there was 'wild excitement'. Bose remembered, 'In utter indignation young and old, rich and poor began to pour in as volunteers. The authorities were alarmed and they converted the city into an armed camp.'[41] The anger spread even to the police: some of the constables swore to Basanti Devi that they would resign from their jobs the next day. The level of anger forced the government to release Basanti Devi around midnight. Thus, one part of the campaign was successful as large numbers came out to join the movement. The prisons were full with volunteers courting arrest, and even camp-prisons were bursting at the seams.[42] Driven to desperation, the government arrested Das and his close associates, among whom was Subhas. Thus on the evening of 10 December 1921, Subhas found himself in jail—the first of his

---

[41] Ibid., p. 71. Bose had objected to the idea of Basanti Devi and other leaders going out as volunteers. His reason for this objection is worth noting: 'We opposed the idea especially on the ground that no lady should be permitted to go out as long as there was a single man left.'

[42] Ibid., p. 72.

eleven imprisonments under British rule.

As if to illustrate how the lives of the two men ran along parallel tracks, Jawaharlal's first imprisonment took place on 5 December 1921, only five days before Subhas's. The latter went into prison with his father figure C.R. Das, and Jawaharlal with his father Motilal. Thus it could be said in a somewhat lighter vein that by the time one was thirty-two and the other was twenty-four, both men could put the honorific 'JB' after their names. 'JB', or 'Jailed by the British', was, according to a famous British television serial of the 1980s, the highest honour in the Commonwealth.[43]

Jawaharlal's path to jail, like Subhas's, was also by way of the Non-Cooperation Movement. Jawaharlal described Gandhi's call for non-cooperation as a kind of intoxicant. Jawaharlal was 'full of excitement and optimism and a buoyant enthusiasm'. He was imbued with a sense of happiness that comes to people 'crusading for a cause'.[44] He became 'wholly absorbed in the movement . . . I gave up all my other associations and contacts, old friends, books, even newspapers . . . In spite of the strength of my family bonds, I almost forgot my family, my wife, my daughter.'[45] This complete absorption did not rule out doubts, however. He was troubled by the growth of the religious element in Indian politics, both on the Hindu and Muslim sides. The religious twist, he felt, hindered clarity of thought. Some of Gandhi's phrases he found jarring, especially his frequent references to Ram Rajya as a golden age that would return. He felt that Gandhi's language was difficult for the 'average modern' person to comprehend. Yet he could not deny that Gandhi 'was a great and unique man and a glorious leader' and therefore he was willing to give 'an almost blank cheque, for the time being at least'. Jawaharlal's allegiance to the doctrine of non-violence, at this stage of his life, was also not absolute nor for ever.[46]

---

[43] James Hacker, 'Doing the Honours' in *The Complete Yes Minister: The Diaries of a Cabinet Minister,* (ed.) Jonathan Lynn and Antony Jay (London, 1984), p. 235.

[44] *An Autobiography*, p. 69.

[45] Ibid., p. 77.

[46] Ibid., pp. 72–73.

It was Jawaharlal's enthusiastic participation that was partially responsible for galvanizing the Non-Cooperation Movement in UP after it got off to a disappointing start. He was an ardent advocate of swadeshi and he devoted himself to the boycott of foreign goods and cloth. In Allahabad, he went from door to door to collect foreign clothes. He believed swadeshi would drive out the British from India. In his speeches, he spoke about the importance of non-violence, of Hindu–Muslim unity and of the removal of untouchability. His campaign was by no means confined only to urban centres. In May 1921, he undertook a tour of the districts of UP, travelling by train, car and horse carriage and on one occasion even running between two places. Like Subhas, Jawaharlal had also worked to build up volunteer units, which had organized hartals in Allahabad, Lucknow and Kanpur, and had effectively picketed shops selling foreign goods. The success of the movement elicited grudging acknowledgement from even the viceroy who wrote, 'The non-co-operators put forward the full strength of an undoubtedly powerful organization and yet, save in Allahabad, have really not succeeded anywhere, although, surveying the situation impartially, I am bound to admit that they have at places managed to prevent the visit [of the Prince of Wales] being the unqualified and triumphant success it would otherwise have been.' By December the volunteer organizations in UP were declared illegal and Jawaharlal and his father were behind bars.[47]

Jawaharlal's prison sentence was curtailed and he was released, for reasons unknown to him, in March 1922. But he was arrested six weeks later and incarcerated for eighteen months. Subhas served his full prison sentence and came out in the middle of 1922. While they were in prison, developments outside altered the trajectory of the political movement that had taken them to jail. Subhas was an eyewitness to some aspects of one development as they involved his mentor C.R. Das. Just before the visit of the Prince of Wales to Calcutta on Christmas Eve, 1921, the viceroy, Lord Reading, sent Madan Mohan Malaviya as an emissary to Das in prison. The deal was that if the Congress lifted the boycott of the visit, the government

---

[47] This paragraph is based on Gopal, *Jawaharlal Nehru*, vol. 1, pp. 61–63.

would release the prisoners arrested for non-cooperation and arrange for a round-table conference to discuss the future Constitution of India. Das was not unwilling and he managed to persuade his young followers like Subhas that this was tactically not a bad position since the swaraj that Gandhi had promised was nowhere in sight. Das sent a message to Gandhi to accept the terms the government was offering but the latter rejected them. The deal fell through much to the annoyance of Das who believed that 'a chance of a lifetime had been lost'. Subhas witnessed these developments as Das's lieutenant and agreed that Gandhi 'had committed a serious blunder'.[48]

Jawaharlal learnt about the deal and its rejection only after he was released in March. By that time, however, far more momentous events had taken place. In early 1922, Gandhi announced that in late February the final phase of the movement—non-payment of taxes—would commence from Bardoli district in Gujarat. However, before this could take place, on 5 February 1922, a gathering of peasants in Chauri Chaura in Gorakhpur district of UP set fire to a police station and twenty-one policemen died. Shocked by this news, Gandhi unilaterally called off the Non-Cooperation Movement. Both Jawaharlal and Subhas in their respective prison cells were angry and devastated that the movement they had worked for had been forced to beat an unexpected retreat.

In the aftermath of the withdrawal of the Non-Cooperation Movement certain changes took place within the Congress party. The party came to be divided into two distinct groups. One group led by Gandhi continued to oppose entry into the legislatures that had been made possible by the Montagu–Chelmsford reforms of 1919. The others led by Das favoured entry into the legislatures and the councils. The former group came to be called the 'no-changers' and the latter the 'pro-changers'. As a logical sequel to this, Das, with the support of Motilal, formed the Swaraj Party. But by September 1923, a compromise had been arrived at between the two groups, and Congress candidates were allowed to contest elections for entry into the councils under the banner of the Swaraj Party. Not unexpectedly,

---

[48] Subhas Chandra Bose, *The Indian Struggle*, pp. 73–75.

the Swarajists, under Das's leadership, did well in the elections to
the Bengal Legislative Council. The Swarajists had the support of
both the Hindus and the Muslims of the province. Subhas, as Das's
acolyte, worked tirelessly both for the Swaraj Party and the Congress.

One aspect of the triumph of the Swaraj Party in Bengal was
the control it established over the Calcutta Municipal Corporation.
The Calcutta Municipal Act had been amended in 1923 largely at
the initiative of Surendranath Banerjee. Under the amended Act the
municipality had larger powers, the franchise had been enlarged
and the elected component strengthened. These changes and a
powerful campaign enabled the Swaraj Party to capture the Calcutta
municipality in 1924. One feature of this victory was the significant
presence of a large number of Muslim candidates.[49] Das was elected
mayor, Saheed Suhrawardy was made deputy mayor, and Subhas,
then barely twenty-seven years old, was appointed the chief executive
officer. This put him in charge of the entire administration of the
Calcutta Municipal Corporation.

Subhas, as was his wont, immersed himself in his new work and
responsibilities; such was his commitment that he was 'forced to give
up politics altogether'.[50] Under Das's leadership, the new councillors,
all dressed in khadi, decided to dedicate themselves to the uplift of
the poor, especially in the spheres of health and education. Subhas
was complimented by Gandhi for his efforts to employ Muslims
in the municipality.[51] There was one area in which the Swarajists
in the municipality were unknowingly a trendsetter. They began
to rename streets and parks of the city after India's greatest men.
Subhas approved of such renaming.[52]

Detailed research on the workings of the municipality during
this period does not, however, present as rosy a picture as Subhas
painted in his book, *The Indian Struggle*. The findings of Rajat

[49] Ibid., p. 104.

[50] Ibid., p. 118.

[51] Sugata Bose, *His Majesty's Opponent*, p. 54.

[52] Subhas Chandra Bose, *The Indian Struggle*, p. 105.

Ray reveal some very unseemly features of Das's mayoralty and of Subhas's tenure as chief executive officer. 'From the very beginning,' Ray writes, 'there was a tendency towards bribery and corruption . . . [C.R. Das] needed funds for the Swaraj Party and was not particularly scrupulous as to how they were obtained.'[53] In one case, obtaining of such funds was facilitated by Subhas. He arranged for the corporation to accept a tender from Messrs Kar and Company, Engineers, Contractors and Builders, to the tune of Rs 12,75,000 in connection with the Palta Water Works extension scheme. In return, Kar and Co. paid Rs 75,000 into the Swaraj Party funds; Kar and Co. also contributed Rs 3600 to the expenses of sixty-three Swarajists who accompanied Das as representatives to the AICC meeting in Allahabad in 1924.[54] It is of course difficult to establish if Subhas knew about these dealings, but given his closeness to Das, it is hard to believe that he was totally ignorant. Another shadow on the reputation of both Das and Subhas is the campaign that was mounted to defeat B.N. Sasmal for the post of chief executive officer. According to Ray, Sasmal's 'low caste was touched upon repeatedly during the campaign against him'.[55] Subhas could not have been unaware of the terms of this campaign. Perhaps he was not unwilling to be a party to a mode of faction politics that used caste to defeat a rival.

Subhas's work in the Calcutta municipality came to an abrupt halt when in the early hours of the morning of 25 October 1924, he was arrested. There were secret Intelligence reports that he was one of the principal organizers of the revolutionary movement in Bengal and that he had links with 'Bolshevik propagandists'.[56] The charges were unfounded and never established. Subhas was sent to Alipore Central Jail where he remained till January 1925 when he was transferred to a jail in Mandalay in Burma.

---

[53] Rajat Ray, *Urban Roots of Indian Nationalism: Pressure Groups and Conflict of Interests in Calcutta City Politics, 1875–1939* (Delhi, 1979), p. 106.

[54] Ibid.

[55] Ibid., p. 107.

[56] Sugata Bose, *His Majesty's Opponent*, p. 55.

During Subhas's long imprisonment in Burma, two events occurred which affected him. One was the sudden death of C.R. Das in June 1925. This naturally affected Subhas profoundly and, sitting in prison, he wrote a long essay on Das.[57] The other was a fifteen-day hunger strike that he undertook from 18 February 1926 with some of his fellow prisoners. The ostensible reason for the hunger strike was the refusal of the government to sanction funds for the celebration of Durga Puja. The jail superintendent had given the prisoners the necessary facilities. But the government, on hearing this, withdrew the sanction and censured the superintendent. The prisoners wrote to the government informing it of their decision to go on a hunger strike if the order was not rescinded. In spite of the best efforts of the government to stop the news of the strike leaking out, news of it reached Calcutta and there was a furore in the legislative assembly and a great deal of indignation among the public. The government had to withdraw from its position and it allocated thirty rupees per prisoner per annum to enable the prisoners to perform their religious rites. There was something more to the incident. Subhas told his brother, Sarat, that the full story behind the strike could only be told after their release. He added that the decision to go on strike had been taken only after 'mature deliberation'. This suggests that under the pretext of the freedom to perform religious rites, the prisoners were attempting to exert pressure on the authorities.[58]

The hardship of prison life combined with the hunger strike had broken Subhas's health. Realizing this, the government said that it would release him if he went at his own expense straight from jail to Switzerland and recuperated there. Subhas rejected this offer, treating it with the contempt that he thought it deserved. On 11 April 1927, he wrote to the superintendent of Insein jail: 'Much as I value my life—I love honour more and I cannot for the life of me barter away those sacred and inviolable rights which will form the future body politic of India.'[59] Given the condition of his health,

[57] Ibid., p. 59.

[58] Subhas Chandra Bose, *The Indian Struggle*, pp. 152–3; and ibid., p. 65.

[59] Sugata Bose, *His Majesty's Opponent*, p. 69.

the government had very little option save releasing him, which it did in May 1927. The long spell in prison and his enforced exile had only strengthened Subhas's patriotism and his resolve to serve his motherland.

Jawaharlal's life after his release from prison in the anti-climactic years following Chauri Chaura and Gandhi's arrest did not have any of the drama and excitement that pursued Subhas's career during these years. The feeling of exhilaration that was inevitable after being released from prison gave way very swiftly to a sense of despair. Jawaharlal found the state of the Congress to be 'discouraging'. The cliques and intrigue within the party 'made politics a hateful word to those who are at all sensitive'.[60] His father joined Das in forming the Swaraj Party but Jawaharlal refused to join his father though he knew that Motilal would be very pleased if he did. He found solace in family life. But 'mentally,' he wrote, 'I was at a loose end'.[61] Under these circumstances, when Jawaharlal was in a kind of vacuum, a new avenue of work opened up for him. Like Subhas, he found himself drawn to municipal work when he was made head of the Allahabad municipality. He noted later that around this time many leading Congressmen had become heads of municipalities in various parts of India—C.R. Das in Calcutta, Vithalbhai Patel in Bombay and Vallabhbhai Patel in Ahmedabad.[62]

Thus both Subhas and Jawaharlal took to municipal administration around the same time. There was, however, a slight difference in the attitudes of the two men to the work they undertook. Subhas by his own admission was so overwhelmed by his responsibilities as chief executive officer of the Calcutta municipality that he gave up politics altogether. Jawaharlal could not see the two as being separate. To the collector of Allahabad he wrote on assuming his new office, 'I regret that I cannot split myself up into various compartments—one for "general politics", another for "municipal affairs" and so on.' He added that he would have to tender his resignation if the Congress

---

[60] *An Autobiography*, p. 98.

[61] Ibid., p. 100.

[62] Ibid., p. 100.

committee so desired it.[63] In a circular to Congress workers in UP, he confessed that he had accepted the chairmanship of the municipality 'with considerable misgivings'. In the same circular he clarified his priorities: 'The great work that lies before every Congressman is to fight for Swaraj unceasingly, to strengthen the Congress and not to rest till we have achieved our goal. Everything else is secondary. We have gone to the municipalities to help our primary object . . . Let us be careful that we do not forget this or else our capturing the municipalities will become a curse to us rather than a blessing . . . On no account can we allow the Congress to take a back seat . . . the chairmanship is to me only the means for serving the nation for hastening Swaraj . . . If anyone imagines that I am going to function as Chairman of the Allahabad Board for the next three years and to let my other duties suffer he is grossly mistaken . . . I shall fight and hit hard whenever I may. That is my main function till Swaraj is attained.' He described his mentality as 'revolutionary': 'I believe in revolution and in direct action and in battle.' But he also recognized that revolutions require training and discipline.[64]

One of the hallmarks of Jawaharlal's chairmanship was the emphasis he gave to work and discipline. He cracked down on idleness and absenteeism and made efficiency the yardstick of success. He said, 'It is impossible for a person who is slack to be efficient and I desire no slackness in the municipal employ.' To the Public Health Committee he wrote, 'Has the Committee ever heard of discipline?' He fought against sectarian prejudices; under his guidance the board rejected the suggestion to prohibit cow slaughter. Jawaharlal could command loyalty because of his impeccable integrity. On one occasion he had accepted the oral resignation of a colleague; he realized that he had erred in doing so and asked the board to censure him. He worked to improve the level of instruction in schools, as also the state of sanitation, water supply and roads.[65]

[63] Letter to the Collector of Allahabad in Nehru, *Selected Works*, vol. 2, pp. 2–3.

[64] Circular to UP Congressmen on Municipal Work in Nehru, *Selected Works*, vol. 2, pp. 4–5.

[65] See Gopal, *Jawaharlal Nehru*, vol. 1, pp. 88–94.

While serving as the chairman of the Allahabad Municipal Board, Jawaharlal had gone to the princely state of Nabha where he was arrested on the flimsiest of charges and had a harrowing experience in jail and in the law courts there.[66] After his release he was ill with typhoid, which affected his health. What was even more worrying was the deterioration in the health of his wife, Kamala. For her treatment, Jawaharlal, his wife and daughter set sail for Europe on 1 March 1926. Subhas was then still in jail in Burma. He would return a year later in May 1927, a few months before Jawaharlal came back to India in December 1927.

The two men had by 1927 won their spurs in politics and served their terms in British Indian prisons. Nationalism had called them and they had both responded without the slightest hesitation. Both had accepted the leadership of Gandhi, one with more reservations than the other. They were poised to take on important responsibilities in the Congress. Yet the available evidence suggests that during this period, Jawaharlal and Subhas had met only once, and it was a meeting that neither recalled in their memoirs. Jawaharlal came to Calcutta, along with Gandhi, Motilal and other Congress leaders, to attend the special session of the Congress in September 1921. Subhas was back in Calcutta working as Das's lieutenant. Most of the Congress leaders were staying as Das's guests and it is highly unlikely that Jawaharlal and Subhas did not meet in the course of those few days. Subhas recalled that during this session he came into contact with the prominent leaders of the Congress and he mentioned by name Motilal Nehru, Lala Lajpat Rai and Mohammad Ali. He did not say he had met Jawaharlal but wrote, 'And in 1921, Nehru Junior (Pandit Jawaharlal Nehru) was not so well known or experienced that he could have replaced his father.'[67] On his part, Jawaharlal, when he remembered this visit to Calcutta, wrote about the Congress session as the one that inaugurated the Gandhi era in Indian politics. He wrote about his visit, along with Gandhi, to see Motilal Ghosh, the editor of the *Amrita Bazar Patrika*, and about

[66] *An Autobiography*, pp. 109–16.

[67] Subhas Chandra Bose, *The Indian Struggle*, p. 66.

his visit, again with Gandhi, to Santiniketan to meet Rabindranath
Tagore, and the poet's 'most lovable elder brother'.[68] That neither
men remembered meeting each other is an indicator that both were
then apprentices in the Congress—in fact, Subhas in his reference to
'Nehru Junior' hints at this. There was nothing in this first meeting
in 1921 to suggest that the two men together in a few years' time
would be providing a new ideological thrust to the Congress. It was
not a relationship that was foretold.

---

[68] *An Autobiography*, pp. 65–66.

3

Immersion in the Congress

Jawaharlal arrived back from Europe in time for the 1927 Congress session in Madras. He had wanted to keep himself free from accepting an office but was reluctantly drawn into the whirl of Congress politics. This was because his ideas and ideology had undergone a radical transformation during his European sojourn. In his own words, 'My outlook was wider, and nationalism by itself seemed to me definitely a narrow and insufficient creed. Political freedom, independence, were no doubt essential, but they were steps in the right direction; without social freedom and socialistic structure and the State, neither the country nor the individual could develop much.'[1] It was this altered understanding, derived from his study and observation of European developments and world affairs, that informed Jawaharlal's work in the Congress.

Jawaharlal had come round to the view that the Congress should commit itself to the goal of independence. To this end, he had a resolution passed in the Congress in Madras; the resolution declared 'the goal of the Indian people to be complete independence'.[2] A few days later in January 1928, he wrote to Gandhi, '[I]t passes my comprehension how a national organization can have as its ideal and goal, dominion status. The very idea suffocates and strangles me.'[3]

---

[1] *An Autobiography*, p. 166.

[2] 'The Resolution on Independence' in Nehru, *Selected Works*, vol. 3, p. 5.

[3] Letter to Gandhi, 11 January 1928 in ibid., p. 12.

Even though the independence resolution was passed in the Congress, it did not have a smooth passage after it had been adopted. Gandhi was present in Madras and had attended the open sessions but had kept himself away from the formulation of policy. He absented himself from the meetings of the Working Committee of which he was a member. Jawaharlal had the suspicion that Gandhi did not approve of the independence resolution that he had moved. This was confirmed when Gandhi declared on the pages of his journal *Young India* on 5 January 1928 that the resolution had been 'hastily conceived' and 'thoughtlessly passed'; he commented that 'we [the Congress] have almost sunk to the level of the schoolboys' debating society'.[4] The previous day, writing to Nehru, he had been even more harsh and condemning: 'You are going too fast. You should have taken time to think. Most of the resolutions you framed and got carried could have been delayed for one year. But I do not mind these acts of yours so much as I mind your encouraging mischief-makers and hooligans.'[5]

Gandhi believed that the resolution demanding independence was a 'tragedy'.[6] Similar views were echoed by other members of the Congress old guard.[7] Gandhi's criticism upset Jawaharlal who retorted that the resolution commanded a fair amount of support. He attacked Gandhi's leadership as being hesitant and ineffective.[8] Gandhi agreed with Jawaharlal that their differences were too vast and radical, and he offered to publish their correspondence on the subject. This would have meant a public break between them. Fearing this, Jawaharlal, not for the last time, drew back from a complete rupture with Gandhi. He admitted his debt to and dependence on Gandhi, and asked him: '[E]ven in the wider sphere am I not your

---

[4] 'The National Congress: Irresponsiblities', *Young India*, 5 January 1928, in *Collected Works of Mahatma Gandhi*, vol. 35, p. 438.

[5] Letter to Jawaharlal Nehru, 4 January 1928, in ibid., pp. 432–33.

[6] 'Independence v Swaraj', *Young India*, 12 January 1928, in ibid., p. 456.

[7] 'On the Resolution of Independence' in Nehru, *Selected Works*, vol. 3, pp. 3–4.

[8] Letter to Gandhi, 11 January 1928, in ibid., pp. 10–15.

child in politics, though perhaps a truant and errant child?'[9]

That Jawaharlal's independence resolution had not been taken seriously by the Congress was evident in the party's reaction to the Simon Commission. The British government had announced a seven-member all-white commission, headed by John Simon, to decide on India's future. The Congress considered another resolution condemning the Simon Commission and appealing for its boycott. It was proposed to set up an all-party conference to draw up a Constitution for India. The conference appointed a committee under Motilal Nehru to carry out the task of drawing up such a Constitution. Jawaharlal was not a member of the committee but he did take part in the deliberations while also helping his father with the secretarial work. His heart, however, was not in what the committee was doing; he was utterly out of tune with the attempts to compromise and strike a bargain. He wrote to Gandhi, 'One of the wisest things I have done was to withdraw my name from the membership of the committee . . . It is certainly painful to me to have to put up with all that is said and done there and I am sure my occasional intrusions are not welcomed . . . The fault must be mine but anyway it results in my feeling always that I do not fit in with anything. I am always the square peg and the holes are all round. I feel very lonely.'[10]

His proposal that the new Constitution should aim to set up a democratic socialist republic was not considered seriously by the committee, which favoured Dominion Status. The committee as a concession to the Muslim League recommended reservation of seats and not separate electorates. Here, too, Jawaharlal suffered a setback because he had proposed that the reservation of seats be ended after ten years or earlier with the agreement of all the parties concerned. What jarred most, however, was the acceptance of Dominion Status. This was an issue on which he often spoke publicly—even on occasion against his father. He wanted to keep

---

[9] Letter to Gandhi, 23 January 1928, in ibid., p. 19.
[10] Letter to Gandhi, 30 June 1928, in ibid., p. 50.

alive the demand for complete independence to which the Congress had committed itself.[11]

Subhas was not as disheartened as Jawaharlal with what happened in the Congress session in Madras and what ensued immediately after. He had not been able to attend the session even though he together with Jawaharlal and Shoaib Qureshi had been appointed general secretaries of the party. He saw the Madras session as being significant as it stood for a 'definite orientation towards the Left'.[12] He believed that the resolution for complete independence that had been passed was the 'logical fulfilment of a process going on within the Congress for a long time'. This process had been initiated by the enthusiasm of the younger elements within the Congress that had been exerting pressure on the Congress leadership to adopt a more radical and extremist position.[13] According to Subhas, one event that added to the significance of the Madras session was the return of Jawaharlal who, '[s]ince his return to India [had given] expression to a new ideology and declared himself to be a socialist, which was extremely welcome to the Left wing in the Congress and to the youth organization in the country'.[14] Subhas from afar welcomed Jawaharlal as an ideological peer.

Subhas was a signatory to the report (the Nehru Report) that the committee under Motilal Nehru submitted. This would suggest that he had worked with Jawaharlal on this matter, especially as both of them belonged to the minority that did not accept Dominion Status and had pressed for complete independence as the basis of the new Constitution. On this, he and Jawaharlal were in complete agreement. It would have been logical for the two of them to oppose the Nehru Report at the All Parties Conference in Lucknow. But prudence prevailed over ideology. At a private meeting of the Congress left wing, both Subhas and Jawaharlal proposed that instead of wrecking the conference and thus bringing joy to the

---

[11] Gopal, *Jawaharlal Nehru*, vol. 1, pp. 112–13.

[12] Subhas Chandra Bose, *The Indian Struggle*, p. 162.

[13] Ibid., p. 161.

[14] Ibid., p. 162.

British, they should be content to voice their protest at the conference and then proceed to establish the Independence for India League to propagate the idea of complete independence.[15]

Jawaharlal used the forum of the Independence for India League not only to spread the idea of complete independence but also to spread his own ideas of a socialist India. In his eyes, independence from British rule would have meaning only if it came with economic equality. That equality could only come by way of socialism. The League aimed, he declared, for a 'socialist democratic state in which every person has the fullest opportunities of development and the state control of the means of production and distribution'.[16] He recognized that this could not be achieved from within the fold of the Congress. The people would have to be organized on a large scale to carry the programme to its fruition.[17] It did not take very long for Jawaharlal to realize that the Independence League could not meet these aspirations.

It is revealing that in their memoirs neither Jawaharlal nor Subhas devoted much space to the Independence for India League. Evidently, neither thought it worthy of recollection. The significance of the activities of the League probably lies elsewhere. In Bengal, a provincial branch of the League had been set up with Jawaharlal's encouragement. But the revolutionaries in Bengal did not want Jawaharlal to dominate the provincial branch of the Independence for India League and, according to a member of the Jugantar group, they prevailed upon Subhas to promote a rival India for Independence League. The Bengal revolutionaries feared that by joining Jawaharlal's organization they would lose their own voice, and so would Subhas.[18] It would thus appear that very early in the relationship between Jawaharlal and Subhas there existed groups in

---

[15] Ibid., p.169; also Nehru, Speech at the All Party Conference, 29 August 1928, in Nehru, *Selected Works*, vol. 3, p. 61.

[16] To the members of the central council and provincial organizers and secretaries of the League, 10 April 1929, in Nehru, *Selected Works*, vol. 3, p. 287.

[17] Gopal, *Jawaharlal* Nehru, vol. 1, p. 114.

[18] Reba Som, *Differences within Consensus: The Left–Right Divide in the Congress, 1929–39* (Delhi, 1995), p. 88.

Bengal who for their own vested and provincial interests wanted to foment an artificial rivalry between the two. Subhas allowed himself to be sucked in by this provincialism. Jawaharlal noticed this and resented it. He wrote to a colleague that even though Subhas was the president of the Hindustan Seva Dal, he was 'taking no interest in the matter and he is keeping Bengal volunteers aloof from it. I do not like this provincial separatism.'[19] Even before the cement of their relationship had dried, cracks had begun to appear.

These petty differences evaporated, however, in the course of the boycott of the Simon Commission. Both Jawaharlal and Subhas joined the boycott and worked to make it a success. In Bengal under Subhas's leadership, there were demonstrations against the Simon Commission with cries of 'Simon Go Back'; there was also a boycott of British goods. A campaign for the boycott of British goods started in Calcutta on 1 March 1928: thirty-two meetings were simultaneously held in thirty-two wards of the city where the message of boycott was spread. Two days later at a meeting,10,000 ladies took a vow to boycott British goods.[20] At the Madras Congress at the end of 1927, Jawaharlal had not been too enthusiastic about the boycott of British goods because 'I felt,' he wrote to Gandhi, 'that it would meet with your strong disapproval and the boycott would not succeed unless a more or less unanimous effort was made.' He had been aware, though, of 'the wonderful effectiveness of the boycott in China'. He felt that there was nothing in China that could not be replicated in India. Therefore, he told Gandhi there was nothing to ridicule in the idea of a boycott of British goods.[21] The response to the boycott that Subhas had organized in Calcutta made Jawaharlal write to him to find out the details of the movement, especially of its organizational side. He believed that such information 'will enable us to do something on more or

---

[19] Letter to K.L. Ganguly, 5 March 1929, in Nehru, *Selected Works*, vol. 3, p. 285.

[20] See Nehru, *Selected Works*, vol. 3, p. 161 note. The note is added by the editor of the volume to a letter that Jawaharlal wrote to Subhas on 15 March 1928.

[21] Letter to Gandhi, 11 January 1928, in ibid., p. 12. The editor of the volume adds in a footnote to the letter that in 1925 there had been a boycott of British goods in China and this had caused heavy losses to British traders.

less similar lines elsewhere'. He warned Subhas that though 'the political effect of boycott propaganda is of course considerable but unless it is backed by an efficient organization and a well thought out scheme, the economic effect may not be marked, and after a short while there may be a reaction.'[22]

While Jawaharlal saw Subhas's work in organizing the boycott as something that was worth emulating, his own life in the course of the protests against the Simon Commission went through an experience that helped mould his nationalist persona. He had thrown himself completely into the protests but his objection to the commission was of a very fundamental nature. In a speech delivered in Allahabad in early 1928, he had said, 'We should not only boycott the Simon Commission, but at the same time decide to boycott now and forever the whole conception behind it, the whole conception that the British Parliament is there to give us what it wills and to keep away from us what it likes, and the whole conception that we are parts forever and ever of the British Empire . . . The only honourable and self-respecting reply to the Simon Commission is for us to say that not only are we not prepared to accept any commission of whatever composition, which the British Parliament is going to appoint.'[23] Freedom was the inalienable right of India and as long as that right was denied to India any commission coming out of England would receive no quarter in India.[24] It was decided that the commission would be greeted by a countrywide hartal on 3 February 1928, the day it landed in India. According to Jawaharlal, that was 'not . . . a day of mourning but it should be treated as a day of rejoicing, for on that day will commence afresh in India our war for "independence".'[25]

The experience referred to above occurred when Jawaharlal was part of a demonstration against the commission in Lucknow at the end of November 1928. He arrived there on 25 November when tension was high, as the report of the death of Lala Lajpat

[22] Letter to Subhas, 15 March 1928, in ibid., pp. 161–62.

[23] Speech at Allahabad, 10 January 1928, in ibid., vol. 3, pp. 83–84.

[24] Statement to the Press, 24 January 1928, in ibid., p. 87.

[25] Message to the citizens of Allahabad, 19 January 1928, in ibid., p. 86.

Rai, who had been severely beaten by the police while leading the protest in Lahore, had raised tempers. Jawaharlal asked the young men and women to give the government a fitting reply.[26] There was a huge demonstration on 26 November and this forced the authorities to acknowledge that when the commission actually arrived in Lucknow on the 30th, the scale of the protests would be even larger. On the 28th, there was another procession which had refused to alter its route in defiance of an official order. This procession was lathi-charged. On hearing this, Jawaharlal who had left Lucknow came back on the 29th. The authorities decided not to risk any other procession and on the 29th a small group of twelve led by Jawaharlal and Govind Ballabh Pant proceeded to a public meeting which was again lathi-charged by the mounted police. The group refused to disperse. Jawaharlal received two blows. A large crowd gathered and the police, fearing further trouble, allowed the group to proceed to the meeting with the mounted police going before them 'as a kind of guard of honour'.[27] The next morning when the commission arrived in Lucknow the Congress staged a black-flag demonstration. They were not allowed to go near the station but had been allotted a site 500 yards away. The procession was huge—Jawaharlal estimated it was 50,000 strong. The police carried out a cavalry charge; policemen on foot also freely used lathis and stones. The crowd stood its ground. Jawaharlal received half a dozen blows on his back. He told the press that the violence of the police on a peaceful crowd had brought 'the real issue before the people of the country . . . that issue is that British rule in India means the policeman's baton and the bayonet and the real problem is how to overcome them.'[28]

---

[26] 'They have dared', November 1928, in ibid., pp. 104–5.

[27] Statement to the Press, 1 December 1928, in ibid., pp. 108–15.

[28] Ibid. In Poona in December 1928 talking about a situation where 'there is a clash between the popular will and the will of the government . . . the government meets them [the people], not by argument and reason, but by the bayonet and the policeman's baton, by shooting and sometimes by martial law. The fundamental fact of the situation is the bayonet and the baton.' See Presidential Address at the Bombay Presidency Youth Conference, 12 December 1928, in ibid., p. 208.

These two incidents together represent the first time that Jawaharlal was beaten up by the police—probably it was the first time in his life he had ever been physically assaulted. In his autobiography he wrote a vivid account of the two beatings he received and of his feelings. Of the first, he remembered, 'The bodily pain I felt was quite forgotten in a feeling of exhilaration that I was physically strong enough to face and bear lathi blows. And a thing that surprised me was that right through the incident, even when I was being beaten, my mind was quite clear and I was consciously analyzing my feelings.' The battering next day was more severe, and Nehru recalled, 'the clearness of vision that I had had the evening before left me. All I knew was that I had to stay where I was, and must not yield or go back. I felt half blinded with the blows, and sometimes a dull anger seized me and a desire to hit out. I thought how easy it would be to pull down the police officer in front of me from his horse and to mount up myself, but long training and discipline held and I did not raise a hand except to protect my face from a blow.'[29]

Jawaharlal's commitment to nationalism had been tested in the laboratory of colonial violence. His analysis made immediately after the event had been that the ultimate sanction of British rule in India was dependent on the batons of the police and the bayonet of the soldier. The Indians had to overcome this. From Gandhi, his chosen leader, he had learnt that the only way to subvert the sanction was by resisting it through non-violence. In pursuing this goal, he had suffered bodily pain inflicted on him by an alien State. The infliction of pain had not weakened him; on the contrary, he had emerged physically stronger and morally tougher out of the violence to which his body had been subjected. A few years before, far away in a prison in Burma, Subhas had also undergone physical suffering. To protest against repression, he had starved his body of food for fifteen days. That deprivation had left Subhas feeling morally superior as well as triumphant. The welts that the lathis left on Jawaharlal's back and the pangs of hunger that Subhas had endured were signs of the

---

[29] *An Autobiography*, pp. 178–80.

sacrifice the two young men were willing to make for the cause of nationalism. Pain, in Subhas's case bodily mortification, had leavened their patriotism. Their physical sufferings had also bestowed on both of them the aura of heroes.

The boycott of the Simon Commission in Calcutta and the rest of Bengal was organized by Subhas. Events in Calcutta may not have had the drama of those in which Jawaharlal became a leading participant but the protests were very effective. Bose had made extensive preparations for the hartal that had been planned for 3 February. Police arrangements to prevent trouble on the day of the hartal were also elaborate. The police patrolled the city from dawn to dusk and the city was kept under aerial surveillance. Calcutta assumed the atmosphere of a besieged city. A few trams ran under police escort but buses were absent from the streets. Shops had their shutters down and the streets were deserted. In large parts of Calcutta, people led by Congress volunteers clashed with the police. The students of Presidency College 'stoned the police for several hours'.[30] The protests were not restricted to Calcutta alone; some of the smaller towns, both in east and west Bengal, also responded to the boycott call.[31]

This exhibition of popular anger against the Simon Commission was Subhas's personal triumph. This did not escape the notice of the authorities. The governor of Bengal, F.S. Jackson, wrote to the viceroy, Lord Irwin, 'I am afraid that Bose is the real cause of the trouble.'[32] From the government's attempts to quell the protests, Subhas drew the same conclusions about the nature of British rule in India as Jawaharlal had done in Lucknow. In a speech in Calcutta on 4 February, he said, 'We may call it Goonda Raj, Police Raj or Military Raj . . . The type of Raj as was evinced by the British

---

[30] These details are taken from *Ananda Bazar Patrika*, 3 February 1928; also see Tanika Sarkar, *Bengal, 1928–1934: The Politics of Protest* (Delhi, 1987), p. 16. The words 'stoned the police for several hours' (cited by Sarkar) were written by Jackson to Irwin on 12 February 1928.

[31] Ibid.

[32] Jackson to Irwin, 13 February 1928; cited in Sarkar, *Bengal 1928–1934*, p. 16.

raj today is a bigger edition of goondaism.'[33] Both Subhas and
Jawaharlal were articulating their growing conviction that Britain
had no moral right to rule over India; that it ruled India through
coercion and violence.

There was tremendous excitement over Subhas's programme to
boycott foreign cloth, and the burning of foreign cloth in a bonfire
made a great spectacle. Subhas's efforts, as already noted, were
seen somewhat approvingly by Jawaharlal but they did not have
the approval of Gandhi. The latter wrote to one of his followers in
Bengal that he had heard of 'the sensational reports about boycott'
but he thought the programme was 'perfectly useless'.[34] He may
not have been completely off the mark in this assessment: though
the import of cotton-piece goods and liquor did show a decline
after the boycott, the import of tobacco, sugar and machine goods
marked a rise. Officials believed that the fall in the import of cotton-
piece goods was due to sluggish demand that had been caused by
an accumulation of stocks from the previous year. The boycott,
according to the government version, had nothing to do with it.[35]

Jawaharlal and Subhas were also involved at this time with youth
and workers' movements. Immediately after the assault in Lucknow,
Jawaharlal travelled to western India to speak to students and the
youth. He participated in the Bombay Presidency Youth Conference
in Poona where he spoke to the students about the links between
imperialism and capitalism. Gaining political freedom, he told them,
was only the immediate problem—what was actually required was
'the destruction of all imperialism and the reconstruction of society
on another basis. That basis must be one of cooperation, and that
is another name for socialism. Our national ideal must, therefore,

[33] Speech at hartal meeting, 4 February 1928, in *Netaji: Collected Works*, (ed.)
Sisir Bose (Calcutta, 1985), vol. 5, pp. 236–37.

[34] Gandhi to Satish Dasgupta, 10 March 1928, in *Collected Works of Mahatma
Gandhi*, vol. 36 (Ahmedabad, 1970), p. 93. To Subhas, Gandhi wrote on 31 March
1928: 'Will you kindly tell me why you have preferred the cry of boycott of British
goods, principally British cloth, to boycott of foreign cloth and why also boycott of
British cloth . . .' Ibid., p. 166.

[35] Sarkar, *Bengal 1928–1934*, p. 15.

be the establishment of a cooperative socialist commonwealth and our international ideal, a world federation of socialist states.'[36] Not surprisingly, the reaction of the government was a trifle exaggerated: the home secretary interpreted the speech as the preaching of a violent insurrection that would be ushered in by an organized body.[37] In the middle of December, Jawaharlal travelled to Jharia to attend the annual session of the All India Trade Union Congress. It was his first trade union congress and he felt an outsider.[38] The police walked into the meeting to arrest W.J. Johnston, who had come as a fraternal delegate from the League Against Imperialism. Jawaharlal turned the police out from the precincts and made a fiery speech. The next day Johnston was arrested outside the venue. This resulted in another denunciation of British rule and imperialism from Jawaharlal.[39]

During this period, Subhas was also fully involved in youth and working-class movements. At the end of 1928, speaking at the All India Youth Congress, he drew attention to the fact that across the world there was a 'renaissance of youth'. Youth associations, he said, should be dedicated to change; they must be informed by 'a feeling of restlessness, of impatience with the present order'.[40] He acknowledged in a footnote in *The Indian Struggle* that he and Jawaharlal 'were among the few public men who encouraged the students at the time to organize themselves'.[41] At the Maharashtra Provincial Conference in Poona, in May 1928, he delivered a long speech which he recalled in *The Indian Struggle*. In the speech he expounded some ideas that he had formed during his imprisonment in Burma. He told the audience that '[D]emocracy is by no means a Western institution; it is a human institution.' He also put forward new lines of activity for Congressmen who, he said, should take

---

[36] Presidential Address at the Bombay Presidency Youth Conference, 12 December 1928, in Nehru, *Selected Works*, vol. 3, p. 206.

[37] Gopal, *Jawaharlal Nehru*, vol. 1, p. 120.

[38] *An Autobiography*, p. 186.

[39] Gopal, *Jawaharlal Nehru*, vol. 1, p. 120.

[40] Speech at the third session of the All India Youth Congress, 25 December 1928, in *Netaji: Collected Works*, vol. 5, pp. 270–74.

[41] Subhas Chandra Bose, *The Indian Struggle*, p. 170n.

up the task of organizing labour and that the youth and students should begin to establish their own organizations for serving their own interests as well as those of the country's. He also advocated separate organizations for women.[42]

Subhas's enthusiasm for working-class movements led him to get involved in at least three strikes that occurred around this time. There was a strike of railway workshop workers at Liluah and other parts of Eastern Indian and Bengal Nagpur Railways; another was the first major strike of jute workers in Bengal; and then came the strike at the Tata Iron and Steel Corporation in Jamshedpur.

At Liluah, in early 1928, the railway authorities announced that they would retrench 2600 workers. This resulted in a strike and around 14,000 workers were locked out. Trade unionists rushed to help the workers. The absence of a central railway workers' union proved to be a weakness and the workers were defeated. Even the death of two workers and injuries to several from police firing in Bamangachi failed to arouse sympathy and solidarity. Subhas espoused the cause of the workers by giving speeches and making appeals to raise funds for their relief. According to the *Amrita Bazar Patrika,* in a speech in Kharagpur he told a gathering of 6000 workers that those who were working for the political freedom of the country were also working for labour. He added that the latter in any dispute with their employers were always at a disadvantage because the employers had all the resources of the State behind them. The government, in its turn, was aided by the employers in its efforts to put down the movement for freedom. He thus urged labour to be united and close its ranks to face the common enemies.[43]

This rhetoric became sharper in the context of the strike by jute millworkers because many of the jute mills were owned by foreign companies. In the course of a visit to one of the jute mills, Subhas noted perceptively, 'Mill authorities were practically the zamindars

[42] Ibid., p. 168; and Presidential Address at Maharashtra Provincial Conference, Poona, 3 May 1928, in *Netaji: Collected Works*, vol. 5, pp. 242ff.

[43] *Amrita Bazar Patrika*, 17 April 1928: cited in Leonard Gordon, *Brothers Against the Raj: A Biography of Indian Nationalists, Sarat and Subhas Chandra Bose* (Delhi, 1990, repr. 2012), p. 172.

of surrounding villages . . . [the] poor villagers are living in another "raj".[44]

The strike in Jamshedpur was a little different.[45] The grievances were of long standing and the demands of the workers had even brought Gandhi to Jamshedpur in 1925. As the 1927–28 strike unfolded, the trade unionist N.M. Joshi came to unify the workers and work towards a settlement. When their efforts failed, the Strike Committee invited Subhas to Jamshedpur. Subhas arrived there in August 1928. His presence in Jamshedpur was not entirely unwelcome to the management. Subhas did succeed in working out a settlement; by the terms of the agreement, the workers would receive no pay for the strike period but would be entitled to loans repayable in easy instalments. But the management retained the right to retrench any worker who was considered redundant at the end of twelve months. Subhas believed that this was 'an honourable settlement'.[46] But a section of the workers refused to see it as one and under the leadership of Maneck Homi, formed a rival union called Labour Federation whose members attacked the office of the Labour Association. The management played on this split and argued that the Labour Association (that had invited Subhas) represented only the Bengalis.[47] The workers turned so hostile to Subhas that when he came to address the workers, he was booed by them and could deliver his speech only under police protection.[48] Looking back on the strike in Jamshedpur and on his involvement in it, Subhas wrote that the split 'had disastrous consequences' but the strike had for him served 'as an initiation into the workers' movement'.[49] It will

[44] Statement on Bauria Jute Mill strike, 27 November 1928, in *Netaji: Collected Works*, vol. 5, pp. 266–67. Jawaharlal wrote to Subhas on 24 January 1929 to provide the strikers with some financial aid as their condition 'is becoming more and more critical'. Nehru, *Selected Works*, vol. 4, p. 29.

[45] A history of this phase of the movement is available in R. Mukherjee, *A Century of Trust: The Story of Tata Steel* (Delhi, 2008), pp. 52–57.

[46] Subhas Chandra Bose, *The Indian Struggle*, p. 170n.

[47] R. Mukherjee, *A Century of Trust*, p. 57.

[48] Gordon, *Brothers Against the Raj*, p. 174.

[49] Subhas Chandra Bose, *The Indian Struggle*, p. 170n.

not be unfair to conclude that his efforts in Jamshedpur were not marked by any great success.

Subhas's espousal of the cause of the working class should be placed in the context of what one leading Indian capitalist thought of him in this period. G.D. Birla wrote to Purushottamdas Thakurdas in July 1929: 'Mr Bose could be relied upon to help the Tata Iron and Steel Works whenever necessary, provided properly handled . . . Mr Bose is a very sincere and scrupulous man and appreciates the necessity of co-operation with reasonable and advanced types of capitalists. He himself belongs to the aristocratic class, although he voluntarily renounced many luxuries. His main object in labour matters no doubt is service to the labour but not necessarily inimical to the capitalist. He is one of those who think industrialization in many directions [is the] quintessence of modern civilization and therefore is ready to help the industries by protection and other methods . . . [H]e is a shrewd man with a wide outlook and understands very well that hitting the Tata Iron and Steel Works does not necessarily mean hitting the Tatas.'[50]

This assessment of Subhas's commitment to working-class causes runs counter to the interest he took in the Meerut Conspiracy Case, in which thirty-two labour leaders, many of whom were communists, had been involved. He visited those who had been arrested a number of times and, on 6 July 1929, he called for their release along with the other political prisoners held in Bengal and Punjab. It was perhaps this link with the communists that made the government describe him as 'the most dangerous of the extremist leaders in Bengal'.[51] In *The Indian Struggle*, Subhas rather underplayed his own sympathies for those accused in the Meerut Conspiracy Case. It is possible that there was some ambivalence in his mind: according to one report, when a demonstration at the Congress session in Calcutta in 1928 marched up to the venue to demand that the Congress adequately

[50] Letter from G.D. Birla to Purushottamdas Thakurdas, 16 July 1929, in Purushottamdas Thakurdas Papers, Nehru Memorial Museum and Library (NMML), File No. 42 (Part 1).

[51] Quoted in Gordon, *Brothers Against the Raj*, p. 209.

represent the case of those accused in the Meerut case, Subhas, as the head of the volunteer corps, refused them entry.[52]

Jawaharlal, too, became involved in the Meerut Conspiracy trial. The Congress had formed a defence committee of which he was a member. One of the tasks of this committee was to engage lawyers. Finding lawyers provided Jawaharlal with an insight into the 'cupidity of men of my own profession' because 'lawyers would only sell their services for a full pound of somebody's flesh'. Some of the lawyers who were approached 'seemed to look upon the case as a means of making as much money as possible'.[53] Jawaharlal's involvement in the trial and his enthusiasm for the ideology of communism made him a prime suspect in the eyes of the authorities who tried in vain to pin him down as an agent of Moscow and also regularly intercepted his correspondence.[54] Jawaharlal was convinced that the government was deliberately creating a bogey of communism. He wrote, 'There is a lot of shouting about communists and communism in India. Undoubtedly there are some communists in India but it is equally certain that this cry of communism is meant to cover a multitude of sins of the government. Of the thirty-one accused in the Meerut case, now thirty-two since Hutchinson's arrest, the majority know little about communism. People connected with any kind of labour or peasant activity have been arrested and are being tried. Eight of those included in the Meerut case are members of the All India Congress Committee—the Central Executive Committee of the National Congress. It is patently absurd to say that the government is confining its attention to communists.'[55]

Jawaharlal campaigned for the rights of the prisoners in jail

[52] N.P. Banerji, *At the Crossroads* (Calcutta, 1950), p. 212: cited in Sarkar, *Bengal: 1928–1934*, p. 18.

[53] *An Autobiography*, p. 189; also see his letters to Motilal dated 24 April 1929 and 1 May 1929 in Nehru, *Selected Works*, vol. 3, pp. 334–35 and 337–40.

[54] Gopal, *Jawaharlal Nehru*, vol. 1, pp. 124–5.

[55] Letter to Walter Citrine, 22 June 1929, in Nehru, *Selected Works*, vol. 3, pp. 349–53. On his first visit to see the accused in Meerut jail, Jawaharlal is said to have remarked: 'How little do these accused persons know about the Communist International. I know a lot more than they.' Quoted in Gopal, *Jawaharlal Nehru*, vol. 1, p. 125.

and accused the government of denying them 'the most ordinary amenities'.[56] His efforts, however, did not win him any friends among the communists. One of the accused wrote to a comrade that Jawaharlal was no more than 'a timid reformist'.[57] A writer in the *Comintern* journal described him as a person 'who promises all the blessings of socialism without a revolutionary struggle'.[58] There are no reasons to believe that for all his attraction for communism, Jawaharlal would not have disagreed with the criticism that he was not a revolutionary in the communist sense of the word.

Subhas's and Jawaharlal's involvement in the Meerut case was something of a sideshow compared to what was happening within the Congress and their role in those events. The Congress met in Calcutta at the end of 1928 under the presidentship of Motilal Nehru. Subhas had been one of those who had endorsed Motilal's candidature. He had the responsibility of organizing the volunteer corps that would ensure that the session ran smoothly and all the delegates were well looked after. He gave himself the fancy title of 'general officer commanding'. Subhas made the session a grand affair bearing his own personal stamp. To the press, he announced, 'The Committee which has been given the charge of the volunteer corps is training up the volunteers in a way very similar to military training. Many of those persons from India who joined the First World War have joined the corps as leaders. Volunteers are doing regular parades in different parks of Calcutta.'[59] An eyewitness left behind the following account: 'Bose organized a volunteer corps in uniform, its officers being even provided . . . with steel-chain epaulettes . . . his uniform was made by a firm of British tailors in Calcutta, Harman's. A telegram addressed to him as GOC was delivered to the general in Fort William.' There was a lot of 'strutting, clicking of boots and

[56] Statement on Meerut Prisoners, 22 May 1929, in Nehru, *Selected Works*, vol. 3, p. 343.

[57] Muzaffar Ahmed to P.C. Joshi, 9 March 1929: quoted in Gopal, *Jawaharlal Nehru*, vol. 1, p. 126.

[58] Ibid.

[59] Quoted in Gordon, *Brothers Against the Raj*, p. 190.

saluting'.[60] He led this corps on a brown horse. Motilal was received in Howrah station in Calcutta with a 101-gun salute and was taken away from the station in a carriage pulled by twenty-eight white horses.[61] Recalling this welcome, Subhas wrote, 'The President . . . on the day of his arrival was given an ovation which would excite the envy of kings and dictators.'[62] And indeed, the Intelligence department of the government of Bengal saw the display as Subhas's attempt to ape the honours heaped upon the King Emperor and the viceroy.[63] Obviously, welcoming the president of the Congress in the manner of a king or a dictator did not strike Subhas as incongruous. Neither did the fact that yesterday's advocate of boycotting and burning foreign cloth was today's wearer of a uniform tailored by a British firm. Predictably, Gandhi scorned at this spurious military display and likened it to a Bertram Mills circus.[64] This fascination of Subhas with military discipline and ritual, traceable to his adolescent years, acquired meaning and significance later on in his life. It was an integral part of his future vision.

Things military were overtaken by things ideological in the proceedings of the Congress. It was the common expectation that the Calcutta session would see a conflict between the proponents of the Nehru Report who had advocated Dominion Status and those who had pushed the resolution for complete independence at the previous session in Madras. Motilal was aware that this could cause a breach within the Congress as the moderates would never accept the demand for independence. To prevent such an occurrence, he persuaded Gandhi to attend the Calcutta meeting. Gandhi was aware

---

[60] Nirad C. Chaudhuri, *The Continent of Circe* (London, 1965), pp. 103–4.

[61] For these details, see Gordon, *Brothers Against the Raj*, pp. 191–2; and Som, *Difference within Consensus*, p. 93.

[62] Subhas Chandra Bose, *The Indian Struggle*, p. 175.

[63] Som, *Differences within Consensus*, p. 93, citing a file in the Home Political series in the West Bengal State Archives.

[64] Chaudhuri, *Continent of Circe*, pp. 103–4. In an article in *Young India* on 10 January 1929 ('Overhaul Congress'), Gandhi had written, 'The Congress *pandal* was constructed as an adjunct to and in the midst of an enlarged edition of Filis's circus.' Gandhi, *Collected Works*, vol. 38, p. 237.

of the importance of avoiding a split. He favoured Dominion Status but his heart was not entirely with the Nehru Report. In August 1928, he had written to a correspondent, 'The way to constitutional *swaraj* may lie through Lucknow [read the Nehru Report]; the way to organic *swaraj*, which is synonymous with Ramrajya lies through Bardoli [read satyagraha, no-tax campaign].'[65] He argued that this controversy between Dominion Status and independence was no more than a quibble. He urged the members not to make the 'grievous blunder' of pitting independence against Dominion Status under the assumption that the former represented a triumph and the latter humiliation. He conceded, however, that 'I do not want a Dominion Status that will interfere with my further growth, with my independence.'[66]

Those opposed to Dominion Status, led by Jawaharlal and Subhas, saw the controversy as being fundamental. In a speech, Jawaharlal articulated their position. He confessed that 'energy oozes out of me at the very thought of Dominion Status'. He then went on to present the real issues involved: 'The real thing in the world is not so much the question of struggle between India and England, the real conflict is between two sets of ideals; and the question is, which set of ideals are you going to keep before the country? This is a conflict between imperialism and all that is not imperialism and if you look at it from that point of view, you cannot for one moment think of Dominion Status so long as Great Britain has the empire around her . . . By accepting Dominion Status you show to the world that you are prepared to accept the psychology of imperialism and this is a very dangerous thing.' He also pointed out that while the Congress spoke of Dominion Status, 'there is no mention of this on the other side'.[67]

---

[65] Letter to B.G. Horniman, 28 August 1928, in Gandhi, *Collected Works*, vol. 37, p. 212.

[66] Speech on the resolution on the Nehru Report, Calcutta, 31 December 1928, in Gandhi, *Collected Works*, vol. 38, p. 308.

[67] 'On Independence', 27 December 1928, in Nehru, *Selected Works*, vol. 3, pp. 270–74.

Gandhi realized the need for some sort of compromise.[68] The concluding line of Jawaharlal's speech probably provided him with an opening. Jawaharlal had said, 'prepared as this House should be for any compromise on any lines it should not be prepared to give up this definite and clear idea of independence for any length of time'.[69] Gandhi's compromise proposal said that the Congress would accept the Nehru Report but if the government did not act upon it within two years, the Congress would move towards seeking full independence. He later reduced the time limit to one year as a placatory gesture to Jawaharlal and other leftists. But Subhas refused to accept this compromise and moved an amendment that said the Congress should stay with the goal of independence. He began by noting that the very fact that he was moving the amendment was 'a clear indication of the cleavage, the fundamental cleavage between the elder school and the new school of thought in the Congress'. He admitted that he was voicing the views of the Bengal delegates, the majority of whom wanted the amendment to be moved. The youth of the country, he said, was gripped by a new consciousness and 'they are no longer prepared to follow blindfold'. He said nobody believed that the British would grant Dominion Status within one year; even Motilal Nehru in his speech had confessed that he did not believe this. The demand for independence would help to develop a 'new mentality'; this would enable India 'to overcome the slave mentality, which was at the root of India's political degradation'. He was convinced that '[T]he talk of dominion status does not make the slightest appeal to our countrymen.' He ended with the following: 'Respect and love, admiration and adoration for leaders is one thing; but respect for principle is another thing.'[70]

Jawaharlal spoke in favour of Subhas's amendment. He reminded Congressmen that Dominion Status 'is meant for those who originally belonged to Britain but established colonies elsewhere. The

---

[68] Speech on the resolution on the Nehru Report, 31 December 1928, in Gandhi, *Collected Works*, vol. 38, pp. 307–10.

[69] 'On Independence', 27 December 1928, in Nehru, *Selected Works*, vol. 3, p. 274.

[70] *Netaji: Collected Works*, vol. 5, pp. 275–78.

situation in our country is quite different. India can never become their colony. Has any nation ever sacrificed her sons for such a sort of state? Dominion Status can never be liked by any Indian ... If you wish that India be free and our country rid of this slavery as soon as possible, then our goal can only be independence.'[71] Having made this speech, Jawaharlal, possibly out of deference to his father and Gandhi, stayed away from the final session when Gandhi's resolution and Subhas's amendment were put to the vote.[72]

Subhas's amendment was defeated: there were 973 votes in its favour and 1350 against. Subhas believed that the voting was not fair as Gandhi had made it clear prior to the voting that if his resolution was defeated he would retire from politics. Most people therefore did not want to precipitate that outcome. They voted for Gandhi's resolution but not out of conviction.[73] What is important is that Subhas had openly challenged Gandhi. He had shown the courage to stand up for his principles and had not allowed respect for age or personal loyalties to stand in the way. Gandhi, in his view, had merely temporized and lost precious time since '[O]nly madness or folly could have led one to hope that the mighty British government would concede even Dominion Home Rule without a struggle.'[74]

The Calcutta congress brought Subhas and Jawaharlal closer to each other: the latter had supported Subhas even though he was absent when the voting took place. What is remarkable is also the similarity of their approach while arguing against Dominion Status and in favour of independence. They echoed each other's ideas and even used the same words and phrases. In March 1929, Jawaharlal wrote to a trade union leader in Bengal that he was coming to

---

[71] Nehru, *Selected Works*, vol. 3, pp. 276–77.

[72] Gandhi explained his absence thus: 'He thinks this resolution itself falls far short of what he wants but, a high-souled man as he is, he does not want to create unnecessary bitterness ... how can he help feeling dissatisfied? He would not be Jawaharlal if he did not strike out for himself an absolutely unique and original line in pursuance of his path. He considers nobody, not even his father, nor wife, nor child. His own country and his duty to his own country he considers and nothing else.' 28 December 1928, in Gandhi, *Collected Works*, vol. 38, pp. 284–85.

[73] Subhas Chandra Bose, *The Indian Struggle*, p. 175.

[74] Ibid., p. 175.

Calcutta at the end of the month and he was hoping to stay with Subhas.[75] The bonds between the two had grown stronger and they could see themselves as confrères in the left wing of the Congress. The British government in India noted this; the home secretary observed on 21 February 1929: 'If the experience of the Calcutta Congress is any guide, the decision of future policy appears to be almost entirely with the younger men notably Pandit Jawaharlal Nehru and Babu Subhas Chandra Bose, and on their intentions and activities future developments may be expected largely to depend.'[76]

This growing friendship between the two men experienced its first stress in the course of 1929. The tension was rooted in Jawaharlal's appointment as Congress president for the session in Lahore at the end of the year. Jawaharlal's elevation came, not unexpectedly, at the behest of Gandhi. It was Subhas's firm conviction that Gandhi had done this to drive a wedge into the left opposition that was emerging in the Congress. The Calcutta session had demonstrated that this opposition could not be trifled with. According to Subhas, Gandhi recognized the left as the principal challenge to his leadership and proceeded to divide the left. To quote Subhas, 'The Left Wing opposition at the Calcutta Congress had indeed been formidable and if his leadership was to be retained, he would have to deal with the opposition in a diplomatic manner. The tactics employed by the Mahatma . . . were indeed superb . . . [He] divided the ranks of the opposition by winning over some of the Left Wing leaders.'[77] It will not be unfair to conclude that the phrase 'some of the Left Wing leaders' referred to Jawaharlal.

The situation, however, was a little more complex than the motives that Subhas ascribed to Gandhi. Motilal was very keen to see his son as the president of the Congress and had discussed such a possibility with Gandhi in 1927. The latter had then felt that the time was not suitable for Jawaharlal to take over. Motilal renewed his efforts in 1928 but that year the views of the Congress

---

[75] Letter to M.K. Basu, 22 March 1929, in Nehru, *Selected Works*, vol. 3, p. 331.

[76] Quoted in Gopal, *Jawaharlal Nehru*, vol. 1, p. 123.

[77] Subhas Chandra Bose, *The Indian Struggle*, p. 176.

leaders in Bengal, where the session was held, had to be taken into account and they insisted that Motilal be the president.[78] Subhas had endorsed this move. Jawaharlal had then been quick to note that the 'real objection to me is not youth or jealousy but fear of my radical ideas'. Jawaharlal was clear that he would not 'tone down my ideas for the presidentship'.[79] In 1929, when his name came up for the presidentship, the two other contenders were Gandhi himself and Vallabhbhai Patel; ten Congress committees voted for Gandhi, five for Patel and three for Jawaharlal. Gandhi was declared elected but he resigned and a substitute had to be found. Gandhi wanted a younger person to lead, to inspire the youth of the country.[80] And he chose Jawaharlal.

Jawaharlal had been unwilling all along to be president. In early July, he admitted to Gandhi, 'I am very nervous about the matter and do not like the idea at all.'[81] Elaborating on his disinclination, a few days later he wrote to Gandhi: 'My personal inclination always is not to be shackled down to any office . . . I represent nobody but myself. I have not the politician's flair for forming groups . . . Most people who put me forward for the presidentship do so because they want to keep someone else out . . . This kind of negative backing is hardly good enough . . . If I have the misfortune to be president you will see that the very people who put me there, or many of them, will be prepared to cast me to the wolves.'[82] He urged Gandhi to become the president: 'There can be no doubt it will make all the difference in the world,' he wrote to him, 'whether you lead it or not. Of course you can lead, as you have done in the past, without being Congress President. But it would help matters certainly if you are also the official head of the organization. I feel that it would be a great gain

[78] Gopal, *Jawaharlal Nehru*, vol. 1, pp. 126–27.

[79] Letter to Syed Mahmud, 30 June 1928, in Nehru, *Selected Works*, vol. 3, p. 51.

[80] B. Pattabhi Sitaramayya, *The History of the Indian National Congress* (Bombay, 1935; repr. 1946), vol. 1, p. 347.

[81] Letter to Gandhi, 9 July 1929, in Nehru, *Selected Works*, vol. 4, p. 155.

[82] Letter to Gandhi, 13 July 1929, in ibid., pp. 156–7.

if you would preside.'[83] About a month later he sent a telegram to
Gandhi begging him not to press his name for the presidentship.[84]
Gandhi assured him that he would not be 'unduly pressing your
name on the country'; then he added, '[I]t is an ugly business for
anybody this time.'[85] Even Motilal, who dearly wanted to see his son
as Congress president, seeing Jawaharlal's reluctance overcame his
personal wishes and observed to Gandhi that forcing Jawaharlal to
be president would be unfair to him and to the country.[86]

But Gandhi prevailed and Jawaharlal was elected president of the
Congress in September 1929. Gandhi, in an article in *Young India*,
meaning to compliment Jawaharlal, wrote that making Jawaharlal
president was as good as making Gandhi the president—Jawaharlal
was Gandhi's alter ego.[87] It did not occur to him that such a statement
could be humiliating for Jawaharlal by making him out to be no
more than Gandhi's creature or merely his mirror image. Jawaharlal
was deeply unhappy with the outcome. He believed that he had been
elected 'simply because somebody had to fill the vacuum created.
I have been placed during the last few months in a very difficult
situation but now it is even worse. I realize thoroughly that few
people are keen on me but somehow or other, without many people
wanting it, I have been pitchforked into the Congress chair.'[88] In
despair, he wrote to someone who had offered his congratulations,
'I feel in spite of my scientific spirit and outlook that after all we are
to some extent playthings of fate.'[89] Looking back on this episode, he
commented candidly in his autobiography: 'I have seldom felt quite
so annoyed and humiliated as I did at that election. It was not that
I was not sensible of the honour, for it was a great honour . . . But

---

[83] Ibid.

[84] Telegram to Gandhi, 21 August 1929, in ibid., p. 158.

[85] Letter to Nehru, 22 August 1929, in Gandhi, *Collected Works*, vol. 41, p. 314.

[86] Gopal, *Jawaharlal Nehru*, vol. 1, p. 127.

[87] 'Who should wear the crown?', *Young India*, 1 August 1929, in Gandhi, *Collected Works*, vol. 41, pp. 239–41.

[88] Letter to Shiva Prasad Gupta, 1 October 1929, in Nehru, *Selected Works*, vol. 4, pp. 160–61.

[89] Letter to S.A. Brelvi, 7 October 1929, in ibid., p. 161.

I did not come to it by the main entrance or even a side entrance; I appeared suddenly by a trap-door and bewildered the audience into acceptance. They put a brave face on it, and, like a necessary pill swallowed me. My pride was hurt, and almost I felt like handing back the honour. Fortunately I restrained myself from making an exhibition of myself, and stole away with a heavy heart.'[90]

Within a month of having had the Congress presidentship thrust upon him, Jawaharlal found himself facing another situation that caused him immense discomfiture. From March 1929, the viceroy, Lord Irwin, had been eager to convey the impression to some Congress leaders that he was not completely deaf to the demands of the Congress. He attempted to do this by speaking through an intermediary, Grimwood Mears, the chief justice of the Allahabad High Court, to Motilal Nehru and Tej Bahadur Sapru. The suggestion was made by Mears that the British would call a Round Table Conference at which the case for Dominion Status for India could be mooted. Neither Motilal nor Sapru was averse to the idea.[91] During his furlough in London, Irwin discussed the matter with the leaders of three British political parties and in spite of intense opposition from various political groups came back to India in early October determined to issue what he termed the Declaration.[92] It stated that His Majesty's Government had come to the conclusion that 'the natural issue of India's constitutional progress . . . is the attainment of Dominion Status'. It was now the government's intention to invite 'representatives of different parties and interests' to a Round Table Conference in London to arrive at new constitutional proposals for India in consultation with British political leaders.[93]

The Congress had to formulate its response to this declaration. This was not as easy as it seemed. As the general secretary of the party, Jawaharlal informed all the members of the Working Committee

[90] *An Autobiography*, pp. 194–95.

[91] D.A. Low, *Britain and Indian Nationalism: The Imprint of Ambiguity, 1929–1942* (Cambridge, 1999), pp. 44–5.

[92] Andrew Roberts, *'The Holy Fox': The Life of Lord Halifax* (London, 1991; repr. 2004), pp. 26–29.

[93] Low, *Britain and Indian Nationalism*, p. 45.

not to issue conflicting statements till the Working Committee met informally to take a view of the matter.[94] Gandhi was convinced of the viceroy's sincerity and saw the declaration as a gesture of conciliation, but he was not clear about how he should respond to the announcement.[95] He wanted certain guarantees—conditions precedent. Jawaharlal drafted a response to the declaration. He began by recalling the resolution adopted at the Calcutta session of the Congress. He accepted the tone and the language of the declaration but he noted, 'there is no assurance in it that our demands will be acceded to in the near future'. He reiterated that '[T]here can be no common ground if even Dominion Status is considered a distant objective to be arrived at by successive stages', because the minimum demand was that of Dominion Status by the end of 1929. Failing this the Congress would move towards complete independence. He also pointed out that there would have to be changes in the way of administering the country through 'the abandonment of autocracy and an adherence to democratic methods'.[96] He was sceptical about Irwin's intentions. He was to observe later, 'It was an ingeniously worded announcement, which could mean much or very little, and it seemed to many of us obvious that the latter was the more likely contingency.'[97]

But at a meeting of some of the members of the Working Committee on 2 November at Gandhi's insistence a different draft—known as the Delhi Manifesto—was adopted. Contrary to what Jawaharlal believed or wanted, the Delhi Manifesto announced: 'We hope to be able to tender our cooperation to His Majesty's Government in their effort to evolve a scheme of Dominion constitution suitable for India's needs.' The manifesto laid down three conditions: (a) a more conciliatory policy to be adopted; (b) political prisoners should be granted amnesty; and (c) the representation of political organizations

---

[94] To all members of the Working Committee, 29 October 1929, in Nehru, *Selected Works*, vol. 4, p. 163.

[95] Gandhi, *Collected Works*, vol. 42, p. 64.

[96] The Congress and the viceroy's statement, November 1929, in Nehru, *Selected Works*, vol. 4, pp. 175ff.

[97] *An Autobiography*, p. 195.

be secured for the forthcoming conference, with the Congress having the predominant representation. The manifesto took it as a given that 'the conference is to meet not to discuss when Dominion Status is to be established but to frame a scheme of Dominion constitution for India'.[98]

It was not easy for Jawaharlal to sign this manifesto. At first, he refused, as did Subhas. According to one witness, Gandhi told Jawaharlal that he was entitled to his views but he could not remain a member of the Working Committee and president of the Congress if he differed from his other colleagues over as important a matter as the manifesto. Another report said, 'When Jawaharlal was signing he was in tears and Gandhi said, "Jawahar think well. If you put your signature honour the responsibility."'[99] Subhas felt let down by Jawaharlal and expressed his disappointment to Mrs C.R. Das: 'Jawaharlal has now given up Independence at the instance [sic] of the Mahatma.'[100]

If Subhas was disappointed by Jawaharlal's action, the latter was dejected and heartbroken. In his letter to Gandhi, two days after the signing, he expressed his anguish. He confessed that '[S]omething seems to have snapped inside me evening before last and I am unable to piece it together . . . the fever in my brain has not left me.' Gandhi had appealed to him on the ground of discipline and he had not been able to ignore that appeal. He added, 'I am myself a believer in discipline. And yet I suppose there can be too much of discipline.' He told Gandhi that his allegiance to the Congress as its general secretary had to be seen in the context of his 'other capacities and other allegiances' like his presidentship of the Indian Trade Union Congress, the secretaryship of the Independence for India League and his close links with the youth movement. 'What shall I do,' he asked, 'with the allegiance I owe to these and other movements I am

---

[98] The Delhi Manifesto, November 1929, in Nehru, *Selected Works*, vol. 4, pp. 165–66.

[99] Both these accounts are given in Low, *Britain and Indian Nationalism*, p. 51. The witness was Dr Moonje who recorded the incident in his diary which Low cites. The other account was Sapru's.

[100] Letter to Basanti Devi, 5 November 1929, in *Netaji: Collected Works*, vol. 4, pp. 273–74.

connected with? I realize now more than I have ever done before that it is not possible to ride a number of horses at the same time. Indeed it is hard enough to ride one. In the conflict of responsibilities and allegiances what is one to do except to rely on one's instincts and reason? I have therefore considered the position apart from all outside connections and allegiances and the conviction has grown stronger that I acted wrongly day before yesterday. I shall not enter into the merits of the statement or the policy underlying it. I am afraid we differ fundamentally on that issue . . . I shall only say that I believe the statement to have been injurious and a wholly inadequate reply to the Labour Government's declaration . . . I believe that we have fallen into a dangerous trap out of which it will be no easy matter to escape.' It was Jawaharlal's contention that the Delhi Manifesto had attempted 'to soothe and retain a few estimable gentlemen' and in so doing it had 'ruffled and practically turned out of our camp many others who were far more worth having'.[101] Jawaharlal could not have been unaware that Subhas belonged to the latter group. It will not be wrong to take that comment as an indicator of how much Nehru valued Subhas as a colleague and fellow patriot at this point of time. Subhas's disappointment was also an expression of his expectations of Nehru in this matter.

In the middle of the two individuals stood Gandhi. On the same day that Nehru wrote to him, Gandhi, having heard from others about Jawaharlal's troubled state of mind, tried to offer solace. 'I said to myself,' Gandhi told Jawaharlal, '"have I been guilty of putting undue pressure on you?" I have always believed you to be above undue pressure. I have always honoured your resistance.' He wondered why Jawaharlal was dejected if he had done nothing wrong. Offering justification for Jawaharlal's signature to the manifesto, Gandhi wrote, 'As an executive officer now and President for the coming year, you could not keep yourself away from a collective act of the majority of your colleagues. In my opinion your signature was logical, wise and otherwise correct.'[102] Probably because the two

---

[101] Letter to Gandhi, 4 November 1929, in Nehru, *Selected Works*, vol. 4, pp. 166–67.

[102] Letter to Nehru, 4 November 1929, in Gandhi, *Collected Works*, vol. 42, p. 96.

letters—Jawaharlal to Gandhi and the latter to Jawaharlal—were written on the same day and thus crossed each other, Gandhi did not know that Jawaharlal had already sent in his resignation as the general secretary of the Congress and the Working Committee. To the president of the party, his father Motilal, he pointed out that he had signed the statement to 'carry out the wishes of the majority' in spite of his disagreement with the statement. Under the circumstances, he felt that '[I]t would be most unfair to the Committee and to me if I continued to occupy a responsible position in the AICC and in the Working Committee when my views are opposed to those of the majority of its members.'[103] Gandhi, of course, would have none of this. On 8 November, he replied to Jawaharlal: '[Y]ou must not resign just now . . . it will affect the national cause.'[104]

Subhas's reaction to the Delhi Manifesto was straightforward. He rejected it and, together with S. Kitchlew and Abdul Bari, put forward an alternative manifesto. He also sent in his resignation from the Working Committee of the Congress. In his resignation letter he wrote, 'At today's conference I made my position clear with regard to the Viceregal pronouncement. I feel it is my duty to express my views publicly to explain the attitude of the Independence School. After hearing Mahatmaji's remarks at the conference this afternoon I feel convinced that I should not do so while I am a member of the Working Committee. I therefore beg to tender my resignation from the Working Committee.'[105] The manifesto that Subhas prepared with Kitchlew and Bari opposed the acceptance of Dominion Status as well as the idea of participating in the proposed Round Table Conference. In terms that echoed Jawaharlal's letter to Gandhi (at this point of time Subhas could not have known the contents of that letter), the manifesto warned that the viceroy's declaration was 'a trap laid by the British government'.[106]

---

[103] Letter to the President of the Congress, 4 November 1929, in Nehru, *Selected Works*, vol. 4, pp. 168–69.

[104] Letter to Nehru, 8 November 1929, in Gandhi, *Collected Works*, vol. 42, p. 116.

[105] Letter from Bose to President of AICC, 1 November 1929, AICC Papers, File No. G 117.

[106] Subhas Chandra Bose, *The Indian Struggle*, pp. 190–91.

Events, however, made both Jawaharlal's anguish and Subhas's disappointment irrelevant. Motilal had anticipated this, and given his political predilections, even apprehended it. Writing to Jawaharlal to persuade him to stay his hand on the resignation, Motilal had correctly predicted that the debate in the House of Commons would demonstrate that the British government would not accept the conditions contained in the Delhi Manifesto. He said that the Working Committee would have no other alternative but to take this as a rejection of its offer and thus recommend to the Congress to launch a civil disobedience campaign.[107] The debate in the Commons on 7 November was indeed acrimonious and weakened Irwin's position in India since his declaration had intended to assure Indians about the good faith of the British government.[108] Gandhi, either because he was influenced by Jawaharlal's opposition or because he had heard about the lack of enthusiasm in Britain regarding Irwin's declaration, was changing his tune. He had initially offered cooperation to the government but on 8 November, the day after the Commons debate, he said, '[U]nless there is a full response to what must be frankly considered to be the conditions enumerated in the leaders' manifesto there can be no peace.'[109] Irwin had caught on to the changed mood. On 13 November, he wrote to the secretary of state for India, William Wedgwood Benn: 'Jawaharlal thinks he has sold his soul by signing the leaders' manifesto . . . his path is again quite clear to carry Congress with him in a policy of rejection and of renewed advocacy of civil disobedience.'[110] Even Vallabhbhai Patel was apprehensive that 'Mahatma Gandhi surrounded as he is

---

[107] Letter from Motilal to Jawaharlal, 7 November 1929: cited in Low, *Britain and Indian Nationalism*, p. 54.

[108] Roberts, 'The Holy Fox', p. 30. Also see S. Gopal, '"Drinking Tea with Treason": Halifax in India', in S. Gopal, *Imperialists, Nationalists, Democrats: The Collected Essays*, (ed.) Srinath Raghavan (Ranikhet, 2013), p. 86.

[109] Letter to editor of *Kaiser-i-Hind*, 8 November 1929, in Gandhi, *Collected Works*, vol. 42, p. 123. On 14 November in *Young India*, he wrote, '[I]t is highly likely that the Labour government has never meant all the implications mentioned by me.' Gandhi, *Collected Works*, vol. 42, pp. 150–51.

[110] Letter from Irwin to Benn, 13 November 1929: cited in Low, *Britain and Indian Nationalism*, p. 57.

at present by the Nehrus . . . may be prevailed upon to repudiate the Delhi manifesto.'[111] Gandhi found himself exposed to twin pressures—one from Jawaharlal and the other from men like Sapru who were in favour of the Delhi Manifesto. Gandhi's resolution accommodated both views; it said in its last and crucial part, 'the working committee confirms the action taken by Congressmen at Delhi, it being clearly understood that this confirmation is constitutionally limited to the date of the holding of the forthcoming session of the Congress.'[112] At the same meeting, both Jawaharlal and Subhas (who had been persuaded to attend by Jawaharlal)[113] withdrew their resignations.[114]

The controversy over the Irwin declaration and the Delhi Manifesto showed that both Jawaharlal and Subhas were not unwilling, when required, to climb down from their stated positions. It is important to underline this since Subhas had been quick to criticize Jawaharlal for deserting the cause of independence at the behest of Gandhi. It would now appear that Subhas was susceptible to influence even when it came from quarters with which he was not entirely in agreement. On 22 November, Subhas issued a statement explaining the withdrawal of his resignation. He said that when Gandhi had stated at the Delhi conference that the decision of the Working Committee should be binding on all members, he had 'felt the force of the argument' and had thought that it would be better to resign from the Working Committee. By resigning, he had felt, he would be free to carry on his campaign for independence and his criticism of Irwin's declaration without causing any embarrassment to the other members of the Working Committee. But in the middle

---

[111] Ibid. Low does not cite any source for this quotation he attributes to Patel.

[112] Quoted in ibid., p. 61.

[113] Letter from Subhas to Jawaharlal, 11 November 1929, and from Jawaharlal to Subhas, 14 November 1929, AICC Papers, File No. G 117. Subhas's letter to Jawaharlal of 11 November was typewritten; it had the following handwritten postscript: 'Kindly tell Panditji [meaning Motilal] that his desire in the matter is a command to me . . .'

[114] AICC Papers, File No. G 117, 1929. At the bottom of Subhas's letter of resignation dated 1 November is the note dated 19 November: 'Resignation withdrawn in response to WC's resolution.' The signature is illegible.

of November, in the Working Committee, Motilal had explained to him that it was not necessary for him to resign since the Working Committee had room for various shades of opinion. That explanation and the resolution requesting Jawaharlal and Subhas to withdraw their resignation had made Subhas take back his resignation letter. Subhas felt that '[A]s long as the working committee gives me the liberty of speech and action, there is no reason why I should not serve on the Committee.'[115] What is remarkable is that when both of them recalled this phase of their lives, they did not mention the fact that both had in fact resigned from the Working Committee and had later withdrawn their resignation letters. Their radicalism was sincere but it could also be tempered in response to circumstances.

Irwin had no assurances to offer when on 23 December he met Gandhi, Jinnah, Patel, Motilal and Sapru. The path was now set for the Lahore congress. But, for Subhas, before that important Congress session, there was another contretemps concerning yet again a resignation letter. When Subhas heard that Motilal with the support of the Working Committee had prohibited the newly elected members of the AICC from Bengal, he dashed off a resignation letter to Motilal. He described the decision as 'arbitrary, unconstitutional and unprecedented'.[116] Dr B.C. Roy, a renowned physician and a powerful figure in Bengal politics who in the 1950s would become chief minister of the state, interceded to sort things out. Subhas realized that he had perhaps allowed his anger to get the better of him and that he had nothing to gain by alienating Motilal. He offered his apologies to Motilal and rejoined the Congress Working Committee. He even remarked that Motilal was like a father to him.[117] This was

[115] Statement explaining withdrawal of resignation, 22 November 1929, in *Netaji: Collected Works*, vol. 6, pp. 60–61.

[116] Letter from Bose to President of the Working Committee (AICC), 27 December 1929, AICC Papers, File No. G 120.

[117] Gordon, *Brothers Against the Raj*, p. 218, recounts this episode, and Subhas's description of Motilal as being like a father, without giving any source. Also see Subhas's statement in an interview with *Free Press*, 7 January 1930: *Netaji: Collected Works*, vol. 6, pp. 102–3. There are some differences in Gordon's account of the incident and Subhas's. The latter said that thanks to the efforts of B.C. Roy there was a

Subhas's second resignation in two months. Was he earning for himself a reputation for throwing resignation tantrums whenever things did not go to his liking? On both occasions he withdrew his resignation. It is also remarkable that in *The Indian Struggle* he did not recollect this resignation and its withdrawal just as he did not mention the withdrawal of his first resignation.

The 1929 Lahore session of the Congress was momentous for Jawaharlal. He was conscious of the honour that had been bestowed on him and of the fact that the triumph was not personal. A few years later, looking back on that 'vivid patch' of his memory, he commented, '[I] occupied the centre of the stage; . . . I knew well that this overflowing enthusiasm was for a symbol and an idea, not for me personally; yet it was no little thing for a person to become that symbol, even for a while.'[118] For Subhas, however, the session saw a series of setbacks.

Jawaharlal rode into the Congress session, amidst tumultuous applause, on a white charger. It is ironic that both Jawaharlal and Subhas, while showing their outward allegiance to Gandhi and his creed of non-violence, when it came to the choice of symbols to demonstrate the new spirit of independence and freedom, opted for things associated with military valour. Subhas donned a resplendent military uniform for the session in Calcutta, and Jawaharlal appeared in Lahore as India's gallant knight. Gandhi had found Subhas's exhibition risible; his thoughts on Jawaharlal's entry à la Sir Galahad are not known.

Jawaharlal had begun to draft his presidential address at the beginning of December[119]; he was convinced then that the meeting

---

compromise and the Working Committee agreed to admit the newly elected members. Subhas felt vindicated and did not mention about any apology to Motilal. Gordon writes, 'Dr B.C. Roy stepped in and persuaded all parties to allow an election disputes panel working with Motilal Nehru to confront this matter after the Congress session. In effect, he made Bose back off from his sweeping charges against the president and the Working Committee and rejoin the Congress executive.'

[118] *An Autobiography*, p. 201.

[119] Gopal, *Jawaharlal Nehru*, vol. 1, p. 133.

of the Congress leaders with the viceroy before Christmas would yield nothing. The address, not unexpectedly, began by placing the Indian situation in an international context. He was confident that '[t]he brief day of European domination' was fast nearing its end and 'Europe has ceased to be the centre of activity and interest'. The future lay with America and Asia. India was thus part of a world movement in which China, Turkey, Persia, Egypt and even Russia were participants. India could not remain in isolation. India had her own problems, 'difficult and intricate', but she could 'ignore the world . . . at [her] own peril'. While India had a message to give to the world, 'she has also to receive and learn much from the messages of other peoples'.

Turning to India's internal problems, Jawaharlal held that the country needed to find a solution to the problems of economic liberty and equality. Without these, India's social structure would not have stability. But the solution to the problem of economic inequality would have to 'be based on the genius of her people and be an outcome of her thought and culture'. He was confident that once this solution was found 'the unhappy differences between various communities, which trouble us today and keep back our freedom, will automatically disappear'. He turned to the subject of British rule in India and to what Dominion Status would mean. 'It would mean,' he said, 'the shadow of authority to a handful of Indians, and more repression and exploitation of the masses.' Under the circumstances, Indians had one goal before them: independence. About his own creed, Jawaharlal spoke frankly: 'I am a socialist and a republican, and am no believer in kings and princes, or in the order which produces the modern kings of industry, who have greater power over the lives and fortunes of men than even the kings of old.' He admitted that it would not be possible for the Congress, as it was constituted, to adopt a full socialistic programme. He added, however, 'that the philosophy of socialism has gradually permeated the entire structure of society the world over, and almost the only points in dispute are the pace and the methods of advance to its full realization'. India, too, would have to go through the socialist process if she sought to end her poverty and inequality, he held, though this process may have to adapt the ideal to the genius of the Indian race.[120]

The address was vintage Jawaharlal 1929. There was the uncompromising commitment to independence and the dream of socialism. Jawaharlal knew the dream had no place in the agenda of the Congress but he needed to state his own personal creed. Still, he had to lace the creed with a concession to the genius of India and the Indian people. He could not have been unaware of the contradictions and also of the fact that barely a month and a half ago he had put his signature to the Delhi Manifesto. Compromises were not welcome but there were times when they were unavoidable. He was conscious of the discipline that a membership and the high office of a party imposed on him. He occasionally strained at the leash but never to a breaking point.

Once the Congress session was over, Jawaharlal spent some time organizing the Independence Day celebrations that had been scheduled for 26 January 1930 and in drafting the pledge to be taken that day. He had wanted the day to be celebrated on 'a big and impressive scale'—the national flag would be unfurled in the morning and in the evening there would be processions and public meetings under the flag.[121] In the event, the plans had to be modified because Gandhi was not in favour of processions and speeches as he did not want to precipitate a crisis before he was ready with his plans for civil disobedience.[122] Jawaharlal conceded that too much stress should not be put on processions but he was aware that 'it is difficult to prohibit them'. He feared that if the government attempted to prevent the demonstrations on 26 January through the imposition of Section 144 or by other means, the dilemma would be whether to obey the order or to defy it.[123] In his instructions to the Congress Provincial Committees, Jawaharlal tried to convey this dilemma and then left the ultimate decision in the hands of the local

---

[120] Presidential Address, 29 December 1929, in Nehru, *Selected Works*, vol. 4, pp. 184–198.

[121] Letter to secretaries of PCCs, 6 January 1930; and statement to the press, 6 January 1930: Nehru, *Selected Works*, vol. 4, pp. 203–4.

[122] Letter to Nehru, 12 January 1930, in Gandhi, *Collected Works*, vol. 42, p. 392.

[123] Nehru to Gandhi, 17 January 1930, in Nehru, *Selected Works*, vol. 4, pp. 214–15.

committee with the caveat that if 'the meeting has to be held in the face of prohibition, care should be taken that everything is done in a peaceful and disciplined way'.[124] The Independence Day pledge was drafted jointly by Gandhi and Jawaharlal. It could be said that the celebrations around the first Independence Day on 26 January 1930 inaugurated the collaboration of Gandhi and Jawaharlal: they had together planned the event and had drafted the pledge.[125]

Subhas's experience in Lahore, in sharp contrast to Jawaharlal's heady one, was a trifle rough. It began, as noted earlier, with a resignation letter and its withdrawal. Early on in the session, Gandhi moved a resolution strongly condemning a bomb attack on the viceroy and congratulating him on his escape. The resolution was passed with a narrow majority. Subhas did not agree with Gandhi's and he wrote later, '[T]he feeling in the Congress was that the clause was uncalled for in a political resolution, but the Mahatma insisted on retaining it, probably because he wanted to placate Lord Irwin and prepare the ground for a rapprochement in future . . . the Mahatma made it a question of confidence.'[126] Subhas got his chance of expressing his disagreement with Gandhi when the latter moved the resolution for complete independence. On 31 December, Subhas made two speeches, both pushing Gandhi's resolution for complete independence a little further than Gandhi intended. In an amendment before the Subjects Committee, Subhas argued that Gandhi's programme would not carry the country to the goal of complete independence. 'I cannot see,' Subhas told the Congressmen, 'how we can reach our goal except by setting up a parallel government based on the goodwill of the people.' He advocated complete boycott of all bodies and, further, he wanted the Congress to identify itself with the cause of the oppressed classes. Essentially, Subhas believed

---

[124] Nehru's circular to PCCs, 17 January 1930, in Nehru, *Selected Works*, vol. 4, pp. 217–18.

[125] The joint nature is manifest in the flurry of letters and telegrams that passed between the two on this subject between 10 and 17 January 1930. These can be found very conveniently in *Together They Fought: Gandhi–Nehru Correspondence, 1921–1948*, (ed.) Uma Iyengar and Lalitha Zackariah (Delhi, 2011), pp. 103–11.

[126] Subhas Chandra Bose, *The Indian Struggle*, p. 193.

that boycott of the legislatures, and Gandhian constructive work were not adequate to bring forth independence.[127] The amendment was defeated. Subhas moved another amendment proposing an all-round boycott. While moving this amendment, he articulated what was perhaps a very important article of his creed and beliefs. He said, 'I am an extremist and my principle is—all or none.'[128] This amendment, too, was defeated.

Subhas had possibly expected the amendments to be defeated. But he was not quite prepared for what happened when the new Working Committee was selected on 1 January 1930. When the committee was announced, he discovered he and his ally, Srinivasa Iyengar, had been dropped while most of the older members had been retained. The authorized history of the Congress records that the Working Committee was formed by preparing two independent lists—one by Motilal in consultation with Gandhi and the other by Jamnalal Bajaj. There was a difference over one name (the name is not mentioned); this difference was resolved and the committee was formed. Subhas and Srinivasa Iyengar, however, wanted an election, and when their proposal was thrown out, there was 'a dramatic exit'. In 'less than ten minutes the news was broadcast that a new party was formed . . . which was [to] be known as the Congress Democratic Party'.[129]

What is implied in this account is that Subhas had come to the meeting prepared to form a separate party. In a statement made on 7 January, Subhas had said it was J.M. Sengupta, a former mayor of Calcutta and a rival of Subhas in Bengal politics, who had 'insinuate[d] that we walked out as a pretext for forming a

---

[127] Counter resolution at a Subjects Committee meeting on 31 December 1929: *Netaji: Collected Works*, vol. 6, pp. 94–97. Also see Subhas Chandra Bose, *The Indian Struggle*, p. 193.

[128] Speech at the Lahore session of the Congress, 31 December 1929, in ibid., pp. 97–100.

[129] Sitaramayya, *History of the Congress*, vol. 1, p. 360. He adds that soon after forming the new party, Subhas sent the following telegram to Mrs C.R. Das: 'Circumstances and tyranny of majority forced us to form separate party . . . named Congress Democratic Party.' Sitaramayya does not cite any source for this telegram but the text of the telegram was printed in the *Hindustan Times* of 5 January 1930. The clipping is preserved in NMML: AICC Papers, File No. G 126, 1930.

new party'.[130] Subhas's version thus differed from what was written
up as the authorized version some years later without taking into
account Subhas's two statements on the subject.[131] In his statements,
Subhas claimed that he and his group had reacted to the decision of
Jawaharlal, Gandhi and other leaders 'to form what they regarded
as a homogeneous party' and had thus 'resolved to exclude old
and tried members of the Working Committee on the ground of
incompatibility of temperament'. He alleged that this violated the
Congress constitution and existing practices. He said that if he and
his allies had been consulted, 'in all probability we would have
stepped aside'.[132]

There are two things that stand out in the statements of Subhas.
One is that the walkout and the decision to form a new party could
not be treated in isolation to what had taken place during the session
in Lahore. Subhas said, '[T]he fact is that the AICC meeting of 1
January proved to be the proverbial last straw. Throughout the
session of the Congress, members of our party had been shabbily
treated by the President and the Working Committee far from helping
us had virtually supported the President.'[133] The other, evident in the
above quotation, is Subhas's resentment towards Jawaharlal. Both
statements are peppered with criticisms of Jawaharlal, of which the
following is the most telling and perhaps representative as well: 'It
will be surprising to many that Mahatmaji and Pandit Jawaharlal
Nehru are now of one mind and there is no incompatibility of
temper between them. We do not know how the younger generation
in India will receive this news. It will be news to many. Pandit
Jawaharlal Nehru has now more in common with his erstwhile
friends of Dominion Status school than his erstwhile colleagues of

---

[130] Statement in an interview with *Free Press*, 7 January 1930: *Netaji: Collected Works*, vol. 6, pp. 102–05.

[131] Apart from the above, Subhas issued another statement, on 8 January 1930, as President of the Bengal Provincial Congress Committee (BPCC): *Netaji: Collected Works*, vol. 6, pp. 105–110.

[132] Statement to the *Free Press*, in ibid., p. 103.

[133] Ibid.

the Independence League.'[134]

Jawaharlal could not have been unaware of Subhas's ire against him, but he appeared unperturbed by it. His comments on the incidents in the Lahore session involving Subhas were only in passing. To a correspondent from Bengal, Jawaharlal wrote, 'I can assure you that I have not least bitterness against anybody. How can I have bitterness against people who have been my valued colleagues for years past?' He wrote that he failed to 'appreciate the inclusion of the personal factor in politics' but admitted that people's temperaments could differ. He could not see the latter as something that should stand in the way of working together. In the same letter, he took up the issue of forming a parallel government that Subhas had put forward in one of his amendments, and commented, 'I have no doubt that a time will come when a regular parallel government will have to be established in India . . . At the same time I feel that vague and tall talk often defeats its very purpose. Any campaign for independence must necessarily aim at parallel government at some stage. Civil disobedience and non-payment of taxes in a particular area practically means the organization of a parallel form of government.' Jawaharlal added that he could not see any 'vital difference' in the programmes of the Congress Democratic Party and the Congress. He wished that there was more clarity in the talk about left wing and right wing within the Congress.[135]

Perhaps the crucial difference in the approaches of Jawaharlal and Subhas at this stage was in the emphasis on what the former called 'the personal factor'. For Subhas, whatever had happened in Lahore was the outcome of Gandhi's attempts to drive a wedge between Jawaharlal and the radical elements in the Congress represented among others by Subhas. He believed that his amendments had been defeated because they became a 'question of confidence in the Mahatma and as the House did not want to repudiate him [Gandhi], it had no option but to give in to his demand'. He thus saw the

---

[134] Statement as President of BPCC, in ibid., p. 108.

[135] Letter to Abdur Rahim, 7 January 1930, in Nehru, *Selected Works*, vol. 4, pp. 205–06.

Lahore congress as 'a victory for the Mahatma' even though for 'the general public, unacquainted with the intricacies of politics or with the differences in the inner councils of the Congress, the Lahore Congress was a great inspiration'.[136]

What of the Congress Democratic Party? It sank almost without a trace. Subhas did not even mention it in *The Indian Struggle*. It had travelled very briefly in the van of Subhas's defiance and then had been consigned to the large collection of Indian nationalism's lost luggage.

To some extent, Subhas's pique with the Congress leadership was a reflection of the squabbles within the Bengal Congress.[137] Subhas was involved in these factional quarrels that divided the provincial leadership. Its origins went back to the untimely death in 1925 of C.R. Das, the first mentor of Subhas. When Das died, Gandhi suggested that J.M. Sengupta, a barrister-at-law who came from Chittagong, succeed Das in all the three posts he had held: mayor of Calcutta, head of the BPCC and the leader of the Swarajists in the Bengal Legislative Council. It was difficult to fathom the reasons for this suggestion since Sengupta at that time had not distinguished himself as a politician, nor was he one of Das's principal lieutenants. Sengupta served in all the three posts till 1927 when he gave up the presidentship of the BPCC to Subhas. Sengupta was often at odds with the 'Big Five' of Bengal politics—B.C. Roy, Tulsi Goswami, Nirmal Chandra, Nalini Sarkar and Subhas's brother, Sarat Bose— who saw him as an outsider in Calcutta because of his origins. There was no problem with Subhas on this score, and he could easily have been the sixth if the quintet had become a sextet. The problem began in 1928 when Sengupta stepped down as mayor. Subhas was a candidate for the post and when he lost, he blamed it on the lukewarm support he had received from Sengupta. The next year Sengupta was re-elected as mayor. Thus Sengupta ran the Calcutta Corporation and was the leader in the Legislative Council but the

---

[136] Subhas Chandra Bose, *The Indian Struggle*, p. 194.

[137] The broad contours of my account of the squabbles in the Bengal Congress are taken from Gordon, *Brothers Against the Raj*, pp. 213ff.

party was run by Subhas. The moot question was: who was more important in Bengal politics, Sengupta or Subhas? Sengupta was not without ability but he lacked Subhas's charisma.

In August 1929, the attention of the Congress high command was drawn to the divisions within the Bengal Congress when serious controversies arose over elections to the BPCC and the AICC. Sengupta found these controversies to be the result of a 'nefarious conspiracy'. He wrote to Jawaharlal to allege that 'there is a determined attempt on behalf of a group of men with which the executive is in league, to exclude people from membership of the Congress in the fear that the group would lose its power and would not be able to run the Congress according to their group ideas'.[138] Without naming Subhas, he was pointing an accusing finger at him. Subhas wrote to Jawaharlal in November 1929: 'As you may be aware Mr Sengupta is up in arms against me and is at the moment busy organizing his party for the purpose of hounding me out of the Bengal Provincial Congress Committee.'[139] Under the circumstances in which conflicting allegations were coming in from Bengal, Motilal, as the president of the Congress, sent Sitaramayya as his representative to Calcutta in late 1929 to make inquiries and to suggest ways to resolve the dispute. Unfortunately, Subhas and his brother Sarat did not take to Sitaramayya and accused him of favouring Sengupta. Sitaramayya was shocked by the state of affairs and the role played by leading Congressmen. He commented, 'It gave me an insight into the character of the leading men in the province.'[140] Moreover, in terms of organization the BPCC under Subhas left a lot to be desired. In 1929, the AICC auditor had complained that the cash books had not been balanced; payments had been made on voucher systems but these had not been passed by any authority; details of travel expenses had not been recorded; there was no salary register and all salaries had been paid through vouchers; not one

---

[138] Sengupta to Nehru, 15 August 1929, in AICC Papers, File No. P 6 (Part II).

[139] Subhas to Jawaharlal, 11 November 1929, in AICC Papers, File No. G 117.

[140] Sitaramayya to Motilal, 16 December 1929, in AICC Papers, File No. G 120.

district out of the thirty-two in Bengal had submitted accounts.[141]

Caught in this controversy and seeing the failure of the Bengal leaders to work out a solution to the disputes, on the eve of the Lahore session, Motilal decided that the sitting members of the AICC should continue until the Lahore session, after which he would try to resolve the issues. It was this decision that debarred the newly elected members from Bengal from the AICC—prompting Subhas's resignation and his strongly worded letter to Motilal, to whom he was devoted. He made the allegation in that letter that Motilal's decision 'was directly influenced by representations from Mr J.M. Sengupta and his party who have opposed the present BPCC'.[142] Subhas thus made his factional quarrels a cause for his resignation from the Working Committtee, a resignation that he later regretted and withdrew. Similarly, when Subhas issued his statement protesting against being dropped from the Working Committee at the Lahore congress, he brought in the name of Sengupta who he said had insinuated that he had already decided to form a new party.[143]

These episodes seem to suggest that Subhas was fully implicated in the unpleasant faction fighting that initiated the decline of the Congress in Bengal.[144] It is important not to see this factionalism as merely a leadership struggle or as only a clash between Subhas and Sengupta. There was also emerging a division within the Bengal Congress regarding its relationship with the Gandhi-led Congress, which dominated national politics. C.R. Das till his death had maintained his supreme position within the Bengal party and had not been subservient to the high command. Sengupta, appointed by Gandhi after Das's death, failed on both counts. Subhas, as Das's cup-bearer, began to emerge as the critic of Gandhian politics. This

---

[141] AICC Papers, File No, P 28 (Part II), 1929.

[142] Bose to President of the Working Committee (AICC), 1929, in AICC Papers, File No. G 120.

[143] Statement in an interview with *Free Press*, 7 January 1930: *Netaji: Collected Works*, vol. 6, p. 103.

[144] J. Gallagher, 'Congress in Decline: Bengal, 1930 to 1939' in J. Gallagher, *The Decline, Revival and Fall of the British Empire* (Cambridge, 1982; repr. 2004), pp. 155–211.

put him at odds with the Congress national leadership and with Jawaharlal. He was, however, unable, in spite of his popularity in Bengal, to establish his dominance within the Bengal Congress. In terms of the path that Subhas's political career was to take in the late 1930s, this point merits underlining. But these aspects of his life were swept aside by his arrest on his thirty-fourth birthday on 23 January 1930, immediately after his return from Lahore. Charged with sedition and unlawful procession, Subhas became His Majesty's guest in Alipore Central Jail for one year. Gandhi hailed his arrest but did not forget the divisions within the Congress in Bengal: 'My congratulations to Sjt Subhas Bose and his companions on one year's rigorous imprisonment for having dared to serve the country. Bengal may be rent into many divisions and parties. But Bengal's bravery and self-sacrifice can never wane.'[145]

Subhas was thus forced to learn in prison about the momentous events that occurred in early 1930: Gandhi's Dandi March and the launch of the Civil Disobedience Movement. Gandhi had been authorized by the Working Committee of the Congress to decide on the timing and the method of the Civil Disobedience Movement. He chose to do so by marching from his ashram in Sabarmati to the sea in Dandi to manufacture salt in defiance of the government's salt monopoly. He began his march on 12 March with a band of seventy-one dedicated disciples, and on 6 April he violated the salt law. Thus the Civil Disobedience Movement was inaugurated. The Dandi March has become the stuff of legend in the history of liberty across the world. Jawaharlal confessed later that he was at first 'bewildered' and 'could not quite fit in a national struggle with common salt'. But, salt, in the hands of Gandhi, 'suddenly became a mysterious word, a word of power'.[146]

Jawaharlal spent a few hours with Gandhi at Jambusar in the course of the march and recalled seeing him 'stride away with his party to the next stage in the journey to the salt sea. That was my last glimpse of him then as I saw him, staff in hand, marching along

[145] *Young India*, 30 January 1930, in Gandhi, *Collected Works*, vol. 42, p. 438.
[146] *An Autobiography*, p. 210.

at the head of his followers, with a firm step and a peaceful but undaunted look. It was a moving sight.'[147] More than two decades after the Dandi March, he wrote even more evocatively about the moment: 'Many pictures rise in my mind of this man, whose eyes were often full of laughter and yet were pools of infinite sadness. But the picture that is dominant and most significant is as I saw him marching, staff in hand, to Dandi on the Salt March in 1930. He was the pilgrim on his quest of truth, quiet, peaceful, determined and fearless, who would continue that quiet pilgrimage regardless of consequences.'[148] These recollections are important to understand Jawaharlal's relationship with Gandhi. As S. Gopal, Jawaharlal's biographer, has written, '[A]fter this experience it was not perhaps to be expected that, whatever the ideological and temperamental strains, Jawaharlal would ever completely break away from his leader.'[149]

Subhas remembered the Dandi March and the launch of the campaign as being among 'some of the most brilliant achievements of his [Gandhi's] leadership and they reveal the height to which his statesmanship can ascend in times of crises'. Gandhi's march to the sea to manufacture salt, Subhas placed through some bizarre logic 'at the same level [as] Napoleon's march to Paris on his return from Elba or Mussolini's march to Rome when he wanted to seize political power'.[150] Subhas, because he was in prison, never had the opportunity, like Jawaharlal, to see Gandhi in one of the greatest moments of his life. It was perhaps Subhas's misfortune that more often than not he encountered Gandhi in Congress meetings and in negotiations. He thus missed the more charismatic moments of Gandhi's personality and leadership.

Jawaharlal watched as Gandhi progressed to the sea and the government did not arrest him. He continued to prepare the party

---

[147] Ibid., p. 212.

[148] Written on 30 June 1951: Foreword to D.G. Tendulkar, *Mahatma*, vol. 1 (Bombay, 1951).

[149] Gopal, *Jawaharlal Nehru*, vol. 1, p. 141.

[150] Subhas Chandra Bose, *The Indian Struggle*, pp. 199 and 201.

workers and the youth for the coming movement. He campaigned intensively in the rural areas of UP. To a correspondent, he wrote a few days before Gandhi actually broke the law: 'There is no doubt that India is awake and astir and we are going to give a good fight to the British government . . . Somehow I cannot help thinking that the days of the British Empire are numbered now.'[151] Once the Civil Disobedience Movement commenced, Jawaharlal proceeded with his own selling of salt; and in Rae Bareli he formed associations of tenants for the non-payment of rent. The expected happened on 14 April when he was arrested and sentenced to six months' simple imprisonment in Naini Central Prison for assisting in the illegal manufacture of salt.

Thus, by April 1930, both Subhas and Jawaharlal were back in prison. The routine of life in jail took over. Both read; to keep himself fit, Jawaharlal ran a couple of miles every morning within the compound; Subhas meditated. But, for both, this routine was soon to be interrupted. On 22 April, Subhas, along with others, was severely beaten up by the police within the jail. Subhas's plight was particularly severe: he had head injuries and was unconscious for about an hour.[152] In the case of Jawaharlal, the assault was emotional. Within a month of his imprisonment, his father was arrested and lodged in the same compound as him, known in the jail as the *kuttaghar*—the doghouse.[153] He was shocked to see his father, as Motilal was in poor health and in no condition to bear the conditions of a prison. With the arrival of his father, Jawaharlal's principal occupation lay in looking after him.

Outside the prison walls, civil disobedience proceeded apace. Movements outside the folds of Gandhian non-violence stirred the country and struck fear in the corridors of power. One happened in Chittagong where under the leadership of Surya Sen, a group

[151] Letter to Roger Baldwin, 4 April 1930, in Nehru, *Selected Works*, vol. 4, pp. 298–99.

[152] Sugata Bose, *His Majesty's Opponent*, p. 79; and Gordon, *Brothers Against the Raj*, pp. 230–31.

[153] *An Autobiography*, p. 218.

of armed revolutionaries seized the local armoury, issued an Independence Proclamation and fought a pitched battle on 23 April. Their violent methods notwithstanding, the revolutionaries announced their triumph with the cry, 'Gandhi raj has come'. On the same day as the battle in Chittagong, a popular upsurge in Peshawar took the city out of British control, with Hindu soldiers refusing to fire on Muslim crowds. It took the British ten days to bring Peshawar under control. In Sholapur in Maharashtra, the news of Gandhi's arrest sparked off a textile strike on 7 May; crowds attacked liquor shops, police outposts and government buildings. It required the imposition of martial law before order could be restored on 16 May. The news of all this did not penetrate the walls of the prisons though Jawaharlal did get to know of the incident in Peshawar and of the one in Sholapur.[154]

These tumultuous events increased repression on the opponents of British rule; it also may have set in motion attempts to arrive at a truce. Before he was arrested, Motilal may have been instrumental, unwittingly, in raising hopes of such a peace. In jail, he expressed regret to Jawaharlal for having spoken in terms that suggested that the Congress was open to a compromise.[155] Motilal's words had galvanized the liberals, especially Sapru and Jayakar, to initiate a dialogue between the government and the Congress leaders. Sapru and Jayakar appointed themselves intermediaries and interviewed Gandhi in Yerwada jail on 23 and 24 July. Gandhi gave them a note for the Nehrus, then lodged in Naini prison. In this note, Gandhi said that the Round Table Conference should be restricted to a discussion of the safeguards necessary in connection with full self-government during the period of transition.[156] In a separate covering letter to Motilal, Gandhi admitted that he had grave doubts if the time was ripe for an honourable settlement. But he wanted Jawaharlal's to

---

[154] Gopàl, *Jawaharlal Nehru*, vol. 1, p. 144, and Prison Diary, May 17, in Nehru, *Selected Works*, vol. 4, p. 349.

[155] *An Autobiography*, p. 227.

[156] Gandhi's note to the Nehrus, 23 July 1930, in Sitarammaya, *History of the Congress*, vol. 1, pp. 637–38.

be the final voice in this decision. 'You and I,' Gandhi told Motilal, 'can only give our advice to him.' He added that the note he had given to Sapru and Jayakar represented 'the utmost limit to which I can go'. But he was open to a 'stronger position'.[157] The response of the Nehrus to the Sapru–Jayakar initiative was far less positive. Jawaharlal, particularly, had nothing but contempt for the liberals.[158] In a joint memorandum, both father and son made it clear that it was impossible for them, from within prison, to take any definite steps without consulting their colleagues, especially Gandhi.[159] Jawaharlal in a separate letter to Gandhi wrote more frankly. He confessed that neither he nor his father quite accepted Gandhi's position on the constitutional issue. But both of them agreed with Gandhi's statement that they could not be 'parties to any truce which would undo the position at which we have arrived today'. Jawaharlal was not optimistic about any truce and he did not want to issue any statement that could be interpreted as weakness on the Congress's part. Speaking about himself, he told Gandhi, 'I delight in warfare. It makes me feel that I am alive. Events of the last four months in India have gladdened my heart and have made me prouder of Indian men, women and even children than I had ever been, but I realize that most people are not warlike and like peace and so I try to suppress myself and take a peaceful view.'[160]

As a fallout of all this, Motilal, Jawaharlal and Syed Mahmud were taken by special train to Yerwada where a meeting was held where other than the three mentioned above, Sapru, Jayakar, Gandhi, Vallabhbhai Patel, Sarojini Naidu and Jairamdas Doulatram were present. The Congress leaders signed a memorandum on 15 August

---

[157] Gandhi to Motilal, 23 July 1930, in Nehru Papers, File No. 125.

[158] In his Prison Diary on 31 May 1930, Nehru noted: 'Some of the moderates are waking up, but some behave like old women—weeping and howling and feeling terribly oppressed about everything! . . . It is enough to sicken one to hear them sing the praises of Irwin & Benn & Co! It is difficult to imagine a greater babe at the political game than the moderate in India.' Nehru, *Selected Works*, vol. 4, pp. 357–58.

[159] Memorandum by Motilal and Jawaharlal Nehru, 28 July 1930, in Sitaramayya, *History of the Congress*, vol. 1, p. 639.

[160] Letter to Gandhi, 28 July 1930, in Nehru, *Selected Works*, vol. 4, pp. 369–70.

that stated that the time was not yet ripe for a settlement honourable for India. The signatories underlined the fact that they had seen 'no symptom of conversion of the English official world to the view that it is India's men and women who must decide what is best for India'. In spite of this, they said, a solution could be possible if the British government: (a) recognized the right of India to secede from the British Empire; (b) gave to India a complete national government responsible to her people, including the control of defence forces and economic control; and (c) gave to India the right to refer if necessary to an independent tribunal such British claims, concessions, etc. that are seen by the national government to be unjust or not in the interests of the people of India.[161] The viceroy, Lord Irwin, found the points raised by the Congress leaders unacceptable, and the Nehrus, now back in Naini prison, informed Gandhi on the last day of August that the efforts of Sapru and Jayakar to broker a truce had been in vain.[162]

There was one aspect of these talks and exchange of letters that did not escape the notice of the top British officials. The secretary of state for India, Wedgwood Benn, wrote to the viceroy in September that he had been struck by 'Gandhi's deference to Jawaharlal and Jawaharlal's pride in what had been achieved as well as his declaration of belief in non-violence. It was the apparent pride which depressed me, because it did not show the spirit of a beaten man.'[163] British officialdom was slowly beginning to acknowledge that in India they had to reckon with another voice, apart from Gandhi's.

This foray into political negotiations had left Motilal exhausted, and Jawaharlal watched in alarm as his father's health declined. Motilal was released on 8 September and Jawaharlal in early October. The latter's reprieve was for only eight days and he was back in Naini prison on 19 October. This spell in prison was an anxious

---

[161] 'Congress Leaders' Demands', 15 August 1930, in Sitarammaya, *History of the Congress*, vol. 1, pp. 641–42.

[162] Letter to Gandhi, 31 August 1930, in Nehru, *Selected Works*, vol. 4, pp. 379–83.

[163] Letter from Benn to Irwin, 3 September 1930, in Gopal, *Jawaharlal Nehru*, vol. 1, p. 146.

time for Jawaharlal as it was apparent that his father was dying. Motilal breathed his last on 6 February 1931. Jawaharlal felt this loss much more than his undemonstrative nature allowed him to show. He had on occasion strongly differed with his father on political issues but he had always been conscious of his profound dependence on Motilal. Jawaharlal was one of those persons who needed to lean on a father-like figure. He admitted in his autobiography that 'my father's death had brought him [Gandhi] particularly near to me'.[164] In this sense, the death of Motilal had political consequences by bringing Nehru closer to Gandhi than ever before. This closeness almost inevitably left its imprint on Nehru's relationship with Subhas.

When Motilal died, Subhas was in prison.[165] It is thus not clear when he heard the news—in prison as soon as the death occurred or after his release in March 1931, a month or so after the event. What is worth noting is that there does not seem to be any letter of commiseration that he wrote to Jawaharlal on the latter's bereavement. It is possible that he wrote and the letter has not survived. But this appears unlikely since so much of the correspondence between the two has actually survived and has been archived. Neither did Subhas issue any public statement on Motilal, the man whose desire he saw as an order.[166] This failure—if failure it was—to acknowledge a loss, to offer condolences, was not in keeping with Subhas's manners and temperament. Was it his own sufferings in jail and the subsequent tide of political events that made him neglect his personal and social obligations? Or had there been a temporary falling out between him and the Nehrus, father and son, following the dropping of Subhas from the Congress Working Committee in Lahore? The word 'temporary' is used advisedly since the mid-1930s saw a great deal of warmth between Subhas and Jawaharlal, and in *The Indian Struggle*, Subhas wrote

---

[164] *An Autobiography*, p. 255.

[165] During this period, Subhas spent three terms in prison: January–September 1930; January–March 1931; and January 1932–February 1933.

[166] See the handwritten postscript to his letter to Nehru, 11 November 1929: AICC Papers, File No. G 117. Cited above in fn. 114.

with the highest regard for Motilal. He described Motilal's death as 'lamentable' and called him 'the last intellectual stalwart of the Congress . . . a leader among men'—'the one man in the Congress Working Committee who could have influenced the Mahatma for good'.[167] But in a totally uncharacteristic lapse of memory he got the month of Motilal's death wrong.[168]

Between 1930 and 1933, during the periods that Subhas was a free man, he got drawn into Bengal provincial politics and the affairs of the Calcutta Corporation. Neither of these was particularly edifying, marked as both were by factional squabbles and petty-mindedness. These wranglings were rooted in the rivalry between Subhas and J.M. Sengupta, as elaborated earlier. The latter was seen as Gandhi's man and Subhas as the defiant leader from Bengal who did not hesitate to speak his mind, even if he later regretted doing so. Subhas had been particularly irked by the inclusion of Sengupta in the Working Committee when he himself had been dropped. This internecine strife reached such proportions that Bengal actually had two civil disobedience committees. Even Subhas was forced to admit that '[T]hese dissensions lowered the prestige of the Congress.'[169] The same leaders and the same factions fought to dominate both the provincial Congress and the Calcutta Corporation, and there was little to distinguish between the skirmishes of one field from those in the other. In disgust, Jawaharlal wrote, 'It is exceedingly unfortunate that in spite of the fact that the whole country is on the verge of civil disobedience and we are faced with the biggest national struggle of our generation petty election squabbles should go on in Calcutta and should to some extent neutralize the effort of Bengal

---

[167] Subhas Chandra Bose, *The Indian Struggle*, p. 232.

[168] He mentions it as March in ibid. And on p. 221, he writes that on 14 February 1931, Gandhi applied for an interview with Irwin and then proceeded to Delhi to meet the viceroy. Most of the members of the Working Committee went with Gandhi except Motilal who, says Subhas, 'was too ill'. Motilal had, in fact, died on 6 February 1931. After the publication of *The Indian Struggle*, Subhas wrote to Jawaharlal on 4 October 1935: 'Regarding Pandit Motilalji's death, I remember that I taxed my brain for a long time in order to recall the exact date—but I falied.' *Netaji: Collected Works*, vol. 8, p. 109.

[169] Ibid., p. 214.

in the coming fight . . . It has been an amazing sight—on the one side the country ringing with preparations for civil disobedience; on the other Congressmen spending their time and energy and money in attacking each other for the purpose of gaining admittance to the Calcutta Corporation.'[170] It is difficult to comprehend why Subhas allowed himself to become a leading participant in this faction-mongering. Was it because he found it difficult to resist the mantle of Das, his mentor and ideal? Or was it because he resented Sengupta's closeness to Gandhi and the Congress high command? After being removed from the Working Committee and finding his own new party a non-starter, he probably felt left out at the national level. The province and the municipality beckoned as sources and levers of power. He chose for the moment to be the big fish in the provincial pond.

Subhas had been elected mayor of Calcutta while he was still in prison and he assumed office when he was released in September 1930. In his inaugural speech, he made the following observation: 'I would say that we have here in this policy and programme a synthesis of what Modern Europe calls Socialism and Fascism. We have here the justice, the equality, the love, which is the basis of Socialism, and combined with that we have the efficiency and the discipline of Fascism as it stands in Europe today.'[171] This could very well be Subhas's first public utterance about what he saw in 1930 as the positive features of fascism.[172] At this point it is best to flag the statement. There will be occasion in a later chapter to come back to this theme.

At the national level, in March 1931, much to the bewilderment and disappointment of both Subhas and Jawaharlal, the Civil Disobedience Movement was halted by the Gandhi–Irwin pact. Jawaharlal watched the steps leading up to this truce from close

---

[170] Note on the 'Congress Disputes in Bengal', 29 March 1930, in Nehru, *Selected Works*, vol. 4, pp. 263–64.

[171] The Mayoral Address, 27 September 1930, in *Netaji: Collected Works*, vol. 6, pp. 126–33.

[172] Gordon, *Brothers Against the Raj*, p. 235, says that to his knowledge this is the first mention.

quarters as he was actually in Delhi and had the opportunity to spent some time with Gandhi. In his autobiography, he wrote candidly about his feelings regarding the pact: 'The thing had been done, our leader had committed himself; and even if we disagreed with him, what could we do? Throw him over? Break from him? Announce our disagreement? That might bring some personal satisfaction to an individual, but it made no final difference to the final decision . . . in my heart there was a great emptiness as of something precious gone, almost beyond recall. "This is the way the world ends, / Not with a bang but a whimper."'[173]

Apart from their disappointment, there was one other thing about which both Subhas and Jawaharlal were in agreement. Both of them felt that if Motilal had been there, he could have averted the setback that the Gandhi–Irwin pact represented. One year after the truce had been signed, Jawaharlal recorded in his prison diary, '[A]lways when thinking of the truce people start guessing what might have happened if father had been there and there appears to be a general consensus that events would have taken a very different turn. Foolishly I said so in Delhi a few hours after the truce. How Bapu was pained at my remark!'[174] Subhas, too, believed that the presence of Motilal would have made a difference. As we have seen, he regretted the fact that Motilal had not been able to go to Delhi in the middle of February 1931 to be with Gandhi. In a previous paragraph we have already quoted Subhas's belief, written in the context of the Gandhi–Irwin pact, that Motilal was the one man who could influence Gandhi 'for the good'.

Jawaharlal met Gandhi early in the morning the day after the pact had been signed. Gandhi had heard about Jawaharlal's distress and had wanted to speak to him. Jawaharlal found Gandhi's justification of what he had done to be 'forced'. He was not convinced but the talk soothed him. This did not stop Jawaharlal, however, from telling Gandhi that 'his way of springing surprises upon us frightened me; there was something unknown about him

---

[173] *An Autobiography*, pp. 257–59.

[174] Prison Diary, 4 March 1932, in Nehru, *Selected Works*, vol. 5, p. 363.

which, in spite of the closest association for fourteen years, I could not understand at all and which filled me with apprehension.' Gandhi confessed that there was this presence of an unknown element in him and he could offer no assurances about it or predict where it might lead to. The pact left Jawaharlal in 'great mental conflict and physical distress'.[175]

Subhas learnt about the pact in prison. Unknown to him, his name had cropped up, tangentially and in a confusing way, at the very beginning of the talks between Gandhi and Irwin. According to Irwin, Gandhi had said that he would like other Congressmen to be present with him at the meeting and he had mentioned the name of Subhas, among others. But Gandhi's account of the same meeting and conversation is at variance with the viceroy's one. When Subhas's name came up, Gandhi had apparently said that Subhas was not a member of the Working Committee, and added, 'He is my opponent and will denounce me; still, if he wants to attend, we must give him a chance to do so.'[176] What is important about this anecdote is that despite being in jail and preoccupied with provincial and municipal politics, Subhas was seen by others, including Gandhi and Irwin, as a figure of national importance.

Disappointed though he was, Subhas decided not to make any public criticism of Gandhi and the pact. As soon as he was released from prison, he rushed to Bombay to meet and talk to Gandhi. From Bombay he travelled with Gandhi to Delhi. In the course of this trip, he saw for himself the popularity of Gandhi. As large crowds greeted Gandhi, Subhas was led to wonder 'if such a spontaneous ovation was ever given to a leader anywhere else. He [Gandhi] stood out before the people not merely as a Mahatma but as the hero of a political fight.'[177] From Delhi, Subhas moved to Karachi for the Congress session which took place under the shadow of the execution of Bhagat Singh and his comrades. Many believed that Gandhi had been unwilling to break his pact with Irwin to secure a reprieve for

---

[175] *An Autobiography*, p. 260.

[176] Both versions are available in Gandhi, *Collected Works*, vol. 45, pp. 196 and 200.

[177] Subhas Chandra Bose, *The Indian Struggle*, p. 236.

Bhagat Singh. When Gandhi arrived in Karachi, he was met with a black-flag demonstration. One version described the protestors as 'Subhas youths'.[178]

The execution of Bhagat Singh affected both Jawaharlal and Subhas. The latter, in a speech delivered in Karachi a few days after the Congress session, spoke about Bhagat Singh and about the Gandhi–Irwin pact: 'Bhagat Singh was a symbol of the spirit of revolt which has taken possession of the country from one end to the other. The spirit is unconquerable, and the flame which the spirit has lit up will not die . . . These recent executions are to me sure indications that there has been no change of heart on the side of the Government and the time for an honourable settlement has not arrived as yet.' He said that he found the terms of the truce to be 'exceedingly unsatisfactory and highly disappointing'.[179] Jawaharlal's reaction was similarly powerful and poignant: 'Not all of us could save him who was so dear to us and whose magnificent courage and sacrifice have been an inspiration to the youth of India. India today cannot even save her dearly loved children from the gallows . . . when England speaks to us and talks of a settlement there will be the corpse of Bhagat Singh between us, lest we forget.'[180]

For both Subhas and Jawaharlal, time was running out to be free men. Gandhi returned from the Round Table Conference in London at the end of 1931 with nothing gained. Jawaharlal was arrested on 26 December 1931, a few days before Gandhi's arrival back in India; Subhas's arrest followed in early January 1932. These were part of a pre-planned campaign of repression that the government unleashed on the Congress and other freedom fighters. The year 1931, after the Gandhi–Irwin agreement, saw nationalist activity at a low ebb. Subhas toured parts of Bengal and attempted to restore some sort of order in the Bengal Congress. To achieve this, he even resigned as the

[178] Gordon, *Brothers Against the Raj*, p. 242.

[179] Presidential Address at the Karachi Conference of the All India Naujawan Bharat Sabha, 27 March 1931, in *Netaji: Collected Works*, vol. 6, pp. 147–49.

[180] On execution of Bhagat Singh, 24 March 1931, in Nehru, *Selected Works*, vol. 4, p. 500.

president of the Bengal Congress in September 1931.[181] Jawaharlal, on his part, worked among the peasants of UP who were badly hit at this time by an agrarian crisis.

Subhas's imprisonment, made somewhat bearable by the presence of his elder brother Sarat, brought about a sharp deterioration in his health. His removal to a sanatorium did little to improve his condition. He was forced to admit that he would accept the government's offer of allowing him to travel to Europe at his own expense for treatment. The government would on no plea set him free on Indian soil. He was not even allowed to see his parents. Subhas would thus never see his father again. He was put aboard a ship directly from jail. A curtain thus came down on one act of the life of Subhas. He himself was aware of this.[182] The exile in Europe would give to his life, political and personal, unexpected directions.

Jawaharlal remained in India, in and out of prison, till the illness of his wife Kamala also took him to Europe. This point in the lives of the two men—one forced into exile in Europe, and the other only occasionally a free man and soon to depart to Europe—is a convenient point to reflect on their involvement in the Congress and the national movement up to the early 1930s. Both had turned to nationalism sacrificing what could have been lucrative careers. This choice in the case of Jawaharlal had been largely determined by his meeting with Gandhi; Subhas had not fallen under that spell, serving his country had come to him as a calling, in somewhat the same way it had come to Gandhi himself many years ago. The pattern of Jawaharlal's and Subhas's relationship with Gandhi was also set in these years. Both respected and admired him; both saw him as the undisputed leader of the Indian people; but neither, in their respective ways, was blind to his faults. But while Subhas preferred to publicly air his differences with Gandhi and to cast himself, often, as his opponent, Jawaharlal's dissent was more muted and therefore more angst-ridden. He found it difficult to break with Gandhi even

---

[181] Gordon, *Brothers Against the Raj*, pp. 250–51.

[182] 'One chapter of my life has ended': Letter to Satyendra Nath Majumdar, 28 April 1933. *Netaji: Collected Works*, vol. 8, pp. 8–10.

when he differed fundamentally and strongly with him. The nature
of both their relationships with Gandhi was manifest in the way they
addressed him. For Subhas, it was always Mahatmaji, respectful but
distant; for Jawaharlal, it was invariably Bapu, personal, intimate,
almost like a son to his father.

The terms and the pattern of Jawaharlal and Subhas's relationship
with the most important public figure in India as they came to be
established through the 1920s and the early 1930s carried signs
for the future. Even without any retrospective knowledge it was
possible to say in the 1930s that if one of them were to break with
Gandhi, it would be Subhas and not Jawaharlal. Yet there was much
that brought Jawaharlal and Subhas ideologically close. Both had
emerged as champions of independence without any concessions and
compromises; both had come to believe that this independence would
be empty without the participation of the workers, the peasants
and the young; both saw themselves as socialists (the nature of the
socialism they upheld will be discussed in a subsequent chapter);
and both saw the Indian national movement as a part of a global
struggle against imperialism. The bonds between the two were of
political respect and of mutual intellectual recognition. They were
not yet friends but were ideological comrades, though they differed
sharply in their views about the leader.

There was one man, however, for whom both had unalloyed
respect. This was Motilal Nehru. Subhas saw in Motilal a father-
like figure after the death of C.R. Das; Motilal to him was an astute
political person not given to utopian dreams. Jawaharlal grew out
of his father's shadow and criticized his moderate views; but as
Motilal's political views evolved, perhaps as he watched his son's
activities, Jawaharlal came to value his sagacity and missed his
'sheltering wisdom'[183] when he was gone. Their enforced sojourns to
Europe—Subhas's had already begun and Jawaharlal's was about to
commence—represented in a way their flight from their nests, away
from their familiar terrains, their mentors and their paterfamilias.
Europe would help both to come into their own.

---

[183] The phrase is Gopal's. *Jawaharlal Nehru*, vol. 1, p. 150.

4

Two Women and Two Books

It was to Vienna, the emblematic city of the decaying European aristocracy, that Subhas, the advocate of ascendant Indian nationalism, came in March 1933. Subhas was lonely in Vienna. This was not because he was homesick, ill and bereft of friends and family in an alien land. The reasons were more profound. There was a sense of alienation as he was physically in Vienna but 'my mind and entire being' were in India, seeking a method to make India, the 'half-awake nation attain self-fulfilment and be victorious'. He was acutely conscious that he was embarking on a new phase of his life. He believed, as he wrote to a Bengali friend and colleague a month after he had arrived in Vienna, that '[I]n our national history also the old chapter had come to an end. The chapter that started in 1920 is now closed.' It was never to return. A new method, a new sense of power would have to be found 'in our own souls'. In that same letter, he wrote, '[W]here I have taken my stand today, I am alone, friendless. When I look around I feel as if, there is all round me an endless desert of solitude.' He had in his heart the famous song of Rabindranath Tagore: 'If no one hearkens to your call, march ahead alone.' This loneliness was, however, necessary and transient. The path to richness and fulfilment in life was invariably solitary.[1]

The loneliness was perhaps also a symptom of his inner

[1] Letter to Satyendranath Majumdar, 28 April 1933, in *Netaji: Collected Works*, vol. 8, pp. 8–10.

restlessness. Subhas was eager to carve out a role for himself during the period he was forced to be in exile in Europe. He saw himself as the ambassador of Indian nationalism. He wrote to his nephew very soon after his arrival in Vienna to say that 'outside India, every Indian is India's unofficial ambassador'.[2] He could not keep himself distant from what was happening in his own country. In May 1933, he heard that Gandhi had withdrawn the Civil Disobedience Movement. He and Vithalbhai Patel, the elder brother of Vallabhbhai who was also in Vienna for treatment and had become a friend of Subhas's, issued a joint statement. The Bose–Patel manifesto contained some clues about the new message that Subhas was seeking and intended to imbibe among Indians. The statement said, 'We are clearly of [the] opinion that as a political leader Mahatma Gandhi has failed. The time has therefore come for a radical reorganization of the Congress on a new principle and with a new method. For bringing about this reorganization a change of leadership is necessary . . . If the Congress as a whole can undergo this transformation, it would be the best course. Failing that a new party will have to be formed within the Congress, composed of all radical elements. Non-cooperation cannot be given up but the form of non-cooperation will have to be changed into a more militant one and the fight for freedom to be waged on all fronts.'[3]

There was no equivocation on this. Gandhi had failed and his methods were no longer viable for Subhas. The national movement needed militancy and radicalization. Having floated a new party that was stillborn, Subhas was not shy about suggesting the formation of another new party though it would be within the fold of the Congress. The banner of the Congress could not be rejected. Similarly, the radical direction the new party was expected to take remained unspecified. What is significant is that in his mind and in his ideological orientation, by the summer of 1933, he had already broken with Gandhi.

In India, often within prison walls, Jawaharlal was also reviewing

---

[2] Quoted in Gordon, *Brothers Against the Raj*, p. 256.
[3] Ibid., p. 271.

his political and ideological position in the context of Gandhi's withdrawal of the Civil Disobedience Movement, his fasts and his focus on the removal of untouchability. He was seriously upset by Gandhi's decision to halt the Civil Disobedience Movement. In his autobiography, he was to record the sense of loss and vacuum that overwhelmed him when he got the news of the withdrawal. He was frightened by Gandhi's statement that Congressmen should turn to social work—to the spread of khadi, to hand-spinning and hand-weaving. He was appalled, and he wrote, 'This was the political programme that we were to follow. A vast distance seemed to separate him [Gandhi] from me. With a stab of pain I felt that the chords of allegiance that had bound me to him for many years had snapped.'[4] A couple of entries in the diary he kept in prison in 1933 are also revealing. About a month after Gandhi began his self-purificatory fast on 8 May 1933, Jawaharlal wrote, '[A]s I watched the emotional upheaval during the fast I wondered more and more if this was the right method in politics. It is sheer revivalism and clear thinking has not a ghost of a chance against it . . . I am afraid I am drifting further and further away from him mentally, in spite of my strong emotional attachment to him.'[5] A little more than a month after this, his comment was even stronger: 'I am getting more and more certain that there can be no further political cooperation between Bapu and me. At least not of the kind that has existed. We had better go our different ways.'[6]

The views expressed in these statements are in substance no different from the ones expressed by Subhas sitting in Vienna. The issue of Subhas breaking away from Gandhi was an inconsequential one in 1933 since he was away in Vienna, far away from the hurly-burly of Indian politics. But for Jawaharlal it was a live one. In his case, as we know, the deed did not follow the words. The reason he failed to make that break with Gandhi is available in the first of the two diary entries just quoted. In one of them Jawaharlal wrote of

---

[4] *An Autobiography*, p. 506.

[5] Prison Diary, 4 June 1933, in Nehru, *Selected Works*, vol. 5, p. 478.

[6] Prison Diary, 18 July 1933, in ibid., p. 489.

'my strong emotional attachment to him'. He was deeply moved by the letter—a 'typical cry from the heart'—that Gandhi wrote to him as he commenced his fast. Jawaharlal responded by a telegram in which he wrote, '[W]hat can I say about matters I do not understand. I feel lost in strange country where you are only familiar landmark and I try to grope my way in dark but I stumble.'[7] The nature and the depth of this attachment could be seen in his reactions to the fast that Gandhi undertook in 1932.

When Gandhi had announced his fast unto death in September 1932 against Ramsay MacDonald's decision to set up separate electorates for the Depressed Classes, or as Gandhi called them, the Harijans, Jawaharlal had an emotional crisis—'I cried and wept.'[8] He could not bear the thought that Gandhi could die. He was annoyed that Gandhi had chosen a side issue for 'his final sacrifice', and was confused about what this meant for the freedom movement.[9] But what overwhelmed these political considerations was the sense of personal loss. To his daughter Indira, he wrote in September 1932, '[I] am shaken up completely and I know not what to do. News has come, terrible news, that Bapu has determined to starve himself to death. My little world in which he has occupied such a big place, shakes and totters, and there seems to be darkness and emptiness everywhere . . . Shall I not see him again? And whom shall I go to when I am in doubt and require wise counsel, or am afflicted and in sorrow and need loving comfort?'[10]

His sense of loss was no doubt aggravated by the fact that he was in prison. Regaining his composure, he sent a telegram to Gandhi where he confessed his mental agony and confusion but ended with the telling words, 'how can I presume to advise a magician'.[11] Jawaharlal's political differences with Gandhi, as he

---

[7] Prison Diary, 8 May 1933, in ibid., p. 474. This also gives the text of the telegram. For the letter to Nehru, 1 May 1933, see Gandhi, *Collected Works*, vol. 55, p. 96.

[8] Prison Diary, 22 September 1932, in Nehru, *Selected Works*, vol. 5, p. 408.

[9] Ibid., p. 407.

[10] Letter, 15 September 1932, in Jawaharlal Nehru, *Glimpses of World History* (Allahabad, 1934–35; repr. Delhi, 2004), p. 379.

[11] Letter to Gandhi, 25 September 1932, in Nehru, *Selected Works*, vol. 5, pp. 409–10.

himself recorded, were vast and in ideological terms unbridgeable, but Gandhi was his personal anchor—'the only familiar landmark'. There was also the awareness—hinted at perhaps in the use of the word 'magician'—that Gandhi alone of all the leaders had the rare gift of feeling the mood of the people and leading them in a campaign. These factors prevailed upon Jawaharlal and prevented him from chalking out a separate path from that of Gandhi. This was exasperating for some of his ideological comrades, especially for Subhas. The latter expressed his sense of disappointment in *The Indian Struggle*: '[W]ith a popularity only second to that of the Mahatma, with unbounded prestige among his countrymen, with a clear brain possessing the finest ideas, with an up-to-date knowledge of the modern world movements—that he should be found wanting in the essential quality of leadership, namely the capacity to make decisions and face unpopularity if need be, was a great disappointment.'[12] Subhas's summing up of Jawaharlal's dilemma was both pithy and apposite: 'His head pulls one way and his heart in another direction. His heart is with Gandhi.'[13]

One reason for Jawaharlal's growing ideological distance from Gandhi was his attraction to socialism and communism. His intellectual conversion to the Marxist way of looking at history and to socialism was articulated in the articles he wrote around this time and in the statements that he made; the most coherent evidence of this is available, however, in the letters that he wrote to his daughter Indira from prison. These letters were brought together in a book called *Glimpses of World History*. In two of these letters Jawaharlal explicated to his daughter the basic tenets of Marxism and communism and the materialist conception of history.[14] He wrote to her admiringly about planning in the Soviet Union: '[T]he argument about the success or otherwise of the Five Year Plan is rather a pointless one. The answer to it is the present state of the

---

[12] Subhas Chandra Bose, *The Indian Struggle*, p. 293.

[13] Letter to Kitty Kurti, 23 February 1934, in *Netaji: Collected Works*, vol. 8, p. 56.

[14] See especially the two letters dated 14 February 1933 and 16 February 1933, in Nehru, *Glimpses of World History*, pp. 624–37.

Soviet Union. And a further answer is the fact that this Plan has impressed itself on the imagination of the world. Everybody talks of planning now . . . The Soviets have put magic into the word.' In Jawaharlal's mind there were no doubts about the success of the Soviet economy based on socialist principles; and this success 'is itself the most powerful argument in favour of socialism'.[15]

Turning to India, Jawaharlal put forward his views in three articles entitled 'Whither India?' written in October 1933. He placed the Indian situation in the context of a global flux that he thought to be unprecedented 'in the long range of history'; the world was going through a 'continuous process of change and revolution'. He saw this as a product of the crisis of capitalism which in turn was located in 'the essence of capitalism': the 'ill-distribution of the world's wealth, to its concentration in a few hands'. This was destroying the capitalist system and the forces of labour were growing more intense. Understanding this process was more important than looking at 'the gaily-decked official stage of India or England [on which] phantom figures come and go, posing for a while as great statesmen; Round Tablers flit about like pale shadows of those who created them.' The global economic scene was changing swiftly, outpacing the attitudes of governments. From his understanding of Marxism, Jawaharlal knew that this hiatus could only be bridged 'by a sudden change called revolution'. He added confidently that '[T]he tremendous importance of economic events in shaping history and forms of government is almost universally admitted now.' The challenge before Indian nationalism was to rid itself of the 'extraordinary habit of thinking of freedom in terms of paper constitutions'. What was needed in contemporary times was attention to 'the vital economic issues'. He spelt out the implications in no uncertain terms: 'India's immediate goal can therefore only be considered in terms of the ending of exploitation of her people. Politically, it must mean independence and the severance of the British connection, which means imperialist dominion; economically and socially it must mean the ending of all special class privileges

---

[15] Letters, 9 July 1933 and 11 July 1933, in ibid., pp. 989–1005.

and vested interests. The whole world is struggling to this end; India can do no less, and in this way the Indian struggle for freedom lines up with the world struggle.'[16]

Apart from the clear divergence from Gandhi's views, there is one minor aspect of these articles that needs to be noted. This is a quotation towards the end of the concluding article; the quote is from Mussolini and the lines are cited with approval: '[T]he whole world is in revolution. Events themselves are a tremendous force pushing us on some implacable will.'[17] Jawaharlal used this quotation to strengthen his argument that '[I]ndividuals, however eminent, play but a minor role when the world is on the move.' This was perhaps the only time that Jawaharlal quoted from Mussolini; it sits very uneasily with his espousal of anti-fascism and his pro-communist sympathies. The context of the citation is also not without some irony since Mussolini saw himself as an individual who could change the course of history. The use of a line from Mussolini in a piece informed by the Marxist view of looking at historical events is also out of tune with what Jawaharlal had written to his daughter a few months earlier. In the letter devoted to Mussolini and fascism in Italy, he saw Mussolini as 'an instigator of violence opposed to socialism, communism and liberalism who had made himself into a dictator of Italy'.[18]

In a remarkable coincidence, in January 1934—practically three months to the day after the last of Jawaharlal's 'Whither India?' articles appeared—Subhas was also quoting Mussolini with some approval. From Milan, he wrote to a friend in Vienna that he had attended the Asiatic Students Congress in Rome from 22 to 28 December and had heard the Italian leader speak. 'The speech was a fine one,' Subhas wrote. But he added, 'whatever we might think of the speaker'.[19] Subhas thus made a distinction between the speech

---

[16] 'Whither India?', in Nehru, *Selected Works*, vol. 6, pp. 1–16. These were three articles that were published in the Indian press on 9, 10 and 11 October.

[17] Ibid., p. 16.

[18] Letter, 21 June 1933, in Nehru, *Glimpses of World History*, pp. 944–53.

[19] Letter to Naomi Vetter, 12 January 1934, in *Netaji: Collected Works*, vol. 8, p. 45. In the letter Subhas quoted the following lines from Mussolini's speech: 'It is

and the man, and it would appear that he had questions in his mind about Mussolini the man. This ambivalence was in contrast to his views expressed in Calcutta when he had become the mayor of the city in 1930. More importantly, in *The Indian Struggle*—a book he began writing in Vienna in the middle of 1934—he would take a more positive view of Mussolini's march to Rome, and compared, as we have noted, Gandhi's Dandi March to it. He did this even though it was well known in the early 1930s that Mussolini had, in fact, not taken part in the march to Rome; he arrived from Milan by train.[20] Subhas overlooked the fact and this was one of the reasons that made the comparison so very odd.

In Rome, Subhas found that there were very few people with a genuine interest in India but there existed a desire to know. What impressed him was that there was no prejudice—on the contrary, there was sympathy. He found the official attitude to be favourable and there was the desire to establish closer contacts with the East.[21] He actually met Mussolini—the 'big boss' as Subhas referred to him jocularly in a letter to a nephew—twice. The Italian leader asked Subhas whether he preferred revolutionary or reformist methods to free India. On learning that Subhas opted for the former, Mussolini asked him to immediately prepare a plan and to work towards its realization.[22]

This reception was in sharp contrast to the one Subhas had received the previous year in Germany. He arrived in Berlin in July 1933 from Warsaw where he had gone from Prague. He was very keen to meet some of the top officials of the new Nazi regime. He was disappointed. Subhas did meet Alfred Rosenberg, the Nazi

nonsense to say that East and West will never meet. Rome has in the past been the connecting link between Europe and Asia and she will be so once again. On this rapprochement depends the salvation of the world. *Rome has in the past colonized Europe—but her relations with Asia have always been of a friendly kind, based on cooperation.'* (Italics in the letter.)

[20] Nehru in his letter to his daughter (cited above in fn. 18) noted that Mussolini had arrived by train. It is safe to assume that if Nehru in prison was aware of this, then it was common knowledge.

[21] Letter to Naomi Vetter, 12 January 1934, in *Netaji: Collected Works*, vol. 8, p. 46.

[22] Gordon, *Brothers Against the Raj*, p. 278.

ideologue, but the meeting did not go well. This was not surprising given Rosenberg's well-known racist views. In fact, Bose was so annoyed with Rosenberg that he wrote a very critical article that drew the attention of the German foreign office. Subhas also met Curt Prufer, deputy head of Division III of the German foreign office; this section was also dealing with the British Empire. To Prufer, Subhas lamented the attitudes of German politicians towards India. Prufer assured him that Germany was neutral in the battle between India and Britain but this did not mean that Germany lacked in sympathy for Indians. Subhas expressed his keenness to meet Hitler and Goebbels because 'it [was] of great importance to him to be able to say in private negotiations in India that he had it from the mouths of responsible German politicians themselves that they are no enemies of India'. It was explained to him that a meeting with Hitler was out of the question as the latter was too busy but a talk with Goebbels could be arranged.[23] According to one member of the Nazi party, Subhas wanted to 'convince him [Hitler] of his entirely wrong judgement of the Indian people' in their fight for freedom. He also wanted Hitler's statements on Indians to be removed from future editions of *Mein Kampf*.[24] It would be an exaggeration to conclude from these moves and statements of Subhas that already in 1933 he was 'thinking . . . of a German–Indian pact of which he wanted to convince his Indian comrades-in-arms'.[25] As a self-styled ambassador of the Indian national movement and of India in Europe, he was trying to only clear misconceptions about India and Indians that were prevalent in parts of Europe, especially Germany. An alliance with Germany may not have been part of his aspirations in 1933. What needs to be emphasized is that Subhas, his intelligence notwithstanding, was being extraordinarily naïve to believe that any Nazi leader, let alone Hitler, would change his views because of some pleading on his part. Indeed, Subhas's understanding of the nature

---

[23] These details are available in Jan Kuhlmann, *Netaji in Europe* (Delhi, 2012), p. 14; also see Romain Hayes, *Bose in Nazi Germany* (Delhi, 2011).

[24] Hayes, *Bose in Nazi Germany*, p. 11.

[25] Kuhlmann, *Netaji in Europe*, p. 14, makes this suggestion.

of the Nazi regime and the Nazi ideology was deeply problematic. He could not have been unaware of Hitler's open admiration for the British Empire.

Subhas went back to Germany the following year in April. On that occasion his experience was distinctly unpleasant. On the streets of Munich he was openly called 'neger' (nigger) by German children, some of whom even pelted him with stones. Subhas correctly linked these expressions of prejudice to the race propaganda that prevailed in Germany under the Nazis. He prepared a short memorandum on how relations between Germany and India could be improved. In this note, Subhas located the origins of the deteriorating relations between India and Germany in the writings and statements of leading Nazi leaders. He pointed out somewhat euphemistically that Hitler's *Mein Kempf* contained 'unfriendly statements' about India; and that Goering had in an interview described Gandhi as 'an anti-British Bolshevik agent'.[26] By November 1935, he was reconciled to the reality that the Nazi regime would not jettison its racism. In a letter to Franz Thierfelder, the director of the German Academy in Munich, he wrote, 'I do not demand that you give up your race theory, no matter how many scientific reasons we might offer against it. We only want it to be modified so that it wittingly or unwittingly, does not provoke any bad opinion about Indians.'[27] In 1934, during a visit to Munich, Subhas met Karl Haushofer, who was a mentor of the Nazi leader Rudolf Hess and had even been an advisor to Hitler. Subhas and Haushofer befriended each other but the latter could not arrange the meeting with Hitler that Subhas so much desired. Subhas still hoped that he would get to meet Ernst Rohm, the chief of staff of the storm troopers, the SA, but Rohm was branded a traitor and eliminated in the notorious 'Night of the Long Knives' in June 1934.[28] Subhas thus returned empty-handed from Nazi Germany,

---

[26] Letter to C.R. Prufer, 5 April 1934; the memorandum is an enclosure to this letter. *Netaji: Collected Works*, vol. 8, pp. 61–64. The throwing of stones was not mentioned by Subhas but it is in Kuhlmann, *Netaji in Europe*, p. 14.

[27] Letter to Thierfelder, 7 November 1935, in *Netaji: Collected Works*, vol. 8, p. 113.

[28] Hayes, *Bose in Nazi Germany*, pp. 13–14.

but this would not deter his efforts in the future.

In 1934, two incidents profoundly affected Subhas's personal life. One was the death of his father and the other was his meeting with the woman who was to become the second love of his life (the first being his country[29]) and subsequently his wife. He met Emilie Schenkl in the summer of 1934 in Vienna. She had come to be interviewed by Subhas who was looking for someone to help with the preparation of the book that he wanted to write. She was from an Austrian Catholic family, and at that time only twenty-four years old, thirteen years younger than Subhas. Her big advantage was that she knew English, shorthand and typing. It was not exactly love at first sight, certainly not from Emilie's side. She was to say later that 'he started it', referring to their romantic relationship.[30] Subhas was attracted to her gentle, firm, cheerful and honest nature; he also came to respect her will and strength of mind. To him she was always fondly *baghini,* or tigress. This relationship was one of the anchors of Subhas's emotional world, though, given the circumstances of his life, it would not be without anguish for both of them.

In late November 1934, Subhas received the news from his mother that his father was dying. He set out from Vienna immediately and arrived in India, after several halts, on 4 December. His father, whom Subhas had not seen since 1931, had passed away on 2 December. For Subhas this rite of passage must have been particularly poignant. His father had sent him to Cambridge in the hope that he would return home as an ICS officer. The disappointment at Subhas's decision not to join the steel-frame of the British Indian bureaucracy soon turned to pride as Subhas established himself as one of India's leading nationalist leaders known for his courage and commitment. The pride was not free of pain as Subhas was imprisoned time and again and endured physical

---

[29] Bose told Emilie Schenkl in March 1936: 'My country calls me—my duty calls me—I must leave you and go back to my first love—my country': quoted in Sugata Bose, *His Majesty's Opponent*, p. 85. I have advisedly written 'told' because Subhas did not write this to her—no such letter is there in the letters that Subhas wrote to Emilie. The letters that the two of them wrote to each other are available in *Netaji: Collected Works*, vol. 7.

[30] Sugata Bose, *His Majesty's Opponent*, p. 97.

suffering in prison. Then there was the wrench of separation which
meant that father and son had not met for three years before the former
died. There exist photographs of Subhas during the ritual mourning
period and they show him as pensive and deeply introspective. It is
easy to perceive from these pictures the inner grief and desolation as
also the outward calm of the man. The path of sacrifice that he had
chosen when he was barely twenty had made Subhas a hero; it had
also made him comprehend the pain of suffering for a chosen cause.
The year 1934 was thus for Subhas personally an important one.
The irredeemable loss of his father chronologically coincided with
his discovery of love for a woman who provided him his emotional
mooring in the turbulent sea of politics.

The mourning for his father did not mean that Subhas was free
from the rules and surveillance of the British government. He was
kept under house arrest. Within prison walls, Jawaharlal, in his diary,
noted Subhas's bereavement, and his anger that the man could not
be free while he was in mourning.[31] Early in January 1935, Subhas
left again for Vienna; en route, he stopped in Italy to meet Mussolini
to whom he presented a copy of his recently published book, *The
Indian Struggle*. But for some reason, he was a bit shamefaced about
this and he wrote to Emilie to 'treat this matter as strictly private'.[32]

For Jawaharlal while he was 'in and out of prison'[33] in India,
the years 1934 and 1935 were also fraught with a sense of loss and
a rediscovery of love. The first loss he had to bear was his growing
alienation from the views of Gandhi. Out on parole, he wrote a long
letter to Gandhi in August 1934. What had upset him deeply, he
wrote, was not so much the withdrawal of the Civil Disobedience
Movement but the reasons Gandhi had given for it and his
suggestions for future work. Jawaharlal wrote, 'I had a sudden and
intense feeling that something broke inside me, a bond that I valued

[31] Prison Diary, 3 and 7 December 1934, in Nehru, *Selected Works*, vol. 6, pp. 305–06.

[32] Letter to Emilie Schenkl, 25 January 1935, in *Netaji: Collected Works*, vol. 7, p. 12.

[33] 'In and Out of Prison' was the original title of what was published as *An
Autobiography*. See Prison Diary entry, 4 June 1934, in Nehru, *Selected Works*,
vol. 6, p. 256.

very greatly had snapped. I felt terribly lonely in this wide world. I have always felt a little lonely almost from childhood up. But a few bonds strengthened me, a few strong supports held me up. The loneliness never went, but it was lessened. But now I felt absolutely alone, left high and dry on a desert island.'[34] Gandhi replied to 'this passionate and touching letter' to reassure Jawaharlal that he had 'not lost a comrade in me' and that he was the same person that Jawaharlal had known since 1917. There is some evidence though that Gandhi did not take Jawaharlal's letter very seriously.[35]

Politics occupied less and less of Jawaharlal's mind as he received news of his wife's illness. Kamala's health had been a source of concern ever since she was diagnosed with tuberculosis in 1919. This was never eradicated despite long spells of treatment. In 1925, she had lost a son, born prematurely and alive for only two days, and in 1928 she had suffered a miscarriage. Her health continued to be frail but she jumped into nationalist political activity in spite of being stalked by illness. In August 1934, her condition required immediate medical attention; Jawaharlal was let out of prison on parole and sent back to prison after eleven days when Kamala's health showed signs of a little improvement. In October, she had to be moved to a sanatorium in Bhowali. The government made the concession of moving Jawaharlal to a jail in Almora, close to Bhowali.

But the treatment in the Bhowali sanatorium did not improve Kamala's condition. It was decided that she would have to travel to Europe for further treatment. In prison, Jawaharlal, probably for the first time in his life, had to worry about his finances to bear the cost of his wife's treatment and travel. He had an annual income of Rs 9000 that was derived from royalties of books and some shares that

---

[34] Letter to Gandhi, 13 August 1934, in Nehru, *Selected Works*, vol. 6, p. 278. Jawaharlal was reacting strongly to the Working Committee resolution sponsored by Gandhi that condemned socialism and spoke of a better relationship between labour and capital.

[35] Letter to Nehru, 17 August 1934, in Gandhi, *Collected Works*, vol. 58, pp. 317–19. But two days later, Gandhi wrote to Vallabhbhai Patel: 'Jawaharlal's explosion is not as frightening as it seems from the flames. He had a right to let off steam, which he has exercised. I think he has calmed down now.' See letter to Patel, 19 August 1934, in Gandhi, *Collected Works*, vol. 58, pp. 329–30.

he held. From this income he had to maintain the establishment at Anand Bhawan and bear the costs of travel and treatment. Around this time, a member of the Birla family, learning of Jawaharlal's financial difficulties, offered to pay him a monthly subsistence, as indeed they did provide to many Congressmen. Jawaharlal declined the offer.[36] He raised the funds from his savings, and Kamala, Indira and a doctor sailed for Europe in May 1935.

In Berlin, Kamala underwent an operation for the removal of lung adhesions but this did not result in any marked improvement. In his diary, Jawaharlal noted on 28 August 1935: 'K's condition unsatisfactory—nausea and vomiting. I felt thoroughly upset and the bad news seemed as if it was a prelude to something worse . . . She is slipping away and the thought of it is unbearably hellish.'[37] Jawaharlal's foreboding was not ill-founded. Within four days of this entry, Jawaharlal received the news that Kamala's condition was critical; the government also received a similar cable. The government finally agreed to release Jawaharlal and permitted him to proceed to be with his wife. He prepared himself for the worst: he noted in his diary: '[S]o this is the end.'[38] He rushed to Badenweiler in the Black Forest where Kamala was in a clinic. Her condition was bad and fluctuated daily. She was moved to Lausanne in January 1936 where she died early in the morning on 28 February.

Throughout this protracted illness of his wife, Jawaharlal had come to realize how important she was to him and how much he had actually grown to love her. Theirs had not been an easy marriage. Kamala's family did not come from the same social background as Jawaharlal's; her parents had none of the wealth and the westernization that Motilal had brought to his family. It is said that Jawaharlal's sisters never allowed her to forget this. When Motilal selected her to be his only son's bride, Kamala spoke no English, only Hindi and Urdu. Motilal brought her to Allahabad, before the wedding, and arranged to train her to be a proper wife for his son.

---

[36] Gopal, *Jawaharlal Nehru*, vol. 1, p. 190.

[37] Prison Diary, 28 August 1935, in Nehru, *Selected Works*, vol. 6, p. 411.

[38] Prison Diary, 4 September 1935, in ibid., p. 416.

This social distance between Jawaharlal and Kamala remained a part of their life together. There were aspects of her life and attitudes that Jawaharlal found utterly incomprehensible. For example, a diary entry reads: 'What a child K is! That irritates me often enough and yet I think that is partly her charm. How my moods change when I think of her. How much she means to me and yet how little she fits in or tries to fit in with my ideas. That is really the irritating part, that she does not try, and so she drifts apart.'[39] The drifting apart probably began when Jawaharlal plunged into politics leaving Kamala alone in a large and alien house with a young daughter to bring up. It is not that Kamala did not approve of Jawaharlal's commitment—she may have even quietly admired him—but this did not compensate for her loneliness. The stoic acceptance of her husband's frequent imprisonments cracked on occasion; Jawaharlal recorded that on 12 February 1934 when the police came to Anand Bhawan in Allahabad to arrest him for another spell in prison, Kamala 'suddenly broke down'.[40] There is no evidence that Jawaharlal tried to understand her pain and to reach out to her. His introverted nature and training stood in the way of discussing emotional matters. Jawaharlal once wrote to a friend, 'You ought to know me sufficiently to realize that I never discuss them [personal matters] unless the other party takes the initiative. I would not do so even with Kamala or Indu. Such has been my training.'[41] His cultivated stoicism and self-control, possibly imbibed in an English public school, stopped Jawaharlal from being demonstrative and inquisitive. Thus the breach once created was never quite bridged.

The self-erected emotional dam collapsed in prison especially when Jawaharlal learnt about Kamala's deteriorating illness. His prison diary became the vehicle for expressing his innermost feelings and fears. He kept detailed track of her condition and of her progress to Europe; he waited eagerly for her letters or of news about her. This appearance of Kamala in his jail diaries of the 1930s is in sharp

[39] Prison Diary, 19 March 1935, in Nehru, *Selected Works*, vol. 6, p. 331.

[40] Prison Diary, 12 February 1934, in ibid., p. 227.

[41] Letter to Syed Mahmud, 24 November 1933, in ibid., p. 211.

contrast to the contents of the diaries he had kept in prison in the 1920s: there, Kamala is hardly mentioned.[42] In prison, worrying about her, and reduced to a bundle of nerves, Jawaharlal most uncharacteristically became prone to bouts of weeping and to having odd dreams and visions.[43] He grew to respect what Rabindranath Tagore with his poetic insight called Kamala's 'reticent dignity'.[44]

When Kamala was in the sanatorium in Bhowali, Jawaharlal made an attempt to heal the festering wounds of their relationship. During one visit, while he read to her stuff he had written and his favourite bits of poetry, she said that she 'wanted to realize God and give her thoughts to this, and as a preparation for this our relations should undergo some change. Apparently, I was not to come in the way of God.' Jawaharlal was taken aback. In his diary, he put down his reaction: 'I had known for long that she had been religiously inclined for some three years or more but it was all rather vague. It seemed to me very far from religion or search for God, whatever that may be, and much more a type of hysteria. This had long irritated me partly, because this kind of thing did not appeal to me, partly I suppose, my vanity was hurt when I found that I counted for less and less in her mental make-up. I seemed to be losing her—she was slipping away and I resented this and felt miserable. Many of our little tiffs during the past two years were due to this background of conflict . . . Ever since I have been going to Bhowali, I have tried as gently but as persistently as possible to approach her mind, to explain to her my outlook . . . I was beginning to hope that we were drawing nearer to each other . . . I felt attracted to her and a little fascinated by this mental adventure. And then suddenly I saw that all my efforts had been wholly in vain. She was further away than ever from me and an almost unbridgeable chasm stretched out between us. She hardly seemed to realize the significance of what

---

[42] Gopal, *Jawaharlal Nehru*, vol. 1, p. 194.

[43] See, for example, Prison Diary, 6 February 1935, in Nehru, *Selected Works*, vol. 6, p. 319, where Jawaharlal records a dream he had about Kamala leaving him. On 19 May 1935, in ibid., p. 365, he records a dream about his father and his weeping.

[44] Tagore's statement on Kamala Nehru is given in Nehru, *Selected Works*, vol. 7, p. 166.

she had said. But I was struck dumb and an utter loneliness took possession of me.'[45] Jawaharlal's belated discovery of Kamala was best expressed in the last lines of poetry he gave to her: 'Thou wast all that to me, love, / For which my soul did pine— / A green isle in the sea, love, / A fountain and a shrine, / All wreathed with fairy fruits and flowers, / And all the flowers were mine. / And all my days are trances / And all my nightly dreams / Are where thy grey eye glances, / And where thy footsteps gleams— / In what ethereal dances / By what eternal streams.' This was on 3 October 1934, sixteen months before Kamala's death, and for those looking for ironies or coincidences in history, the lines were from a poem by Edgar Allan Poe, called 'To One in Paradise'.[46]

Jawaharlal was devastated by his wife's death. The British communist leader, Rajani Palme Dutt, who met him around this time, told Jawaharlal's biographer S. Gopal in an interview that 'with her death some of his backbone went out of him'.[47] He always kept in his bedroom and in his jail cell a photograph of Kamala and a small portion of her ashes; he left the request that the ashes be mingled with his after his death. He felt bereft without her and his sense of desolation was articulated in the austere but poignant dedication to *An Autobiography*: 'To Kamala who is no more'.[48]

Subhas was among the two or three friends who were with Kamala and Jawaharlal during her illness in Europe and her death. In October 1935, Subhas had written to Jawaharlal to say that if he could be of any service 'in your present trouble', Jawaharlal should not hesitate to send for him.[49] He need not have written this because Jawaharlal knew that when Kamala was on her way to Berlin, Subhas travelled with her up to Prague and reported to a friend that she had stood the journey 'fairly well'.[50] From that point, he followed her illness and her

[45] Prison Diary, 1 February 1935, in Nehru, *Selected Works*, vol. 6, pp. 312–13.

[46] Prison Dairy, 3 October 1934, in ibid., p. 295.

[47] Gopal, *Nehru*, vol. 1, p. 195.

[48] Ibid., pp. 195 and 199.

[49] Letter to Nehru, 4 October 1935, in *Netaji: Collected Works*, vol. 8, p. 109.

[50] Letter to N. Vetter, 17 June 1935, in ibid., pp. 97–98.

treatment, expressing his anxiety as her condition worsened.[51] At the end of October, he travelled to Badenweiler to visit Kamala.[52] At the end of February he was actually in Lausanne with Jawaharlal when Kamala breathed her last. He helped in making the funeral arrangements.[53]

This association strengthened the bonds of friendship between the two men. Subhas overcame some of the reservations he had about Jawaharlal, and wrote to him to say, 'Among the front-rank leaders of today—you are the only one to whom we can look up to for leading the Congress in a progressive direction. Moreover, your position is unique and I think that even Mahatma Gandhi will be more accommodating towards you than towards anybody else. I earnestly hope that you will fully utilize the strength of your public position in making decisions. Please do not consider your position to be weaker than it really is. Gandhiji will never take a stand which will alienate you.'[54] This was in sharp contrast to what he had written four months earlier, when he had already met Jawaharlal in Badenweiler twice: 'Thanks to the Mahatma's kindness, Jawaharlal appears to be set to become President again.'[55] To another correspondent, he had wondered how Jawaharlal could support Gandhism and communism at the same time.[56]

Such doubts were shelved for the time being. He not only endorsed Jawaharlal's presidency of the Congress but also counselled him on what to do,[57] while also seeking his advice. In the first half of March 1936, Subhas received a letter from the

---

[51] Letter to N. Vetter, 6 September 1935 and 1 October 1935, in ibid., pp. 105 and 106.

[52] Letter to N. Vetter, 25 October 1935, in ibid., p. 111.

[53] Letter to E. Woods, 5 March 1936, in ibid., p. 149. It should be noted·that when Nehru wrote about Kamala's death in The *Discovery of India* (Calcutta, 1946, p. 38), he made no mention of Subhas's presence and help though he mentioned Dr M. Atal ('our faithful companion and friend') and a 'few other friends . . . from neighbouring towns in Switzerland'. Was his failure to mention Subhas a lapse of memory or a sign of the ideological distance that had grown between the two of them in the 1940s?

[54] Letter to Nehru, 4 March 1936, in ibid., p. 144.

[55] Letter to Sunil Mohan Ghosh Moulik, 20 December 1935, in ibid., p. 123.

[56] Letter to Satyendra Nath Majumdar, 22 February 1934, in ibid., p. 55.

[57] He wrote to Jawaharlal following up on a talk that the two of them had had that his immediate task was twofold: (a) prevent office acceptance at any cost; and (b) enlarge and broaden the composition of the Cabinet. These two steps would bring the Congress out of a rut and stem demoralization. Letter to Nehru, 4 March 1936, in ibid., vol. 8, p. 144.

British government informing him that if he were to return to India (as he indeed intended) he would be arrested. He wrote to Jawaharlal asking what he should do under the circumstances and he wanted Jawaharlal to keep in mind only what Subhas termed the 'public interest'. He added, 'My only excuse for troubling you on such a matter is that I can think of no one else in whom I could have greater confidence . . . It is no use asking my own relatives because it is possible that they may not look at the matter purely from the public point of view. The only course for me, therefore, is to depend on your advice.' He believed that given the outstanding position that Jawaharlal held in the public life of India, he could not avoid 'the responsibility of having to give advice in such peculiar and unpleasant circumstances'.[58]

Jawaharlal's initial advice to Subhas—by cable and letter—was to postpone his departure, but within four days after having spoken to Gandhi and other colleagues, he advised Subhas that his immediate return was desirable.[59] But before he had received any of Jawaharlal's missives, he had made up his mind to return to India even if it meant immediate imprisonment. To Romain Rolland, he wrote, after having made up his mind: 'I feel that it is my duty to return to India at once, regardless of the official frowns. It is, of course, a tragic thing that the best and the most creative years of one's life should be spent behind prison walls but that is a price which enslaved people always had and always will have to pay in this world.'[60]

For a man who held so much in store by public interest, the most painful thing that Subhas had to consider when he took his decision to return was a personal one: separation from Emilie. He gave to her a love letter which he wanted her to destroy after reading; fortunately, she didn't.[61] Subhas wrote, 'Even the iceberg sometimes melts and so it is with me now.' He was going back to India not knowing what lay in the future: 'Maybe, I shall spend my life in prison, maybe I shall be shot or hanged. But whatever

---

[58] Letter to Nehru, 13 March 1936, in ibid., p. 156.

[59] Letter to Bose, 26 and 30 March 1936, in Nehru, *Selected Works*, vol. 7, pp. 407 and 408.

[60] Letter to Romain Rolland, 25 March 1936, in *Netaji: Collected Works*, vol. 8, p. 163.

[61] Sugata Bose, *His Majesty's Opponent*, p. 111 and n74.

happens, I shall think of you and convey my gratitude to you in silence for your love for me. Maybe I shall never see you again— maybe I shall not be able to write to you again when I am back—but believe me, you will always live in my heart, in my thoughts and in my dreams. If fate should thus separate us in this life—I shall long for you in my next life.' He pondered in the letter over the nature of love and its earthly use and reflected on how love had enabled him to transcend the differences between them: 'We who belong to two different lands—have we anything in common? My country, my people, my traditions, my habits and customs, my climate—in fact everything is so different from yours . . . For the moment, I have forgotten all these differences that separate our countries. I have loved the woman in you—the soul in you.'[62] There was the pull of two very different kinds of love and Subhas made the valiant effort to strike a balance between the two. He could do this by invoking for Emilie a higher calling: 'For your life, never pray for any selfish object or aim. Always pray for what is good for humanity—for what is good for all time—for what is good in the eyes of God.'

'Pray,' he told the woman he loved, 'in a *nishkama* [without expectation of gain; Subhas wrote this word in Bengali] way.'[63] It is difficult to imagine what this love that almost inevitably entailed separation and uncertainty, meant for a young Austrian girl who knew little about India except through the presence of the man who had all of a sudden entered her life and her mental universe.

It could not have been easy for Emilie, given her European background, to come to terms with the fact that in Subhas's life she would always be second to an abstract notion like 'love for my country'. Both accepted from the beginning that theirs was going to be an unusual and difficult relationship. This was best exemplified by the mode of address that they adopted for each other in their letters. It was always, even after they became husband and wife, Mr Bose for Emilie and Miss Schenkl or Frl Schenkl for Subhas.

---

[62] Quoted in ibid., pp. 111–12.

[63] Letter to Emilie, 30 March 1936, in *Netaji: Collected Works,* vol. 7, p. 56.

Circumstances dictated these formal forms of address; but it must have struck both of them, when they were alone together, as odd and funny. The prolonged geographical separation did not diminish their love and ardour for each other. In one particular letter, Subhas, not given to exhibiting his innermost feelings, could not contain his emotions. In late April or May 1937, immediately after his release in March, he wrote to her in block capitals: 'I HAVE BEEN LONGING TO WRITE TO YOU FOR SOME TIME PAST—BUT YOU CAN EASILY UNDERSTAND HOW DIFFICULT IT WAS TO WRITE TO YOU ABOUT MY FEELINGS. I JUST WANT TO LET YOU KNOW NOW THAT I AM EXACTLY WHAT I WAS BEFORE, WHEN YOU KNEW ME. NOT A SINGLE DAY PASSES THAT I DO NOT THINK OF YOU. YOU ARE WITH ME ALL THE TIME. I CANNOT POSSIBLY THINK OF ANYBODY ELSE IN THIS WORLD . . . I CANNOT TELL YOU HOW LONELY I HAVE BEEN FEELING ALL THESE MONTHS AND HOW SORROWFUL, ONLY ONE THING COULD MAKE ME HAPPY—BUT I DO NOT KNOW IF THAT IS POSSIBLE. HOWEVER I AM THINKING OF IT DAY AND NIGHT AND PRAYING TO GOD TO SHOW ME THE RIGHT PATH.'[64] This was a clear and heartfelt declaration of love and commitment.

His prayers were answered and he found the right path: back in Europe in the winter of 1937, Subhas secretly married Emilie on Boxing Day. Their marriage and their relationship remained a secret because, as Emilie said later, an announcement would have caused an 'upheaval'.[65] Perhaps Subhas feared that such an announcement, especially on the eve of his becoming Congress president, would in some way diminish his political charisma. That he may not have been exaggerating is borne out by what the writer Nirad C. Chaudhuri, who served for a while as Sarat Bose's secretary and was one of the most erudite men of letters of his time, had to say on the subject: '[A]n event in his personal life . . . gave me a shock. After the war was over I learnt that he had married a German woman, who was his secretary, and left a daughter in Germany . . . He had

---

[64] Letter to Emilie, undated, in *Netaji: Collected Works*, vol. 7, p. 137. The editors of the volume suggest the date as late April or May 1937.

[65] Ibid., p. xvii.

shaped himself, to my thinking, in the image of the warrior ascetics delineated as ideal patriots in a famous Bengali novel, which was the bible of Bengali revolutionaries at the turn of the century . . . I had no doubt Subhas Bose thought of himself in that way, and I cannot explain how he became different.'[66] Subhas was forty when he married Emilie. If he had chosen a more conventional life of the upper-middle-class Bengali bhadralok, he would have been married long before he was forty. Given that he was a charismatic figure, he must have had his share of female admirers and offers of marriage. But there is no inkling even of any previous relationship. Hence the assumption that he had taken the vow of celibacy, of remaining unmarried, and that he had fashioned himself as an ascetic dedicated to the service of his country.[67] Celibacy had enhanced his charisma.

Reconciled to secrecy and separation, Mr Bose and Frl Schenkl retained their love for each other through the uncertainty of war and a freedom struggle. In their devotion to each other, there was only one discordant note—articulated by Subhas in a letter. Responding to Emilie's request for books on India, a few months before their marriage, Subhas wrote a bit too sharply perhaps: 'You have asked for some books about India—but I do not know if it is any use sending them. You do not read the books you already have with you. Unless you can get into a more serious frame of mind you will never like reading. You have plenty of books at your disposal in Vienna, on so many subjects—but I do not think you ever look at them.'[68] Would it be unfair to read these lines as a statement of intellectual distance or even incompatibility? Somewhere, Emilie must have accepted this as her destiny because she must have known, as she spent the little time they had together, that she had chosen as her

---

[66] Nirad C. Chaudhuri, *Thy Hand Great Anarch: India, 1921–1952* (London, 1987), pp. 797–98.

[67] To Emilie, Subhas had written in March 1936, 'So many did love me before, but I never looked at them.' There had also been innumerable marriage proposals put forward to family elders and to Basanti Devi, C.R. Das's wife who was like a mother to Subhas. Basanti Devi believed that Subhas would never marry; his first priority was his country's freedom. See Sugata Bose, *His Majesty's Opponent*, p. 96.

[68] Letter to Emilie, 12 August 1937, in *Netaji: Collected Works*, vol. 7, p. 157.

life's partner a perpetually restless soul whose quest knew no end. To Khitish Prasad Chattopadhyay, a friend from the Cambridge days who later became a professor of anthropology in the University of Calcutta, Subhas once wrote in a moment of remarkable candour: 'I must go on. The path is long and dreary. At times I feel weary. Darkness overtakes me relieved by occasional flashes of lightning. But what of that? There is pleasure in travelling. I am still a homeless wanderer. Peace. Peace! I have not found peace yet, nor satisfaction. It is not the lightning alone which lures me, but the darkness as well. It is not the bright future alone which calls but the gloomy uncertainty as well. If I should fall before I reach the light—what of that? There is pleasure in travelling—in groping—also in falling!'[69] Subhas, unwittingly of course, may have penned in these moving lines his own epitaph.

Having bid adieu to his beloved, Subhas arrived in Bombay on 8 April 1936 and was promptly arrested. Jawaharlal as Congress president announced 10 May to be All India Subhas Day and asked the entire country to observe it to honour the patriot who had returned home only to be arrested. 'Subhas Bose's arrest,' Jawaharlal told the whole of India, 'is not only a question of denying one of our beloved leaders his liberties but involves the question of principle and every patriotic Indian, no matter what political party he belongs to, should combine together for fighting this growing menace and check the government's high-handedness and protect our civil liberties.'[70]

From prison Subhas was moved to a bungalow in Kurseong near Darjeeling. The bungalow belonged to his brother Sarat and here Subhas was interned. This period from Subhas's point of view marked the high point of his friendship with Jawaharlal. He wrote to Jawaharlal asking for books to read. The list of books had a pronounced Marxist orientation: books by R.P. Dutt, Ralph Fox and J.B.S. Haldane appear on the list. Interestingly, he expected

[69] Letter to Khitish Prasad Chattopadhyay, 9 August 1937, in *Netaji: Collected Works*, vol. 8, p. 218.

[70] Subhas Day, 10 May 1936, in Nehru, *Selected Works*, vol. 7, p. 415.

Jawaharlal to have these books in his library.[71] Letters from Subhas to Jawaharlal from this phase of their lives have two features worth noting. For one thing, many of them have personal queries. For example, in one letter he asks, 'Do you hear from Indu regularly? How is she? It must be very trying for her being all alone in Switzerland.'[72] The other aspect is even more revealing. In the letter he wrote on 30 June 1936, his sign-off to Jawaharlal is not merely the previously used and more conventional 'Yours affectionately', but the word 'Love' is added. This continues till February 1939, when the word 'Love' at the end disappears. There were genuine expressions of camaraderie between the two. On 19 October 1938, he told Jawaharlal, 'You cannot imagine how I have missed you all these months.'[73]

It is possible that the experience of falling in love made Subhas empathize with the loss that Jawaharlal had suffered with the death of Kamala. Subhas extended his friendship. Jawaharlal was, of course, unaware of the new developments in Subhas's personal life. His response to Subhas was far more subdued. This may partly have been due to his preoccupations as Congress president. It could partly have been caused also by the ideological distance growing between Subhas and himself. In prison, he had written in his diary, 'Subhas seems to be writing a deal of nonsense. He can only think in terms of being himself a Mussolini.'[74]

The bonds of friendship were influenced by what both had experienced in Europe at the personal level. But what they had seen in Europe at the political level had also inflected their ideological orientations and this could not but start a process that would increase the ideological distance between the two. Even before Jawaharlal left for Europe, as some of his letters to his daughter in *Glimpses of World History* make evident, he was suspicious and

---

[71] Letter to Nehru, 30 June 1936, in *Netaji: Collected Works*, vol. 8, p. 175.

[72] Letter from Bose to Nehru, 31 July 1936, in Jawaharlal Nehru Papers, NMML, Correspondence, vol. ix.

[73] Letter from Bose to Nehru, 19 October 1938, in ibid.

[74] Prison Diary, 19 March 1935, in Nehru, *Selected Works*, vol. 6, p. 332.

apprehensive about what he had been reading about the rise of fascism and Nazism. As early as 1933, he had declared, 'I dislike fascism intensely and indeed I do not think it is anything more than a crude and brutal effort of the present capitalist order to preserve itself at any cost.'[75] His brief European trips had only aggravated his alarm and his complete disapproval. During his wife's illness, he had shown where his heart was by only patronizing shops owned by Jews.[76] Even in Badenweiler, in the calm and the peace of the Black Forest, he could not forget the presence of the swastika in Germany although it was not much in evidence in his immediate surroundings. A sense of foreboding filled his mind, the idyll notwithstanding.[77] Jawaharlal was drawn to the promise of communism and the economic achievements of the Soviet Union but this admiration was not blind. In 1935, he noted in his prison diary, 'Soviet Russia seems to be changing for the worse. The fine idealism that moved her is no longer apparent.' He was sceptical about the methods and approaches being used by communists.[78] But he did believe that the basic ideology of communism and the way Marxists interpreted history were sound.

Subhas's political views also acquired a pronounced leftward tilt in Europe. Asked to give the presidential address to the Third Indian Political Conference in London on 10 June 1933, Subhas decided to tie his colours to the mast. Apart from critiquing the Gandhian mode of protest which was always ready to make compromises and withdrawing mass struggle, and advocating 'uncompromising, militancy', Subhas used the occasion to spell out his vision for the future. India would need a new party that was not wedded to non-

---

[75] 'Fascism and Communism', 18 December 1933, in ibid., p. 133.

[76] Gopal, *Jawaharlal Nehru*, vol. 1, p. 193.

[77] *An Autobiography* ends with the following lines, written in Badenweiler on 25 October 1935: '. . . here in the Black Forest it is calm and peaceful, and even the swastika is not much in evidence. I watch the mists steal up the valley and hide the distant frontier of France and cover the landscape, and I wonder what lies behind them.'

[78] Prison Diary, 9 June 1935, and 'Fascism and Communism', 18 December 1933, in Nehru, *Selected Works*, vol. 6, pp. 372 and 134 respectively.

violence and one that was capable of making a conquest of power, he said. Under the leadership of this party and its dedicated band of workers—'freedom intoxicated missionaries'—the old order in India would be shown the door. 'The socio-economic conditions of free India will be altogether different from what prevails now. In industry, agriculture, land-tenure, money, exchange, currency, education, prison administration, public health etc., new theories and novel experiments will have to be devised. We know, for example, that in Soviet Russia a new scheme of national (or political) economy has been evolved in keeping with the facts and conditions of the land. The same thing will happen in India. In solving our economic problems, Pigou and Marshall will not be of much help.' He was emphatic that 'Free India will not be a land of capitalists, landlords and castes.' The party committed to this vision would be called the Samyavadi Sangh (The Party of Equality).[79]

The dream of equality came to be intertwined with the need for discipline without which no mission could be accomplished. This drew Subhas to fascism and Mussolini. His fascination for Mussolini began, as noted already, even before he had met El Duce. His views on fascism he elaborated in *The Indian Struggle*. Significantly, he did this by directly contradicting and critiquing the views of Jawaharlal as expressed in the piece 'Fascism and Communism', cited above. He held the views of Jawaharlal, as expressed in that statement, to be 'fundamentally wrong'. To assume that the choice before the world at that time was one between fascism and communism was to assert, according to Subhas, that the process of evolution had come to an end. Subhas's belief was that 'the next phase in world-history will produce a synthesis between communism and fascism. And will it be a surprise if that synthesis is produced in India?' He detected in fascism and communism certain common traits. Both made the State superior to the individual; both believed in the dictatorship of the party and in the ruthless suppression of minorities; and both saw planned industrialization as the road to the future. According

---

[79] 'The Anti-Imperialist Struggle and Samyavada', in *Netaji: Collected Works*, vol. 8, pp. 241–63.

to Subhas, these similarities would form the basis of the synthesis between fascism and communism which he called Samyavada.[80] It did not strike Subhas that the practice of ruthlessly suppressing dissenting minorities could stand in the way of any fulfilment of the promise of equality embedded in the notion of *samya*.

It would not be unfair to suggest that at the time of writing his book, Subhas was more inclined to fascism than to communism. This is indicated by a longish paragraph immediately following the ones summarized above; in this paragraph, Subhas enumerates five factors that go against the adoption of communism in India. There is no such discussion on fascism and its suitability for India.[81] His views on fascism would alter. In an interview given to R.P. Dutt in January 1938, Subhas said that when he wrote his book, 'Fascism had not started on its imperialist expedition, and it appeared to me merely an aggressive form of nationalism.' He also said that his phrase 'a synthesis between communism and fascism' had not been 'a happy one': what he had meant was that 'we in India wanted our national freedom, and having won it, we wanted to move in the direction of socialism'. He clarified that earlier the views of communists in India had seemed to him to be anti-national, and this view had been strengthened by the hostility of several communists to the Congress. But he noted that communists had modified their views. He added: 'I have always understood and am quite satisfied that Communism, as it has been expressed in the writings of Marx and Lenin and in the official statements of policy of the Communist International, gives full support to the struggle for national independence and recognizes this as an integral part of its world outlook.'[82] Subhas's advocacy of communism was predicated upon the views the communists and the Communist International adopted on India's struggle to win freedom. Jawaharlal's was more philosophical, based as it was on the Marxist interpretation of history and its way of looking at the world.

It would be simplistic to leave Subhas's evolving political views

---

[80] Subhas Chandra Bose, *The Indian Struggle*, pp. 351–52.

[81] Ibid., pp. 352–53.

[82] Interview to R.P. Dutt, 24 January 1938, in *Netaji: Collected Works*, vol. 9, pp. 1–3.

without noting one particular point. His disapproval of fascism was grounded on it turning imperialist and not on its internal policies. He did not elaborate the point about suppression of minorities. He had lived in Vienna for some time and had travelled in parts of Central Europe. In his correspondence and in his writings there is scarcely a mention of the growing anti-Semitism in Vienna—the city that has been called 'one of the most virulently anti-Jewish cities in Europe', which moulded the ideology of Hitler.[83] His correspondence with Emilie shows a lively interest in the jokes and gossip circulating in Viennese cafes, but the plight of the Jews does not find a mention. He resented, as we noted, that he had been called a 'nigger' in Berlin but the plight of the Jews in Germany did not bring forth a comment. He was living in neighbouring Austria when Hitler passed in September 1935 the infamous Nuremberg Laws institutionalizing discrimination against the Jews. The laws must have disturbed him, but there is no evidence that he discussed them or protested against them. It is not that Subhas was unaware that anti-Semitism was an integral part of the Nazi ideology and policy. In an article written in September 1937, he wrote, 'The new social philosophy of the Nazis, as expounded by Hitler, advocates the purification and strengthening of the German race through elimination of Jewish influence and a return to the soil.'[84] Subhas obviously took the Nazi ideology at face value since he seemed to believe that the Nazis were only interested in the 'elimination of *Jewish influence*' (my italics). These lines were written fourteen months before Kristallnacht in November 1938. Subhas was astounded when Jawaharlal presented a resolution to the Congress Working Committee proposing that the Congress offer employment in India to Jewish refugees who were experts and specialists. This proposal was in the context of the pogrom in Germany. Subhas's surprise and opposition to the proposal— the proposal was turned down in the Working Committee—was based on the premise that '[F]oreign policy is a realistic affair to

---

[83] See Ian Kershaw, *Hitler, 1889–1936: Hubris* (London, 1998), pp. 65–66.

[84] 'Europe—Today and Tomorrow', *Modern Review*, September 1937: *Netaji: Collected Works*, vol. 8, pp. 397–410.

be determined largely from the point of view of a nation's self-interest.'[85] The sentence bears underlining given Subhas's choice of allies in the future.

*

Both Subhas and Jawaharlal, one in exile and the other in prison, began to write books around the same time in the middle of 1934. The compulsions for writing were different, however. Subhas had a contract from a left-wing London publisher, Lawrence and Wishart, to write a book on contemporary India; Jawaharlal thought that writing a book would be a fruitful way of fighting ennui in prison. These circumstances gave to the two books their different tones even though both were written at great speed. Subhas began writing in earnest in June 1934 and the book was published in January the following year. Jawaharlal, too, began writing in June 1934 and finished a manuscript of 976 pages in the middle of February 1935.

The Indian Struggle was written up as a book of contemporary history. It is a chronological narrative of events that the writer had witnessed or had been part of. The narrative was interspersed with the writer's comments. Subhas tried to create a distance between himself and the narrative he was constructing by forsaking the first personal singular. Throughout the book, he referred to himself as 'this writer'. (The only exception were the few autobiographical pages where Subhas described his first meeting with Gandhi.) This can be read as a sign that Subhas was trying to be objective about the events he was chronicling and commenting upon. The attempt to fashion his book as a history suffered from one major constraint. Situated as he was in Vienna, as he noted in the original preface, he had no access to books and to adequate reference materials.[86] The book was, in fact, a feat of memory. But the dependence on memory

[85] For the controversy on the resolution, see *Netaji: Collected Works*, vol. 9, pp. 198–199 and 219–20. They occur in the course of an exchange of letters between Subhas and Jawaharlal in March–April 1939.

[86] Subhas Chandra Bose, *The Indian Struggle*, Editors' Introduction by Sisir Bose and Sugata Bose, p. ix.

did not in any way diminish Subhas's attempts to make the book read like a piece of historical writing. The book is based on facts, but is not a mere chronicle. The writer gave to it a certain direction which was derived from his own ideology and from his belief in what India needed at that time. One of Subhas's close friends and political associates, A.C.N. Nambiar, once described Subhas, perhaps with ample justification, as a 'one-idea man: singly for the independence of India'.[87] It was this idea that gave the book its impetus from the title to the last page. In *The Indian Struggle*, Subhas narrated what he lived for—and what he would eventually die for—the touchstone of his life.

The book began with a short survey of the main trends of Indian history from ancient times till 1920. This was intended to serve as a kind of backdrop to the historical developments that Subhas was to describe. In this preliminary chapter, it is possible to discern three themes that underlie the narrative. One is the argument that 'democratic republican forms of government existed in India in the ancient times' as did 'a large measure of liberty' in political and other matters. These features of Indian life had been ignored by British historians but had been fully established, Subhas wrote, by the researches of Indian historians.[88] Subhas thus used what was a familiar argument of nationalist historians: India did not need to look westwards to seek out notions of democracy and liberty; they were to be found in and retrieved from India's own past. The second theme, also a part of nationalist writing in India, is the idea of India as a civilizational sponge. In Subhas's words, 'Throughout Indian history all foreign elements have always been absorbed by Indian society. The British are the first and the only exception to this.'[89] The third theme is the emergence of the Indian National Congress as the most important organization in India representing the whole country and standing for all the communities. Subhas named Mahatma Gandhi as 'the undisputed leader of the Congress'. There was, however,

[87] Quoted in Sugata Bose, *His Majesty's Opponent*, p. 102.

[88] Subhas Chandra Bose, *The Indian Struggle*, p. 7.

[89] Ibid., p. 10.

within the Congress 'a powerful Left Wing'. While, according to Subhas, Gandhi adopted a middle position on matters of capital and labour, landlord and peasant and on questions of caste, the left wing worked for 'a more radical and uncompromising policy on social and economic issues'. Subhas identified himself as belonging to this left wing in the Congress.[90]

The prefacing of the presentation of contemporary events—from 1920 to the 1930s—by these three themes help in highlighting the crucial aspects of *The Indian Struggle*. The book was shot through with an uncompromising attitude towards British rule—it had to be overthrown at any cost. The overthrow would come when 'active resistance will develop into an armed revolution'.[91] Gandhi, according to Subhas, 'has rendered and will continue to render phenomenal service to his country. But India's salvation will not be achieved under his leadership.'[92] The inadequacies of Gandhi's leadership, in the eyes of Subhas, grew out of the fact that 'he is fundamentally a reformist and not a revolutionary'. Gandhi had provided India with a new method—passive resistance or non-violent non-cooperation—but he had not given the country a new programme of social reconstruction.[93] The new programme would emerge from a synthesis—synthesis which was the strength of Indian civilization. Subhas wrote confidently that 'all the modern socio-political movements in Europe and experiments in Europe and in America will have considerable influence on India's development'.[94] The instrument for developing this programme of synthesis would be a new party, arising from the Congress but with 'a clear ideology, programme and plan of action—a party that will not only fight for and win freedom, but will put into effect the entire programme of post-war reconstruction.'[95]

---

[90] Ibid., p. 38.
[91] Ibid., p. 360.
[92] Ibid., p. 333.
[93] Ibid., pp. 353–54.
[94] Ibid., p. 353.
[95] Ibid., p. 354.

Subhas's book, apart from being a history, was also explicitly a political and ideological tract. The historical narrative was informed by a political and an ideological agenda. This provides Subhas's narrative with a moral suggested already by the word 'struggle' in the very title of the book; that same word also indicates the absence of a closure. The Indian struggle was an ongoing process.

The book was published to wide acclaim abroad. The British Indian government, with the approval of the secretary of state for India, bestowed on it the honour of having it banned in India. Samuel Hoare, the secretary of state for India, informed the House of Commons that the book had been banned as it tended to incite terrorism and direct action.[96] The *Sunday Times*, as much a voice of the British establishment as its sister publication, the *Times*, made up for the ban imposed on the book by saying in its review that it was 'a valuable book for the enlightenment of opinion. It has a point of view difficult for the British mind to comprehend, but it accurately describes a side of the Indian movement that cannot be ignored.' The reviewer in the *Daily Herald* wrote, 'This is the book of no fanatic, but of a singularly able mind, the book of an acute, thoughtful, constructive mind, of a man who, while still under forty, would be an asset and an ornament to the political life of any country.' Romain Rolland thought Subhas had brought the 'best qualities of the historian to the book—lucidity and high equity of mind'.[97] Subhas had every reason to be pleased with his book written under very trying circumstances—in exile, in ill health and without adequate bibliographical support.

Jawaharlal's book was exactly what its title announced—an autobiography. The dominant voice in it was the personal one. But since the author of the book was also a principal political actor, politics entered as a part of the unfolding story of his life. The political was always the second voice, blending, effortlessly when the occasion demanded, with the personal. The predominance of the personal was indicated in the full title of the book: *An Autobiography*

---

[96] Ibid., Editors' Introduction, p. ix.

[97] These comments are taken from Sugata Bose, *His Majesty's Opinion*, p. 101.

with Musings on Recent Events in India. It was by far the best book that Jawaharlal wrote. Its style was detached, laid-back and austere. Jawaharlal's autobiography, unlike Augustine's, Rousseau's or Gandhi's, is not confessional; it is not a book for the prurient, there are no personal revelations. Any autobiography assumes that readers will be interested in the life of the author or that the life is significant enough to be recorded. Jawaharlal does not bring to his life's story any air of self-importance; rather the impression the book conveys is that his life acquires an interest for the readers because of the context in which it was placed and the historical events in which his life was intertwined. The personal gets a salience because of the historical. Jawaharlal warned his readers not to be misled into believing that it was a work of history. It was an attempt to trace his own mental development. His account of recent events could serve to 'provide a background for the study of hard facts'.[98]

The book was conceived and written in prison. Jawaharlal thought writing a book would be a good way to break the solitude of jail life. He wanted to reflect upon what had happened in India in the recent past and of his own involvement in those events. He wrote in the preface to the book that he had begun writing 'in a mood of self-questioning' and this mood persisted throughout. Indeed, certainty was not a noticeable trait of the book; doubt and ambiguity were. He preferred the shade of grey rather than the clarity of white contrasted with black. His comments were open-ended and nuanced. There was self-criticism and self-scrutiny but there were no regrets. If he offered any justification for his actions it was to explain them to himself rather than to the world at large. Looking back on the way his life had unfolded, he admitted, 'If I were given the chance to go through my life again, with my present knowledge and experience added, I would no doubt try to make many changes in my personal life; I would endeavour to improve in many ways on what I have previously done, but my major decisions in public affairs would remain untouched. Indeed, I could not vary them, for they were stronger than myself, and a force beyond my control drove me

---

[98] *An Autobiography*, Preface.

to them.'[99] He was aware of the forces of history that had propelled his actions in public life and it was this consciousness that perhaps prevailed upon him not to draw up any grand vision for the future. With great insight he commented, 'the future has to be lived before it can be written about'.[100] He had no pre-written script for the future.

Jawaharlal's personal inadequacies, which he said he wanted to overcome given another chance, were rooted in part in his upbringing. He noted a paradox in the nature of his upbringing: 'I have become a queer mixture of the East and West, out of place everywhere, at home nowhere. Perhaps my thoughts and approach to life are more akin to what is called Western rather than Eastern but India clings to me, as she does to all her children, in innumerable ways; . . . I cannot get rid of either that past inheritance or my recent acquisitions. They are both part of me, and though they help me in both the East and the West, they also create in me a feeling of spiritual loneliness not in public activities but in life itself. I am a stranger and alien in the West. I cannot be of it. But in my own country also, sometimes, I have an exile's feeling.'[101] Apart from the poignant honesty of this self-analysis, Jawaharlal, unknowingly, had penned here the mental dilemma and angst of many Indians who were the products of anglophone education and who because of that education had imbibed and nurtured European tastes and sensibilities.[102]

The area where Jawaharlal's western attitudes acted as an obstacle to understanding a vital aspect of Indian life was religion. He saw himself as a modern and rational individual for whom religion had little appeal since, '[A]lmost always it [religion] seems to stand for blind belief and reaction, dogma and bigotry, superstition and

---

[99] Ibid., p. 598.

[100] Ibid., p. 596.

[101] Ibid., pp. 597–98.

[102] Compare Salman Rushdie: 'I, too, have ropes around my neck, I have them to this day, pulling me this way and that, East and West, the nooses tightening, commanding, *choose, choose.* I buck, I snort, I whinny, I rear, I kick. Ropes, I do not choose between you. Lassoes, lariats, I choose neither of you, and both. Do you hear? I refuse to choose.' Salman Rushdie, *East, West* (London, 1994), p. 211.

exploitation, and the preservation of vested interests.' Yet he was
aware that religion had brought solace to 'innumerable tortured
souls'. What troubled him profoundly was the recognition that
his disaffinity with the religious frame of mind alienated him from
large sections of the people of India. He questioned himself: 'I felt
lonely and homeless, and India, to whom I had given my love and
for whom I had laboured, seemed a strange and bewildering land to
me. Was it my fault that I could not enter into the spirit and ways
of thinking of my countrymen?'[103] The issue of religion brought
Jawaharlal inevitably to the figure of Gandhi and his relationship
with him. There will be occasion to discuss this relationship in
subsequent chapters.

Not unexpectedly, *An Autobiography* was hailed as an important
book even by those who did not share Jawaharlal's views. The
Times recommended it as 'a book to read however much one may
disagree with the outlook of the author'. No understanding of India
in the last fifteen years, the reviewer in the *Economist* said, was
possible without reading the book. Readers and reviewers in the
West recognized in Jawaharlal's attitudes, in contrast with those of
Gandhi's, something they could understand and even argue with. It
was seen as a sincere voice exemplifying the problems and aspirations
of a resurgent India. But the praise that must have meant the most
was probably the following from Rabindranath Tagore: 'I have just
finished reading your great book and I feel intensely impressed and
proud of your achievement. Through all its details there runs a deep
current of humanity which overpasses the tangles of facts and leads
us to the person who is greater than his deeds and truer than his
surroundings.'[104] Jawaharlal replied, beginning his letter with his
usual form of address for Tagore, Gurudeva, and going on to say,
'what you have written goes to my heart and cheers and strengthens
me. With your blessings and goodwill I feel I can face a world of

---

[103] *An Autobiography*, p. 374.

[104] Letter from Tagore to Nehru, 31 May 1936, in Jawaharlal Nehru, *A Bunch of
Old Letters* (Bombay, 1958; repr. 1960), p. 187.

opposition. The burdens become lighter and the road straighter.'[105]

The book became a bestseller and ran into many reprints in a few weeks. The publishers, The Bodley Head, however, went into liquidation but were soon taken over by a new management. Fortunately for Jawaharlal, he continued to receive regular royalties.[106]

Thus by 1936, both Jawaharlal and Subhas had emerged as writers of two major books, though of very different kinds: one, strident, assertive and political; the other, wistful, introspective and less certain of political orientations. Their personal experiences of love and loss had also left their imprints on their personalities. It had made Subhas stronger and more confident, and Jawaharlal more aware of his own personal shortcomings. These changes would be reflected in the manner both of them would lead the Congress as presidents and in the way they would deal with their growing differences with Gandhi.

---

[105] Letter to Tagore, 10 June 1936, in Nehru, *Selected Works*, vol. 7, p. 134.

[106] Gopal, *Jawaharlal Nehru*, vol. 1, pp. 196–97.

5

Party Presidents

While Jawaharlal was away in Europe coping with his wife's illness and death, he was elected president of the next Congress session to be held in Lucknow in April 1936. Not surprisingly, the idea to make him the leader of the party had come from Gandhi who wrote to Jawaharlal on the subject the day he was leaving for Europe. 'Unless there is an insuperable bar,' Gandhi said, 'you should take charge of the Congress ship next year.'[1] He followed this up a few days later with a more direct request: 'I would like you to allow yourself to be elected President for the next year. Your acceptance will solve many difficulties.'[2] In another letter, written a few days later, he assured Jawaharlal, '[I]f you are elected, you will be elected for the policy and principles you stand for.' He sought Jawaharlal's permission to propose his name 'for the crown of thorns'.[3] Jawaharlal replied that he realized that his election would ease tension within the Congress; he also admitted that he had 'certain qualifications' for taking on the job. He said that Gandhi knew that he was not an 'over-modest and retiring person' but his conceit notwithstanding, he felt reluctant to say yes. The reason for his reluctance, he told Gandhi, 'is partly my desire to be light and free on my return to politics and the

---

[1] Letter to Nehru, 4 September 1935, in Gandhi, *Collected Works*, vol. 61, pp. 385–86.

[2] Letter to Nehru, 12 September 1935, in ibid., p. 406.

[3] Letter to Nehru, 22 September 1935, in ibid., pp. 438–39.

presidentship is a tremendous burden which might well crush me'.[4]

In spite of such thoughts, Jawaharlal agreed to take on the presidentship of the party to which he was loyal. His decision to accept was not determined only by the fact that the request had come from Gandhi. Jawaharlal explained to Gandhi his reasons for accepting the offer: 'I do not believe in shirking a job because of difficulties or possibilities of failure. In any event on my return to India I propose to take an active part in politics. They are not for me a career or an occupation from which I can retire at will. Even if I had not had an irrepressible urge towards something, which might not be easy to define, loyalty to the past and even more so to the present, with all its tragic suffering and vulgar suppression of the best in our people, would drive me on. I have little respect for quitters and I hope I shall never be of their number.' He accepted but with the warning that he was 'apt to behave like a bull in a china shop'.[5]

Gandhi's proposal to have Jawaharlal as president did raise murmurs of protest within the Congress. There were appeals to Gandhi to allow Rajagopalachari to contest; and the latter expressed his concern at 'having dreamers and sentimental men in charge of the wheel' but hoped that Jawaharlal would be 'reasonable' and that 'Bapu will be firm and be able to take the reins'.[6] Jawaharlal was elected president very comfortably with 541 members voting for him among the 592 who voted.[7] The news of his election came to Jawaharlal around the time of Kamala's death and he was in no mood to react, let alone rejoice.

Jawaharlal was aware that he was taking on an enormous responsibility. The Congress after the Civil Disobedience Movement had lapsed into inactivity. In Gandhi's words, '[I]n your absence we

---

[4] Letter from Nehru to Gandhi, 20 September 1935, in *Together They Fought: Gandhi–Nehru Correspondence, 1921–1948*, (ed.) Uma Iyengar and Lalitha Zackariah, p. 242–44.

[5] Letter from Nehru to Gandhi, 20 September 1935, in ibid., pp. 242–44.

[6] Letter from Rajagopalachari to Rajendra Prasad, 7 February 1936: cited in Som, *Differences within Consensus*, pp. 174–75.

[7] Votes for next President, 1936, in AICC Papers, File No. 17, Miscellaneous.

[the Congress] have been literally trekking.'[8] Echoing this, Jawaharlal wrote to Rajendra Prasad, 'I feel that the Congress today is in a state of ideological flux and does not quite know its own mind . . . Our policy all along the line, even mentally, is becoming more and more one of non-action and non-thought. Non-violent non-cooperation and civil disobedience were not to me mere non-resistance but the height of active resistance to evil doing. This dynamic quality seems to have disappeared now and we have a lifeless body which neither thinks nor acts and over which old incantations are repeated to give it the semblance of life.'[9] Jawaharlal saw his task as reviving the party from this torpor.

One factor he had to consider was the change in the political climate while he had been in prison. In August 1935, the Government of India Act was passed. This was seen by the British as the culmination of the process that was begun with the appointment of the Simon Commission in 1927. At the federal level, the British retained control but at the provincial level, the Act introduced greater Indian participation. The electorate was expanded from 6.5 million to 30 million. Most significantly, the Act did not mention anything about Dominion Status, leave alone independence. Looking back at the Act, Lord Linlithgow, viceroy from 1936 who had been chairman of the joint parliamentary committee, noted privately in December 1939 that the Act was passed because 'we thought that way the best way . . . of maintaining British influence in India'. He added, 'It is no part of our policy, I take it, to . . . gratuitously hurry the handing over the controls to Indian hands at any pace faster than that which we regard as best calculated, on a long view, to hold India to the Empire.'[10] Even in the late 1930s, the illusion of permanence persisted: Linlithgow was only repeating what Gladstone had written to Lord

[8] Letter to Nehru, 22 September 1935, in Gandhi, *Collected Works*, vol. 61, pp. 438–39.

[9] Letter to Rajendra Prasad, 20 November 1935, in Nehru, *Selected Works*, vol. 7, p. 43.

[10] Letter from Linlithgow to Zetland, 21 December 1939: quoted in Sumit Sarkar, *Modern India, 1858–1947* (Delhi, 1983), p. 338.

Northbrook in October 1872: 'When we go, if we are ever to go . . .'[11]

The 1935 Act fooled very few in India. All sections of political opinion, including the liberals and the Muslim League, expressed their disapproval of the Act. The Congress leaders were emphatic in their criticism that the Act represented no advance on what had already existed. Jawaharlal's views on the Act were trenchant and well known. He saw the Act as an attempt to strengthen the reactionary and vested interests in India. Gandhi did not disagree with Jawaharlal but he was less vocal. There existed a strong lobby within the Congress to accept office under the Act; many Congressmen found it difficult to resist the loaves and fishes of office after many years of suffering and sacrifice. Jawaharlal believed that the acceptance of office would result in the disintegration of the Congress and would also prevent the launching of a civil disobedience movement. It was in many ways a different Congress that Jawaharlal was coming home to lead.

The situation was a challenge to him especially as his own political views had been further radicalized by what he had seen in Europe. This process had gained in momentum by his chance meeting in Lausanne with Ben Bradley and R.P. Dutt, the two British communist leaders. It was with Dutt—or RPD as he was referred to in communist circles in India and Britain—that Jawaharlal spent some time. He expressed his admiration for Soviet Russia to RPD and his acceptance of the Marxist view of history but he also expressed his reservations about violence and revolutionary dictatorship. These reservations notwithstanding, Jawaharlal promised, according to RPD, to promote, as the president of the Congress, the fledgling Communist Party of India. After this meeting and also because of the shift in the policy of the Third International to support anti-imperialist movements, the British communists modified their views on the Congress. Bradley and Dutt in an article described the Congress as the principal mass-based party seeking national liberation. But its constitution would have to be revised to properly

---

[11] Letter from Gladstone to Northbrook, 15 October 1872: quoted in Gopal, *Jawaharlal Nehru*, vol. 1, p. 13.

represent the interests of workers and peasants, they said.[12] These ideas were not very different from Jawaharlal's when he assumed the presidency of the Congress.

Jawaharlal's presidential address at the Lucknow session in April 1936 was predictable because he expressed his beliefs that reflected his radical convictions.[13] He began by addressing the assembled Congressmen as 'Comrades' and proceeded to place the Indian freedom struggle in the context of what was happening in the rest of the world, especially in Asia. He said, '[O]ur struggle was but part of a wider struggle for freedom, and the forces that moved us were moving millions of people all over the world and driving them into action. All Asia was astir from the Mediterranean to the Far East, from the Islamic West to the Buddhist East; Africa responded to the new spirit . . . And right across the vast area in Europe and Asia, in the Soviet territories, a new conception of human freedom and social equality fought desperately against a host of enemies.' He urged his audience to keep in mind 'the wider picture' and not 'isolate India or the Indian problem from that of the rest of the world'. The global trends were 'the real forces that are shaping events' and they provided 'the vital energy' embedded in the events. An important component of these trends was a fundamental clash between two rival economic and political systems. One was capitalism of which imperialism was an inseparable part; and the other was the socialist order of the USSR. A new facet of capitalism was fascism 'with all its brutal suppression of what Western civilization had apparently stood for; it became, even in some of its homelands, what its imperialist counterpart had long been in the subject colonial countries'. Fascism and imperialism were the twin faces of 'the now decaying capitalism'. Opposed to fascism and imperialism were socialism in the West and rising nationalism in the East. But Jawaharlal made the distinction between the extreme nationalism that fascism represented and the nationalism

[12] This paragraph is based on Gopal, *Jawaharlal Nehru*, vol. 1, pp. 202–04.

[13] The text of the Presidential Address is available in Nehru, *Selected Works*, vol. 7, pp. 170–95.

that was emerging in many Asian countries: 'Nationalism in the East . . . was essentially different from the new and terribly narrow nationalism of fascist countries; the former was the historical urge for freedom, the latter the last refuge of reaction.' He admitted, though, that the 'nationalism of subject countries has sometimes a tendency to fascism'.

India, Jawaharlal continued, had taken its stand alongside the progressive forces of the world that were fighting fascism and imperialism. There was no common ground between Indian independence and British imperialism; remaining within the British Empire would not only impede the attainment of political freedom but also prevent radical social changes. Jawaharlal expressed his special concern for the 'deprivation of civil liberties in India' and in this context he drew the gathering's attention to the plight of Subhas, 'a dear and valued comrade of ours'. He referred to the warning that the latter had been issued in a letter saying that he would be arrested as soon as he arrived in India. (Subhas had actually been arrested on 8 April 1936 on charges of being 'a menace to the peace and tranquility of the country'.[14])

Turning to the Congress, Jawaharlal painted a dismal picture. 'I have found,' he said, 'a spirit of disunion spreading over the land, a strange malaise, and petty conflicts amongst old comrades growing ever bigger and interfering with all activity. We have forgotten for the moment the larger ideals we stood for and we quarrel over petty issues. We have largely lost touch with the masses and, deprived of the life-giving energy that flows from them, we dry up and weaken and our organization shrinks and loses the power it had.' Congress could rescue itself from this plight by coming closer to the masses. 'The Congress,' Jawaharlal asserted, 'must be not only *for* the masses, as it claims to be, but *of* the masses; only then will it really be for the masses.' The Congress needed to get out of its middle-class outlook, he said. Jawaharlal advocated a broad front of all the anti-imperialist forces in the country. But such a front would not be possible unless Congressmen could see their own movement as

---

[14] See Nehru, *Selected Works*, vol. 7, p. 176n4.

a part of a worldwide trend.

Jawaharlal returned to the question of socialism which he saw as 'the key to the solution of the world's problem and of India's problems'. Socialism, he said, was not just an economic doctrine but 'a philosophy of life . . . a vital creed' that he held 'with all my head and heart'. He wanted the Congress to become a socialist organization and join hands with 'other forces in the world which are working for a new civilization'. He realized and accepted that the majority in the Congress was not prepared to go so far; so Jawaharlal did not want to force the issue. Having said this, he emphasized that he believed in rapid industrialization as the only way to combat poverty. Khadi and village industries he saw as 'temporary expedients of a transition stage rather than as solutions to our vital problems'.

Coming finally to the 1935 Act, a subject on which his audience was most eager to hear his views, Jawaharlal said that the Congress had no other choice but to contest the forthcoming elections. But the Congress should contest the polls with the demand for a constituent assembly at the forefront. After the elections to accept office would be to surrender the revolutionary impulse and go back to reformism. There was little to gain from the acceptance of office.

When Jawaharlal had written this address on 31 March 1936, he had no clear idea how deep the feelings were among Congressmen in favour of office acceptance. His views thus failed to strike a chord among most members of the Congress. His presidential address remained a statement of Jawaharlal's personal creed with little or no impact on Congress policies; Gandhi correctly described it as 'a confession of his faith'.[15] Jawaharlal did not get the Working Committee he wanted and on most critical issues his proposals were defeated. He wrote to Gandhi on 25 May that 'A *hayadar* [Jawaharlal wrote this word in Hindi; it means self-respecting] president would probably have resigned but I being *behaya* [again this word was in Hindi; and it means shameless] stuck on even though the majority of the Congress had decided against me on some vital issues. This

---

[15] Letter from Gandhi to Agatha Harrison, 30 April 1936, in Jawaharlal Nehru, *A Bunch of Old Letters*, p. 182.

peculiar position was reflected in the formation of the WC [Working Committee] which certainly could not be under the circumstances of my choice although technically I was responsible for it.'[16] The Working Committee rejected Jawaharlal's proposal to allow the affiliation of trade unions and peasant leagues with the Congress, and also his efforts to link the Congress more directly with the movements for political reforms in the princely states. The 1935 Act was condemned but the Congress agreed to contest elections while deferring a decision on the question of office acceptance.

Even though Gandhi had suggested that Jawaharlal be the president, the latter received no support from his mentor. Gandhi was not willing to accept that Jawaharlal had no role in the formation of the Working Committee. Privately, he admitted that the majority of the Working Committee represented his view[17] but wrote to Jawaharlal to say, '[Y]ou chose the members because it was the right thing to do for the cause.' He added that Jawaharlal's views had caused 'much pain' to Rajendra Prasad, Rajagopalachari and Vallabhbhai Patel. Gandhi's choice of these three names was significant as these three leaders had come to be known as the bastions of the right wing in the Congress because of their opposition to socialism and any kind of radical programme. It needs to be underlined that even before Jawaharlal assumed the office of president, fears about such differences had been expressed. Rajagopalachari had written to Gandhi, 'I was and still am doubtful about Jawaharlal's fitting in with the parliamentary programme and policy, [even though] I readily agree that on personal and general grounds we could not pitch on a better choice for the Congress president's place this year.' Rajagopalachari expected Gandhi to resolve such differences by giving his support to the policies of Patel and others who stood with him. In the letter quoted above, Rajagopalachari wrote, 'Something should be done by you to see that Vallabhbhai's decisions as regards parliamentary policy are not

---

[16] Letter from Nehru to Gandhi, 25 May 1936, in *Together They Fought*, p. 278.

[17] Letter from Gandhi to Agatha Harrison, 30 April 1936, in Jawaharlal Nehru, *A Bunch of Old Letters*, p. 182.

challenged but given full cooperation from the Working Committee and by the Congress President.'[18]

The differences between these men and Jawaharlal, focused on the Congress's commitment to socialism, came to a head in the meeting of the Working Committee at Wardha on 29 June[19] when seven members of the Working Committee, including of course the three just mentioned, resigned from it. The seven members sent a letter to Jawaharlal in which they elaborated the reasons for their resignation.[20] They later withdrew their resignations at Gandhi's intervention. But Gandhi admitted to Jawaharlal, '[T]he sending of such a letter in place of resignation was my suggestion.'[21] Gandhi had thus done what Rajagopalachari had wished him to do. A very tired Jawaharlal wrote to Gandhi that when he toured the country he found 'a bubbling vitality' among the people, and this filled him with fresh energy. He added, 'But this energy seems to ooze out of me at every meeting of the Working Committee and I return feeling very much like a discharged battery. The reaction has been greatest on this

---

[18] Quoted in Rajmohan Gandhi, *Patel: A Life* (Ahmedabad, 1991; repr. 2011), pp. 353–54.

[19] There was in fact 'an acrimonious verbal duel' in Lucknow between Patel and Nehru: ibid., p. 254.

[20] In this letter they wrote, 'We felt that the preaching and emphasizing of socialism particularly at this stage by the President . . . while the Congress has not adopted it is prejudicial to the best interests of the country and to the success of the national struggle for freedom . . . You also appear to feel and have even expressed that the Working Committee as it is constituted is not of your choice but forced on you and that you accepted it against your own better judgement. Our own impression of the events at Lucknow is contrary to yours. We are wholly unaware of the slightest pressure being put upon [you] by any of us. Anyway the position created by your declarations is highly unsatisfactory and we think we should give you the fullest latitude to work without feeling hampered in any way by the presence of colleagues in the Working Committee whom you regard as a drag . . . We are of opinion that through your speeches . . . the Congress organization has been weakened.' Rajendra Prasad et al. to Nehru, 29 June 1936, in Jawaharlal Nehru, *Bunch of Old Letters*, pp. 190–91. Rajendra Prasad, in a personal letter to Nehru written after the withdrawal of the resignations, reiterated and elaborated on the above points. Rajendra Prasad to Nehru, 1 July 1936, in ibid., pp. 192–94.

[21] Letter to Nehru, 8 July 1936, in *Together They Fought*, pp.287–90

occasion.'[22] He made it clear to Gandhi that he felt utterly isolated. He stated his plight, as he saw it, very clearly: 'For however tenderly the fact may be stated, it amounts to this: that I am an intolerable nuisance and the very qualities I possess—a measure of ability, energy, earnestness, some personality which has a vague appeal—become dangerous for they are harnessed to a wrong chariot.'[23]

Outside the Congress too, Jawaharlal's views were attacked by members of the Indian capitalist class. In the middle of May, twenty-one leading businessmen of Bombay issued a statement condemning Jawaharlal's advocacy of socialism, which they thought was destructive and subversive. The programme that Jawaharlal was putting forward threatened 'not only the institution of private property but peaceful observance of religion and even personal safety'. Some of the signatories to the statement also wrote separately against Jawaharlal. Cowasjee Jehangir described him as 'a wholehearted communist' and Homi Mody warned that Jawaharlal was providing 'a through ticket to Moscow'.[24] Jawaharlal was not to be deterred by all this. He refused to tone down his commitment to his creed. In reply, he said, 'Some captains of industry in Bombay take great exception to my use of the word socialism instead of communism, apparently thinking that thereby I seek to delude our people. They need not excite themselves over this matter. I am not afraid of the word communism. Constituted as I am, all my sympathies go to the underdog and to him who is persecuted most. That in itself would be sufficient to incline me towards communism when all the power of the state and of vested interest tries to crush it.'[25] In a counter-attack he accused the twenty-one signatories of harbouring 'the fascist mentality'.[26]

---

[22] Letter from Nehru to Gandhi, 5 July 1936: ibid, p. 283.

[23] Ibid., p. 284.

[24] All these quotes are from Bipan Chandra, 'Jawaharlal Nehru and the Indian Capitalist Class, 1936', *Nationalism and Colonialism in Modern India* (Delhi, 1979), pp. 187–89.

[25] 'Reply to Critics of Socialism', 5 June 1936, in Nehru, *Selected Works*, vol. 7, pp. 280–84.

[26] 'The Fascist Mentality', 22 May 1936, in ibid., p. 263.

More than Jawaharlal's response what was significant was the reaction of G.D. Birla, one of the most important members of the business community. Birla argued that by entering into a public polemic with Jawaharlal on the issue of socialism and private property, the businessmen had brought humiliation upon themselves. He wrote to Walchand Hirachand, one of the twenty-one, on 26 May, in very strong terms: 'You have rendered no service to your caste men. It is curious how we businessmen are so shortsighted . . . It looks very crude for a man with property to say that he is opposed to expropriation in the wider interests of the country.'[27] Birla suggested that businessmen and capitalists were not the best persons to argue against expropriation. 'Let those who have given up property say what you want to say,' Birla added.[28] The responsibility of capitalists was only to strengthen the hands of such persons. He added that because of the myopia of businessmen 'people like Vallabhbhai and Bhulabhai who are fighting against socialism are not being helped'. Birla obviously expected the right wing of the Congress, or those whom he called 'Mahatmaji's Group'[29] to speak against socialism and for the interests of the capitalist class. One such interest was the acceptance of office after the elections since the 'control of the new legislatures would . . . be crucial'. He added, '[T]he election which will take place will be controlled by [the] "Vallabhbhai Group" and if Lord Linlithgow handles the situation properly there is every likelihood of the Congressmen coming into office.'[30]

Was Gandhi a part of this attempt to have the interests of the capitalists articulated and accepted in the Working Committee? Another letter from Birla strongly suggests that there had been a tacit

---

[27] Letter from G.D. Birla to Walchand Hirachand, 26 May 1936, in Purushottamdas Thakurdas Papers, File No. 177. Birla also wrote to Purushottamdas Thakurdas, another signatory, to say that he had been 'painfully surprised to see your [Thakurdas's] name in the crowd'. The statement was 'liable to be seriously misinterpreted' and had 'given impetus to the forces working against capitalism'. Birla to Thakurdas, 1 June 1936, in ibid.

[28] Ibid.

[29] Letter from Birla to Thakurdas, 20 April 1936, in ibid.

[30] Ibid.

understanding between Gandhi and Birla to counter Jawaharlal's
zeal for socialism and keenness to reject the acceptance of office.
In this letter, written immediately after the Lucknow session, Birla
noted in triumph: 'Mahatmaji kept his promise and without his
uttering a word, he saw that *no new commitments were made*.
Jawaharlalji's speech in a way was thrown into the waste paper
basket because all the resolutions that were passed were against
the spirit of his speech.'[31] Gandhi posed to be an innocent observer
but had in fact circumscribed Jawaharlal by his chosen men who
acted for the capitalists to completely undermine the socialist
vision that Jawaharlal had for the Congress. He further reined in
Jawaharlal by engineering the resignation of his chosen men from
the Working Committee. There can be little doubt that Gandhi had
been disingenuous when he had assured Jawaharlal that he would
be elected president for the policies and principles he stood for.
Jawaharlal's conversion to socialism was no secret in 1936.

Jawaharlal may not have been fully aware of the network of
forces ranged against him within and without the Congress. But
he was no innocent. He recognized what he was up against and
hence he had written about his isolation to Gandhi.[32] He may have
even accepted the isolation as the judgement of his peers. He could
have resigned but he prided himself as being not a quitter. Over and
above everything there was the spell of Gandhi. His closeness to and
dependence on Gandhi had increased after the emotional upheaval
caused by Kamala's untimely death. Gandhi was aware of this: he
wrote to Agatha Harrison at the end of April 1936: 'Though the gulf
between us as to the outlook upon life has undoubtedly widened,
we have never been so near each other in hearts as perhaps we are
today.'[33] It was a bond that neither was willing to snap.

---

[31] Ibid. (Emphasis in original.)

[32] He made the point of his isolation to Syed Mahmud: 'In the Working Committee
meetings,' he wrote, 'I was completely isolated.' Letter to Syed Mahmud, 5 May 1936,
in Nehru, *Selected Works*, vol. 7, p. 214; to Krishna Menon, he wrote, 'It is a tiring
business to carry on wars on numerous fronts and there are few to help.' Letter to
Krishna Menon, 18 June 1936, in ibid., p. 288.

[33] Letter from Gandhi to Agatha Harrison, 30 April 1936, in Jawaharlal Nehru, *A*

What also needs to be highlighted is that Birla had got the measure of Jawaharlal. His summing up in April 1936 is worth quoting: 'He [Jawaharlal] could have caused a split by resigning but he did not . . . Jawaharlalji seems to be like a typical English democrat who takes defeat in a sporting spirit. He seems to be out for giving expression to his ideology, but he realizes that action is impossible and so does not press for it.'[34] The opposition and the absence of action notwithstanding, 1936 remained Jawaharlal's red-vintage year.

The man who could have been Jawaharlal's strongest ally in his attempt to make socialism part of the Congress programme was Subhas; unfortunately, throughout this entire time he was forcibly kept out of all political activity by the British government. Arrested as he stepped on to Indian soil on 8 April 1936, Subhas did two stints in prison: first in Bombay's Arthur Road Prison and then in Yerwada Central Prison in Poona. In May he was moved to his brother Sarat's bungalow in Kurseong, where he spent his time under house arrest. He was not allowed to correspond with Gandhi even on non-political matters like khadi and the Harijan movement. A letter Jawaharlal wrote to Subhas dated 8 July on the formation of the Civil Liberties Union was withheld by the police.[35] There were no formal charges against Subhas, and in the House of Lords, Lord Zetland, the secretary of state for India, admitted that 'nothing was more distasteful for any administrator than to have to resort to measures of this kind', but he added 'in India it was unavoidable'. He recognized Subhas as 'a man of great ability and possibly of genius' who 'had always directed his abilities to destructive rather than constructive purpose'.[36]

With the onset of winter Subhas was moved, still as a prisoner, to the Medical College Hospital in Calcutta. It was a relief for Subhas to be proximate to the familiar noises of his own city. He was allowed

---

Bunch of Old Letters, p. 182.

[34] Letter from Birla to Thakurdas, 20 April 1936, in Purushottamdas Thakurdas Papers, File No. 177.

[35] Sugata Bose, *His Majesty's Opponent*, p. 115.

[36] Ibid.

a few visitors and was especially moved when Rabindranath Tagore came to see him. But this could not compensate for Subhas's enforced distance from his chosen calling, politics and the national movement. He was finally released on the night of 17 March 1937; he came out from the hospital a free man.

The decision of the governor of Bengal, John Anderson, to release Subhas had a political context. In the elections that had been held under the 1935 Act, the Congress had done well and the party had decided to accept office in the provinces in spite of the opposition of Jawaharlal and other radicals. In Bengal, a coalition government was formed with the Muslim League and the Krishak Praja Party as partners. This meant that the Congress was in the opposition. This cleared the path for Subhas's release. But the government was careful not to release Subhas before the crucial Congress meeting regarding office acceptance, fearing that Subhas would only strengthen Jawaharlal within the Congress.

Jawaharlal's vulnerable position within the Congress, partly engendered by the absence of people like Subhas, was evident in his acquiescence to the decision of the Working Committee to accept office. In an interview, he said, 'Every decision of the Working Committee is a right one. Just as the king can do no wrong, the Working Committee also can do no wrong.' This statement can be interpreted as a criticism of both the Working Committee and its decision to accept office. But it would be simplistic to assume that Jawaharlal had not worked hard for the Congress to win the elections and had been non-cooperative within the Working Committee. Jawaharlal's involvement in the election process began with his participation in the drafting of the Congress manifesto. He avoided the mention of socialism in the manifesto. Instead, the focus was on the fight against imperialism. The manifesto rejected the Government of India Act of 1935 and the Communal Award that went with it. Congressmen, it was argued, were going into the legislatures to sabotage and to end the Act; the question of accepting office would be decided after the elections. It spoke for the establishment of civil liberties, the release of political prisoners and to repair the wrongs done to the peasantry and to public institutions.[37]

The socialist members of the Working Committee had no objections to the manifesto; in fact, Narendra Deva, a keen socialist, recommended the manifesto as a revolutionary document.[38] The persons most delighted were Jawaharlal's former critics in the Working Committee. Rajagopalachari wrote to Gandhi to say that he was charmed by the manner in which Jawaharlal had gone through the Working Committee. Patel was more eloquent: 'We have been getting on beautifully this time. The smooth and harmonious working reminds me most forcibly of the Working Committee meetings before 1932. It has been more like a gathering of family members than a formal committee meeting . . . I cannot speak too highly of Jawaharlal. He has done wonderful work, and has been burning the candle at both ends. We found not the slightest difficulty in cooperating with him and adjusting ourselves to his views on certain points. I have an impression that he is also satisfied.'[39] Jawaharlal's enthusiasm for Congress politics was thus not dimmed by the fact of his being circumscribed by Gandhi's men in the Working Committee. If he was indeed dissatisfied and aggrieved, there was no private or public articulation of it.

Jawaharlal threw himself into the election campaign, travelling into the interior of rural India by train, by plane, by car, by bicycle, by cart, by steamer, on camelback, on horseback, on elephant and on foot. He drew huge crowds everywhere. Lal Bahadur Shastri, who many years later was to succeed Jawaharlal as prime minister, recalled that on one occasion the crowd was so packed that Jawaharlal was forced to walk on their shoulders and later felt ashamed that he had done so with his shoes on.[40] His popularity

---

[37] The text of the manifesto is available in Nehru, *Selected Works*, vol. 7, pp. 459–64.

[38] Gopal, *Jawaharlal Nehru*, vol. 1, pp. 214–15.

[39] Ibid., p. 215; the letters of Rajagopalachari and Patel were written to Gandhi and communicated to Nehru by Mahadev Desai: ibid., n3.

[40] Shastri's article in *A Study of Nehru* (Bombay, 1959), (ed.) R. Zakaria, pp. 150–51: cited in Gopal, *Jawaharlal Nehru*, vol. 1, p. 215.

was unquestioned. If Jawaharlal did not discover India in this, the very first of his national campaigns, the people of India certainly discovered him. Reflecting on the campaign, he wrote, while he was still in the middle of it, that 'all this enthusiasm is exhilarating, and one feels intoxicated by it . . . I attract enormous crowds and I evoke an astonishing amount of enthusiasm. Partly this may be due to a certain personal popularity, but largely, I think, it is due to the great prestige and influence of the Congress.'[41] In his speeches he did not refer to individual candidates. He spoke on the problems facing the people of India—poverty, debt, and foreign rule. He made no promises except the promise of ceaseless struggle till independence was achieved. He spoke using simple words and phrases. A British official, reporting to his superiors, wrote after hearing Jawaharlal speak at the end of July 1936 that the 'Pandit is by far the most attractive public speaker whom I have heard in India.'[42]

In the middle of the election campaign, Jawaharlal was re-elected president of the Congress at the session in Faizpur in December 1936. This re-election did not pass without opposition. Dismayed by Jawaharlal's willingness to continue as president, Patel wrote to Mahadev Desai, Gandhi's secretary, 'The decked-up groom-prince is ready to marry at one stroke as many girls as he can find.'[43] He made Gandhi write to Rajagopalachari, and the former in his letter said, 'The Sardar is desperately anxious for you to wear the thorny crown.' When Rajagopalachari declined, Patel suggested the name of Govind Ballabh Pant and went to the extent of saying: 'As far as I am concerned, I would break loose and quit if he [Jawaharlal] continues.' Patel was willing to contest Jawaharlal's candidature. According to J.B. Kripalani, who was present when Jawaharlal spoke to Gandhi about continuing as president, the former made the point that eight months was too short a time to revitalize the Congress and so he

---

[41] 'This Touring Business', 16 September 1936, in Nehru, *Selected Works*, vol. 7, pp. 350–51.

[42] Gopal, *Jawaharlal Nehru*, vol. 1, p. 216.

[43] Letter from Patel to Mahadev Desai, 15 November 1936, in Rajmohan Gandhi, *Patel*, p. 256.

wanted another term. Gandhi responded by saying that he would see what could be done. Gandhi then persuaded Patel not to contest.[44]

Perhaps it was with this background in mind that in his presidential address Jawaharlal steered clear of the subject of socialism except to point out that it helped in understanding the problems facing India. But he was clear that '[T]he Congress stands for full democracy in India and fights for a democratic state, not for socialism.' It is also significant that in his address he mentioned Subhas: 'Soon after the last Congress I had to nominate the Working Committee and I included in this our comrade Subhas Chandra Bose. But you know how he was snatched away from us on arrival at Bombay and ever since then he has been kept in internment despite failing health. Our committee has been deprived of his counsel, and I have missed throughout the year this brave comrade.'[45] The shift from the plural to the singular in the last sentence is perhaps worth noting in the context of the relationship between the two men in 1936.

The Congress performed well in the elections. It had contested 1161 of the 1585 seats and won 716. In six of the eleven provinces it had a clear majority and was the single largest party in three others. Reflecting on the election results, a confident Jawaharlal wrote to Stafford Cripps that '[T]he whole campaign and the election itself have been a revelation of the widespread anti-imperialist spirit prevailing throughout the country. It has also made clearer the class cleavages among the people. The big landlord class and other vested interests were ranged against us. They were swept in the Congress flood, their most determined opponents being their own tenants.'[46] In more practical terms, the question of acceptance of office could no longer be deferred. Here, Jawaharlal found himself in a hopeless minority: he had completely misread the mood of the party. He believed that since the Lucknow session, there had been

---

[44] This account of Nehru's re-election is taken from ibid., pp. 256–57.

[45] Presidential Address, 27 December 1936, in Nehru, *Selected Works*, vol. 7, pp. 598–614.

[46] Letter to Stafford Cripps, 22 February 1937, in Nehru, *Selected Works*, vol. 8, pp. 31–34.

a change in the thinking of Congressmen. On 28 September 1936, he had written to Krishna Menon with a great deal of certainty that 'the whole position in India has changed very greatly during the last six months on this subject [acceptance of office]. At the time of the Lucknow Congress, acceptance of ministries was a dead certainty as far as the Congress was concerned. Today it is a very doubtful proposition.'[47]

The error of Jawaharlal's assessment was revealed to him immediately after the election results. A convention of all Congressmen who had been elected was called. Jawaharlal believed that the purpose of this convention was to present before the elected members three principal aspects of the Congress programme: fight the Government of India Act, hinder the coming or the functioning of federation, and work for the constituent assembly.[48] Before the convention met, there was so much talk among Congressmen about forming ministries and accepting office that Jawaharlal had to remind them as the president that '[W]e are not out for the spoils of office but for bigger, vaster things affecting our millions.'[49] When he addressed the convention, he emphasized that '[T]o win an election is a small matter for us; we are out to win the freedom of our people.' To those who had been elected by the people, he spelt out the significance of the people's verdict: 'They [the people] have given notice to British imperialism to quit. This constitution must therefore go, lock, stock and barrel, and leave the field clear for our constituent assembly.'[50] Jawaharlal obviously believed that the acceptance of office would divert Congressmen from the key goals.

His words fell on deaf years. A circular was issued by the Congress headquarters to the provincial branches asking them to provide their views on office acceptance. Out of the eighteen that responded,

---

[47] Letter to Krishna Menon, 28 September 1936, in Nehru, *Selected Works*, vol. 7, pp. 470–71.

[48] Letter to Cripps, 22 February 1937, in Nehru, *Selected Works*, vol. 8, p. 33.

[49] 'Speculations about Office Acceptance', 8 March 1937, in Nehru, *Selected Works*, vol. 8, p. 57.

[50] Presidential Address to the All India Convention of Congress Legislators, 19 March 1937, in ibid., pp. 60–71.

thirteen were in favour of acceptance of office. Within the Congress leadership, men like Rajagopalachari and Rajendra Prasad were in favour; Patel, ever the realist, acknowledged that 'we might in the course of events be driven to such an acceptance'. He was conscious of the mood of the Congress legislators and of the businessmen who had funded the elections.[51] The Working Committee authorized office acceptance and in the same breath reiterated that the fundamental aim of the Congress was to fight and destroy the Act.

Jawaharlal was totally dejected by this development. Immediately after the meeting, he walked into the room of M.N. Roy, the communist leader, and, in Roy's words, 'threw himself on the bed, a broken man, nearly on the point of crying. "I must resign," he said. I enquired, "Why? Have they rejected your draft?" "No," he exclaimed in impotent rage, "they have accepted the whole damn thing, supplemented by a short paragraph dictated by Gandhiji, which invalidates the rest of the resolution."'[52] Gandhi admitted to the press on 30 March 1937 that he was 'the sole author of the office-acceptance clause of the Congress resolution'.[53]

Once again Jawaharlal was on the verge of resigning but he did not. He did not want to split the Congress. His views and aims were clear: 'Our task is . . . to pool our resources, to tone down our differences as far as we can, to bear with each other even though we may differ on some matters, for ours is the larger agreement on the issue of Indian freedom and independence. We have done so in the past and built up the magnificent structure of the Congress.'[54] He saw himself as a soldier serving the cause of the Congress. It is also worth considering if the Congress leadership, in spite of its differences with him, would have allowed him to resign. There was an acceptance that Jawaharlal's stature and popularity as a leader had grown especially during the election campaign. Men like Patel

[51] Som, *Differences within Consensus*, p. 185.

[52] Quoted in Gopal, *Jawaharlal Nehru*, vol. 1, pp. 218–19.

[53] See *Together They Fought*, p. 299n583.

[54] 'On the choice of the Congress President', 20 November 1936, in Nehru, *Selected Works*, vol. 7, pp. 591–93.

and Rajendra Prasad were not willing to totally alienate him. The latter wrote to Patel: 'Nothing should be done to cut him [Nehru] in such a way as to drive him away from us.'[55] Moreover, there was Jawaharlal's bond with Gandhi, a bond that could take enormous stress and strain. All these factors made the Congress and Jawaharlal inseparable.

Jawaharlal's response was to retreat from Congress affairs. While he was 'out of tune with the Congress',[56] Subhas was recovering his health in Dalhousie. From Dalhousie, Subhas extended the invitation to the Congress to hold the next AICC and Working Committee meetings in Calcutta. This meant that some of the important leaders, like Gandhi and Jawaharlal, would actually stay in Sarat Bose's house. The meetings were scheduled to be held in October 1937. Among the many matters that were discussed and decided in the Calcutta meeting, one affected Subhas directly. It was decided that Subhas would preside over the next session of the Congress to be held at Haripura in Gujarat. This decision was not without reservations. Gandhi wrote to Patel on 1 November 1937: 'I have observed that Subhas is not at all dependable. But there is nobody but he who can be the President.'[57]

It is difficult to understand why Gandhi believed that in 1937 there was no one else save Subhas to be the president of the Congress. Was he implying that having made Jawaharlal president twice, the claims of Subhas could no longer be overlooked? Or did he believe that in spite of all his shortcomings, Subhas had already suffered too much for the nationalist cause and had acquired the stature of a popular leader too clearly not to be made the president? There were other practical considerations. Prasad, Patel and Rajagopalachari— all potential candidates—were busy with ministry formation. It is not clear who Gandhi consulted on this matter. There is no existing correspondence between him and Jawaharlal on the choice of the

---

[55] Letter from Rajendra Prasad to Patel, 6 December 1937: cited in Som, *Differences within Consensus*, p. 191.

[56] The phrase is Gopal's, *Jawaharlal Nehru*, vol. 1, the title of chapter 15.

[57] Letter to Patel, 1 November 1937, in Gandhi, *Collected Works*, vol. 66, p. 284.

president to succeed the latter. The choice did create some dismay. Rajagopalachari told the governor of Madras, Lord Erskine, that 'the election of Bose was a great mistake'. But Rajagopalachari was not 'unduly perturbed' as he believed that the right-wing majority of the Working Committee would be able to control and direct Subhas's activities.[58] Apart from offering to Subhas what to Jawaharlal he had called 'a crown of thorns', Gandhi imparted to him another gift: observing that he was not totally fit, he advised Subhas to take more rest, this time in Europe, before he took on the onerous task of leading the party.

Subhas thus found himself back in Austria in November 1937. Both in personal terms and in terms of the political context, it was to a different Austria that he returned. In personal terms, he was coming back to the woman he loved, who he would marry secretly in December 1937 in the course of this visit. In political terms, the entire atmosphere in Austria had changed under the impact of the Nazi regime in Germany and the activities of the Austrian Nazis. By the second half of 1937, and certainly by the time Subhas arrived in the resort of Bad Gastein near Salzburg where he spent most of his time during this visit, Hitler's intentions regarding Austria were evident. Hitler had spoken many times in menacing terms about moving against Austria. By the beginning of 1938, his intentions were being put into action. Within Austria, the Nazis unfolded a ceaseless agitation.[59] Vienna had always been the cradle of European anti-Semitism; under the growing influence of the Nazis, the campaign against the Jews was heightened, most visibly in Vienna, but in other parts of Austria as well. The repression of the Jews began before the actual annexation of Austria but acquired a ferocious form after it.[60] Yet, in the writings and utterances of Subhas in this period, there is not even a hint of his awareness of what was going

[58] Letter from Erskine to Linlithgow, 19 January 1938, in *Towards Freedom: Documents on Movement for Independence in India, 1938*, (ed.) Basudev Chatterji (Delhi, 1939), pp. 25–26.

[59] For these developments and the *Anschluss* (the annexation of Austria by Hitler), see Ian Kershaw, *Hitler, 1936–45: Nemesis* (London, 2000), pp. 66–79.

[60] Ibid., p. 84.

on in Austria. He could not have been unaware of the events. It has been aptly noted that 'Not talking about anti-Semitism was possible; not hearing about it was impossible.'[61] Was Subhas silent because he wanted to protect Emilie?

This question cannot be answered with a definite yes because a large part of Subhas's time in Bad Gastein was spent in writing his second book, an attempt at an autobiography. He could not finish the book and the incomplete version was published as *An Indian Pilgrim*. This book, as the title indicates, was more introspective than his first book as it traced the author's own mental and spiritual development. In spite of this thrust, Subhas kept his mind away from the brutality he saw or heard about in Austria. The absence of any mention of the persecution of the Jews and the emergence of totalitarianism in parts of Europe conveys the impression that these developments had left no imprint on his intellectual and ideological development. Yet, during his visit to Germany in 1933, he had been sensitive and disapproving of racial prejudice directed towards Indians.

There is no satisfactory answer from Subhas's own writings to two questions. One is why he decided to write his autobiography at this point in his life. And two, why he chose to write it in such haste—he wrote ten chapters in ten days in December 1937 while he was in Bad Gastein. Regarding the first question, one historian has suggested that both Gandhi and Jawaharlal had written their autobiographies and these examples could have inspired Subhas to write an account of his own intellectual development and to come to terms with his own inner self.[62] It is possible that having read Jawaharlal's autobiography, Subhas felt, as Jawaharlal's peer, that he should also tell his own story which was very different from Jawaharlal's. The question of haste was probably related to Subhas's realization that once he went back to India to be president of the Congress, there would be very little time for writing. He used the

[61] Edmund de Waal, *The Hare with Amber Eyes: A Hidden Inheritance* (London, 2010), p. 207.

[62] Gordon, *Brothers Against the Raj*, p. 342.

time at Bad Gastein to finish off as much of the writing as he could. Given the path his life took subsequently, he never went back to finishing the manuscript. Perhaps it was just as well that he wrote what he could during this brief spell in Austria.

An Indian Pilgrim, as readers find it today, consists of Subhas's reflection on his growing-up years and his education in Cuttack, Calcutta and Cambridge; these recollections come to an abrupt end with his resignation from the ICS. This is followed by a chapter entitled 'My Faith (Philosophical)'. Subhas's plan for the book was much more substantial. In the first page of the original manuscript he had made an outline of the work. From this it is clear that he wanted to bring the story of his life up to the time he was writing the book, i.e. 1937. This chronological autobiography would be followed, according to Subhas's original plan, by three chapters on his life's philosophy—'My Faith (Philosophical)', 'My Faith (Political)' and 'My Faith (Economic)'.[63] He managed to write, before India and the Congress claimed him, only the section on his philosophical beliefs. In this chapter, he wrote how his mind had moved away from an initial acceptance of Sankara's doctrine of maya because he discovered that he could not live by that doctrine. His quest moved to other branches of Indian philosophy. He arrived at the conclusion that '[I]t is impossible to comprehend the Absolute through our human intellect with all its limitations.'[64] Subhas described his attitude as one of 'benevolent agnosticism'. By this he meant that while he was not prepared to take anything on trust, he could not also 'rule out as sheer moonshine what so many individuals claim to have experienced in the past'.[65] He thus assumed what he called the position of a relativist: 'Truth as known to us is not absolute but relative. It is relative to our common mental constitution—to our distinctive characteristics as individuals—and to changes in the same individual during the process of time.'[66] From

---

[63] Sugata Bose, *His Majesty's Opponent*, p. 128.

[64] *An Indian Pilgrim*, p. 119.

[65] Ibid., p. 120.

[66] Ibid.

this premise, Subhas could not avoid the question regarding the nature of (relative) reality. He offered three conclusions. First, the reality had an objective existence and was not an illusion; second, the reality was dynamic, ever-changing, never static; and third, and this was the most important, the reality, for Subhas, was the Spirit, working with a conscious purpose through time and space.[67]

Subhas then asked himself the question: 'Why do I believe in Spirit?' His immediate answer was uncomplicated. He wrote that he believed in Spirit because 'It is a pragmatic necessity. My nature demands it.' He discerned, he wrote, an 'increasing purpose' in his own life; he saw a design. He could not accept that he was merely a 'conglomeration of atoms' and that reality was only a 'fortuitous combination of molecules'. He was convinced that creation reflected 'the eternal play of eternal forces—the Divine Play, if you will'. But this still did not answer the question about the nature of the Spirit that is reality. Subhas answered this by recalling a parable of the Bengali saint Ramakrishna Paramahamsa about a blind man trying to describe an elephant. From this, Subhas came to the conclusion that 'most of the conceptions of reality are true, though partially', but the point was to discover the conception that represents the maximum truth. For Subhas, most emphatically, the essence of reality was love; it was also the essential principle of human life.[68]

Subhas thus arrived at the core of his philosophical beliefs. It is a moot question how far this affirmation of love as the essence of life was determined by his own profound emotional involvement with Emilie Schenkl. The other point to note is that this brief sojourn into the terrain of philosophy, however amateurish, distinguished Subhas's autobiographical essay from that of Jawaharlal's. The latter in *An Autobiography* had made no attempt to delve into the nature of truth and reality or to sketch the philosophical foundations of his life. This difference is probably a function of their educational background: Subhas had studied philosophy, and Jawaharlal the natural sciences. The reflections of Jawaharlal were more concerned

---

[67] Ibid., p. 121.
[68] Ibid., pp. 121–23.

with the immediate, with events as they were unfolding around him; while Subhas sought to go beyond the immediate. Subhas, perhaps because he self-consciously styled himself as a pilgrim, as a seeker, could not avoid the cragged and steep path that he knew he would have to take to reach the hill on which stood Truth.[69] Subhas believed that his life had a purpose, but he did not broach the problematic question of predestination and fatalism. He wrote, 'The individual has to go through the experience of his race within the brief span of his own life . . . If we accept an idea, we have to give ourselves wholly to it and to allow it to transform our entire life.'[70] The idea of sacrifice for his motherland had already seized Subhas's identity and destiny. That purpose and design was informed by love. How far was his life, from the time he made this declaration, governed by his philosophical faith?

Subhas had to turn to the immediate as soon as he arrived back in India on 23 January 1938, his forty-first birthday. His work was cut out and he began his preparation to take over as the president of the Congress in Haripura. He wrote his presidential address in two days flat and left for Haripura by train on 11 February. He arrived at Bardoli from where he was taken by car to Haripura. His arrival at the seat of the Congress session, called Vithalnagar, after Vallabhbhai's elder brother, was quite a spectacle. He was brought in on a chariot drawn by fifty-one white bulls. The chariot had been provided by a local maharaja, and a farmer, who had lost all his property in the course of the satyagraha movement, was the charioteer. It is worth recalling, if only as a study in contrast, that Jawaharlal had entered the Lahore congress, of which he was the president in 1929, on a white charger.

Subhas's presidential address was the most important and the lengthiest speech he made to the Congress.[71] He began in a

---

[69] In Bengali, Subhas rendered the word as *pathik*, or 'secular wayfarer'. For the implications of this, see Ranajit Guha, 'Nationalism and Trials of Becoming', p. 522.

[70] *An Indian Pilgrim*, p. 20.

[71] The text of the Presidential Address is available in *Netaji: Collected Works*, vol. 9, pp. 3–30.

conventional mode with 'Mr Chairman and Friends', again in contrast to Jawaharlal's controversial presidential address at Lucknow two years before, which began with the word 'Comrades'. But any illusion that may have been harboured that Subhas would not be too radical was dispelled by his quoting Lenin, once the formalities of offering condolences were done. The quotation from Lenin came in the context of the brief analysis of the British Empire that Subhas presented to Congressmen. He saw the British Empire—'a combination of self-governing countries, partially self-governing dependencies and autocratically-governed colonies'—as an entity that was 'sure to break down under its own strain'. The challenge before the British Empire was to transform itself into a 'federation of free nations'. But this would have been possible only if the British people had become free in their own home, if Britain became a socialist state. Subhas linked the capitalist ruling class in Britain and the colonies. The emancipation of the colonies and the establishment of freedom in Britain had to be part of the same process.

Subhas then moved to the policy of divide and rule which the British had deployed with great skill in India. This made any Constitution for India emanating out of Whitehall open to suspicion. But this policy was not always 'an unmixed blessing for the ruling power'. To explicate this, Subhas asked, 'Will she [Britain] please the Muslim or the Hindu in India? Will she favour the Arab or the Jew in Palestine—the Arab or the Kurd in Iraq? Will she side with the King or the Wafd in Egypt?' These divisions were causing strain at a number of points for the British Empire.

Turning to India, Subhas recognized the problem posed by the question of minorities. He was eager to arrive at a solution that would be consistent with the fundamental principles of nationalism. There existed in India 'common interests, economic and political [that] cut across communal divisions and dissensions'. This demanded that a policy of 'live and let live' in matters religious and an understanding in matters economic and political be the objective. He drew attention to the condition of other minorities that often got submerged because of the importance given to the problem of

Muslims. He reiterated that the Congress stood for the political and economic rights of all Indians.

Already in 1938, Subhas had the glint of political freedom in his eyes. He was certain that after the capture of political power, national reconstruction would take place along socialistic lines. This would mean that 'the "have-nots" . . . will benefit at the expense of the "haves"'. Moreover, the Congress believed in 'complete non-interference in matters of conscience, religion and culture as well as of cultural autonomy for the different linguistic areas'. Therefore, the Muslims had nothing to fear from India gaining independence—'on the contrary', Subhas said, reassuring the Muslims, 'they have everything to gain'. He also put forward an outline of the reconstruction that would follow once freedom was attained. There was no doubt in his mind that the principal national problems—the eradication of poverty, illiteracy and disease, and scientific production and distribution—could all be 'effectively tackled only along socialistic lines'. The country would be unified through a strong Central government but this would not threaten the minority communities and the provinces as they would be allowed 'a large measure of autonomy in cultural as well as governmental affairs'.

He drew attention to the need to develop a lingua franca, a common script, and an education policy. The lingua franca, he said, would be a mixture of Hindi and Urdu since the distinction between the two was an 'artificial one'; he suggested the adoption of the Roman script. He had been convinced about the need of the latter by his visit to Turkey in 1934: it would be a 'great advantage to have the same script as the rest of the world'. For economic reconstruction, he advocated the setting up of a planning commission that would consider and decide which of the home industries could be revived. But the way forward was through industrialization. Modern industrialism brought many evils in its train but there was no going back to the pre-industrial era, 'even if we desire to do so'. These last words were an obvious reference to the views of Gandhi. He wanted the planning commission to advise on adopting a 'comprehensive scheme for gradually socializing our entire agricultural and industrial system in the spheres of both production and appropriation. Extra capital will have to be procured for this, whether through internal or external loans or through inflation.' Here was a thumbnail sketch of Subhas's economic thinking. He clearly wanted the state to be the chief economic actor once political power had been captured.

There are two features of this address that need to be highlighted. One is that except for the clear preference for industrialization, there was no statement that remotely suggested a criticism of or deviation from Gandhi's views and programme of action. In fact, while laying down the course of future political action, Subhas said, 'I believe more than ever that the methods should be Satyagraha or non-violent non-cooperation in the widest sense of the term, including civil disobedience. It would not be correct to call our method passive resistance. Satyagraha, as I understand it, is not merely passive resistance but active resistance as well though that activity must be of a non-violent character.' At the beginning of 1938, Subhas's path to political freedom was very much determined by the methods of Gandhi. He had no doubts about these methods. He saw himself as a loyal Congressman committed to Gandhian modes of struggle, although in Vienna in the early 1930s, he had articulated a strong critique of Gandhi and his methods.

The second point worthy of note is Subhas's emphasis on socialism or socialistic methods as the only way for achieving the goals of national reconstruction once India was free. His views on socialism and its need and efficacy were far more concrete than the ideological terms in which Jawaharlal had spoken about it in his presidential address in Lucknow in 1936. The latter had sent shivers of alarm and displeasure among leading Congressmen like Patel, Rajendra Prasad and Rajagopalachari as well as among members of the capitalist class. But Subhas's speech had no such repercussions. Indeed, the absence of friction between Subhas and Patel was noticeable; consensus seemed to be the spirit of Haripura.[72]

[72] Rajmohan Gandhi, *Patel*, p. 265.

One fallout of the consensus was that when the Working Committee was formed, with the help of Gandhi and Patel, there were no socialists in it. Subhas seemed to have yielded to the spirit of consensus. Jawaharlal recalled this one year later when he wrote to Subhas, '[Y]ou have adopted an entirely passive attitude in the Working Committee . . . In effect, you have functioned more as a Speaker than as a directing President.'[73] One disgruntled Congress chief minister, N.B. Khare, called Subhas 'a puppet in the hands of Mahatma Gandhi'.[74]

Haripura and the year that followed marked the high noon of Subhas's career as a Congressman. He worked hard to give substance to some of the proposals he had put forward at Haripura. He held a meeting in Bombay, attended by heads of Congress ministries and Working Committee members, to discuss the industrial reconstruction of India, the development of power resources, and coordination among Congress-ruled provinces.[75] He held meetings with scientists, especially Meghnad Saha. The latter asked him directly about the future of India—whether it was going back to village life or it was to become a modern industrial nation. Saha's question was obviously aimed at Gandhi's ideas and Subhas's attitude towards them. Subhas did not shy away from answering the question. He said that all Congressmen did not hold the same view on this question but 'the rising generation are [sic] in favour of industrialization'. Industrialization was necessary for solving the problem of poverty. Moreover, according to Subhas, 'the rising generation' was thinking in terms of socialism as the basis of national reconstruction and 'socialism presuppose[d] industrialization'.[76] After discussions at Working Committee meetings, Subhas convened a conference of industries ministers drawn from the Congress-ruled provinces. In his address, he assured his listeners that 'there need not be a conflict between cottage industries and large-scale

[73] Letter to Bose, 4 February 1939, in Nehru, *Selected Works*, vol. 9, p. 482.

[74] Gordon, *Brothers Against the Raj*, p. 357.

[75] Sugata Bose, *His Majesty's Opponent*, p. 144.

[76] 'Science and Politics: answers to questions posed by Meghnad Saha', 21 August 1938, in *Netaji: Collected Works*, vol. 9, pp. 43–48.

industries'. He said he was a 'firm believer in the need of developing our cottage industries, though I also hold that we have to reconcile ourselves to industrialization'.[77] It is evident that in the articulation of his economic philosophy, Subhas was straining at the leash of Gandhian ideas against industrialization.

For much of the time that Jawaharlal had been president of the Congress in 1936–37, Subhas had either been abroad or imprisoned. During Subhas's presidency, when he was busy trying to implement his agenda presented at the Haripura session, Jawaharlal was away in Europe. The decision of the Congress to accept office had jarred, and Jawaharlal in his last months as president had withdrawn from the day-to-day activities of the party. At Haripura, there was pressure on him to become the general secretary, but he refused; he even wanted to opt out of the Working Committee.[78] He was a sad and disillusioned man. He urged a friend, Jal Naoroji, who was in London, not to be in a hurry to come back: 'This is a dull country,' Jawaharlal wrote.[79] Europe beckoned him and in June 1937, he set sail with some relief and glee. Referring to his visit, he wrote to Tagore, 'It is a curious puzzling world but I get on with it to some extent because I like unusual things happening and rather enjoy taking part in them.'[80]

This European trip strengthened Jawaharlal's commitment to anti-fascism and opened up possibilities of dialogue and negotiations with the leaders of the Labour Party in Britain. The Spanish Civil War had captured his attention while he was still in India. He had described the gates of Madrid to be 'the symbols of human liberty'.[81] En route to Great Britain, he visited Spain as a guest of the Republican government. This was akin to a pilgrimage for him. In London, he met Lord Linlithgow who he had refused to meet in India the previous year. Linlithgow had been very eager to meet

---

[77] 'The Industrial Problems of India', 2 October 1938, in ibid., pp. 48–53.

[78] Gopal, *Jawaharlal Nehru*, vol. 1, p. 233.

[79] Letter to J.A.D. Naoroji, 30 August 1937, in Nehru, *Selected Works*, vol. 8, p. 852.

[80] Gopal, *Jawaharlal Nehru*, vol. 1, p. 233.

[81] 'Food for Spain', 20 February 1937, in Nehru, *Selected Works*, vol. 8, p. 700.

Gandhi and Jawaharlal after the Congress assumed office in the provinces. Jawaharlal had refused because he did not want to meet the viceroy when prisoners in Andaman Islands were on a hunger strike. But in the middle of 1938 with the strike over and with the viceroy on leave and away from India, Jawaharlal had no objections. He was to recall that though the conversation was general, he told Linlithgow 'that I gave England at the outside ten years before India was independent'.[82] Significantly, when Jawaharlal was leaving, Linlithgow remarked that 'a wide gap separated us and we would look at each other across it'.[83]

The more substantive meeting was the one Jawaharlal had with some of the leaders of the Labour Party. Clement Attlee had just become the leader of the Labour Party and he was not averse to taking a fresh approach to the Indian constitutional problem. Stafford Cripps, who had developed an epistolary friendship with Jawaharlal, shared Attlee's concerns. Over a weekend in late June 1938, Jawaharlal and Indira stayed with Cripps at his country house in Gloucestershire. Among the guests were Harold Laski, Aneurin Bevan and Attlee. It was here, in the very congenial atmosphere of a weekend in an English country house—aptly named Goodfellows—that the first, albeit informal, terms were discussed of a transfer of power in the not-too-distant future. The Labour leaders conceded one major demand that Nehru and other Congress leaders had been making: India should be allowed to devise a new constitution on the basis of a representative constituent assembly. The concession was subject to two conditions: separate minority representation and the election of representatives from the states that accepted the procedure. Once the constitution was formed, the informal concordat added, the free Indian government would be required to sign a treaty that would guarantee the protection of British interests for at least fifteen years.[84] Thus, while Subhas in

[82] Gopal, *Jawaharlal* Nehru, vol. 1, pp. 236–37.

[83] 'Note to the Working Committee', 1 August 1938, in Nehru, *Selected Works*, vol. 9, p. 98.

[84] R.J. Moore, *Escape from Empire: The Attlee Government and the Indian Problem*

India was putting in place the signposts for national reconstruction after the attainment of freedom, Jawaharlal in Britain was creating the ground for a smooth of transfer of power.

Jawaharlal could not visit the Soviet Union as he could not secure a visa in time. He went to Munich as a private tourist, having spurned the approaches made by the Nazi government to visit Germany as its guest. In various fora in Europe, Jawaharlal made his opposition to fascism and Nazism clear. In Prague he expressed his sympathies with the Czech government in its resistance to Hitler. He was sick with the mollycoddling that Hitler received from the British and the French governments. He wrote in *National Herald* in October that '[I]t was the rape of Czechoslovakia by Germany with England and France holding her forcibly down.'[85] His opposition to fascism and Nazism were unequivocal. He urged the Congress Working Committee to pass a resolution expressing its sympathy with the pro-democracy forces in Europe, condemning Nazi attempts at aggression.[86]

While Jawaharlal was away in Europe he had complained mildly to J.B. Kripalani that 'Subhas has not written to me at all'.[87] Once he was back in India, Subhas wrote to him with great warmth: 'You must be wondering what a strange creature I am, not to have replied to all your letters. I got them all right, however . . . You cannot imagine how I have missed you all these months.'[88] Both Jawaharlal and Subhas had their vision of India's future lit up by the idea of socialism. Both of them therefore laid an enormous amount in store in centralized planning for the development of the economy under an independent state. It was almost inevitable that they would work together to fulfil this part of the agenda as spelt

---

(Oxford, 1983), p. 6; and Peter Clarke, *The Cripps Version: The Life of Sir Stafford Cripps, 1889–1952* (London, 2002), p. 118. Nehru reported this discussion to the Congress Working Committee in his note of 1 August 1938: Nehru, *Selected Works*, vol. 9, p. 99.

[85] Quoted in Gopal, *Jawaharlal Nehru*, vol. 1, p. 238.

[86] Letter to Kripalani, 30 August 1938: Nehru, *Selected Works*, vol. 9, pp. 117–18.

[87] Letter to Kripalani, 1 September 1938, in ibid., p. 129.

[88] Letter to Nehru, 19 October 1938, in *Netaji: Collected Works*, vol. 9, p. 183.

out by Subhas in his presidential address. Soon after Jawaharlal's return from Europe, Subhas invited him to be the chairman of the National Planning Committee, adding, '[Y]ou must if it is to be a success.'[89] Jawaharlal accepted without hesitation. Explaining his decision to a friend, Jawaharlal wrote, '[S]o far as the planning committee is concerned I shall associate myself with it because I am intensely interested in planning.'[90]

On the need for planning and industrialization, Jawaharlal and Subhas were in complete agreement. At the inauguration of the National Planning Committee at Bombay on 17 December 1938, while assuaging fears that the work of the Planning Committee would threaten cottage industries and the work going on since 1921 for the production of khadi, Subhas emphasized the importance of machine-based industries and the development of the power sector and of transport and communication.[91] In a note written immediately after assuming the chairmanship of the committee, Jawaharlal made the same point. He added that there was nothing in the Congress programme to prevent the promotion of large-scale industries. He pointed out various resolutions passed in the Karachi congress in 1931 and in the Working Committee in 1934 which had not decided in any way against large-scale industry. In Karachi, in fact, Jawaharlal noted, it had been resolved that '[T]he State shall own or control key industries and services, mineral resources, railways, waterways, shipping and other means of public transport.' He felt it was the duty of the Planning Committee to seriously consider the promotion of large-scale industries in India; he added, '[T]here can be no planning if such planning does not include big industries.' But in doing this, the committee had also to 'remember the basic Congress policy of encouraging cottage industries'.[92]

---

[89] Ibid.

[90] Letter to Anil Kumar Chanda, 1 December 1938: Nehru, *Selected Works*, vol. 9, p. 367.

[91] Inauguration speech at the first meeting of the All India National Planning Committee at Bombay, 17 December 1938: *Netaji: Collected Works*, vol. 9, pp. 62–64.

[92] Note by Nehru, 21 December 1938, in Jawaharlal Nehru Papers, Subject File No. 135 (Part 1).

Jawaharlal enjoyed the work of the National Planning Committee that Subhas had entrusted to him, even though he found the work was time-consuming and exhausting.[93] It was this work, however, that created a certain amount of discord between the two of them in the middle of 1939. The disagreement centred around H.V. Kamath, who had resigned from the Indian Civil Service in 1938 and had been taken on as one of the secretaries of the National Planning Committee to look after the office work. Some of the members complained that Kamath was taking an aggressive part in controversial political matters. Jawaharlal pointed out to Kamath that 'secretaries of committees should take no public part, by means of speeches, statements etc., in highly controversial issues'. The committee as a whole felt that Kamath should not publicly take a position on controversial politics. Kamath was unwilling to accept such a condition. Jawaharlal informed Subhas of the situation and expressed his helplessness: if Kamath did not accept the terms set by the committee he would have to resign, which Kamath offered to do on 22 June 1939. Jawaharlal had kept Subhas informed because the latter was interested in Kamath.[94] Subhas wrote to Jawaharlal early in July to say that the objections that Jawaharlal had mentioned were his own and not those of the other members of the committee. He accused Jawaharlal of wanting 'to get rid of Kamath because he gave expression to a particular view'. Jawaharlal replied, 'You have attributed a particular motive to me which is fair neither to me nor to yourself.' Explaining his stand on Kamath, Jawaharlal added, '[I]t was totally immaterial to me what views Kamath had in regard to Congress or other politics so long as his views were not aggressively expressed so as to come in the way of the work he was doing in the planning committee.'[95] Subhas's interest in Kamath that Jawaharlal had noted became manifest when Kamath became general secretary of the Forward Bloc later in 1939.[96]

---

[93] Letter to Bose, 21 June 1939, in Nehru, *Selected Works*, vol. 9, p. 397.

[94] Ibid., pp. 397–98 and Notes.

[95] Letter to Bose, 11 July 1939, in ibid., p. 401.

[96] Ibid., p. 397n.

One issue on which both Jawaharlal and Subhas had similar experiences was in their attempt to improve the deteriorating communal situation. Both were eager to establish some sort of accord between Hindus and Muslims. To this end they tried to open up a dialogue with Mohammad Ali Jinnah who by the middle of the 1930s had fashioned himself as the 'sole spokesman' of the Muslims in India. Soon after he had assumed the office of president, Subhas took the step of actually going to meet Jinnah in his house in Malabar Hill in Bombay on 14 May 1938. The meeting was cordial but fruitless. It began with Jinnah suggesting that there should be a clear understanding about the position of the Muslim League and the Congress. Jinnah put forward what in his view was the position of these two organizations: the Muslim League was 'the authoritative and representative organization of the Indian Muslims and the Congress . . . the authoritative and representative organization of the solid body of Hindu opinion'.[97] This assertion on the part of Jinnah was unacceptable to the Congress, as Subhas pointed out to Jinnah. In the note he presented to Jinnah, Subhas emphasized that the Congress did not represent just one community: '[I]ts doors must inevitably be open to all communities and it must welcome all Indians who agree with its general policy and methods.' The Congress would become a communal organization, he said, if it accepted the proposition that it only represented one community, the Hindus.[98]

But Jinnah refused to budge from the point he had made regarding the Muslim League representing all the Muslims of India and the Congress only the Hindus.[99] In October 1938, Subhas complained to Jawaharlal that 'Mr Jinnah is unreasonable and intransigent'.[100] The dialogue was thus stillborn. Jawaharlal faced the same intransigence when he had an exchange of letters with

[97] Note handed over by Bose to Jinnah on 14 May 1938: *Netaji: Collected Works*, vol. 9, pp.110–11.

[98] Ibid.

[99] See the correspondence between Bose and Jinnah in *Netaji: Collected Works*, vol. 9, pp. 110–22.

[100] Letter to Nehru, 19 October 1938, in ibid., p. 183.

Jinnah in December 1938. The latter, on the one hand, expressed a desire to 'create a real united front' between Hindus and Muslims,[101] but on the other, made it clear that 'so long as the Congress is not prepared to treat the Muslim League as the authoritative and representative organization of the Mussalmans of India it was not possible to carry on talks regarding the Hindu–Muslim settlement.'[102] Jinnah had thus shut the door on the face of the two Congress leaders who refused to accept that the Congress was an organization of and for the Hindus.

On another issue Subhas encountered intransigence from a different kind of person: Gandhi. In Bengal, after the 1937 elections, the Congress had sat in the opposition. But a different possibility began to open up for the Congress led by the Bose brothers. It was evident that Fazlul Huq, the undisputed leader of the Krishak Praja Party, and the premier (chief minister) of Bengal, was increasingly unhappy with the way his coalition ministry was functioning.[103] At this point of time the Congress in Bengal was also going through a process of radicalization that was the result of a 'strong element of strategic manoeuvre' masterminded by the party's provincial leadership.[104] The Bose brothers were keen to form a Congress–Krishak Praja–Scheduled Caste coalition.[105] But such a possibility was nipped in the bud by the intervention of Gandhi sitting in Wardha. On 18 December 1938 he dictated a letter to Subhas, which G.D. Birla carried to Calcutta. Gandhi wrote, 'I must dictate this

---

[101] Letter from Jinnah to Nehru, 17 March 1938, in Jawaharlal Nehru, *A Bunch of Old Letters*, p. 279.

[102] Letter from Jinnah to Nehru, 13 December 1939, in ibid., p. 414.

[103] In July 1938 in a confidential note that Huq circulated to his Cabinet colleagues, he lamented thus: 'I have been repeatedly suggesting that something should be done which will catch the imagination of the people and make the Ministry popular but all my suggestions have been turned down as either impracticable or difficult or harmful . . . I wish to emphasize the point that we are a thoroughly unpopular lot. I have heard it said by more than one responsible person that the public impression is that the present Cabinet is a "banker's' Cabinet".' Quoted in Partha Chatterjee, *Bengal 1920–1947: The Land Question* (Calcutta, 1984), p. 253 n361.

[104] Ibid., pp. 172–77.

[105] Gordon, *Brothers Against the Raj*, p. 367.

letter as I am wilfully blind. Whilst I am dictating this, Maulana Saheb, Nalini Babu and Ghanshamdas [Maulana Azad, Nalini Sarkar—a Calcutta businessman-cum-politician—and G.D. Birla] are listening. We had an exhaustive discussion over the Bengal Ministry. I am more than ever convinced that we should not aim at ousting the Ministry. We shall gain nothing by a reshuffle; and, probably, we shall lose much by including Congressmen in the Ministry. I feel, therefore, that the best way of securing comparative purity of administration and a continuity of a settled programme and policy would be to aim at having all the reforms that we desire, carried out by the present Ministry.'[106]

This letter came as a 'profound shock' to Subhas. He wrote to Gandhi that in the course of the many discussions the two of them had on the subject, Subhas had the impression that Gandhi agreed with the idea of a coalition ministry for Bengal. Gandhi had completely altered his views and Subhas's guess was that he had done so after talking to Azad, Birla and Sarkar. Subhas rightly pointed out to Gandhi that the latter was giving more importance to the views of the above-mentioned trio than to the views of those who were actually responsible for running the Congress organization in Bengal. Gandhi had taken the decision unilaterally without consulting either of the Bose brothers. Subhas believed that the policy Gandhi was advocating was 'wholly wrong', and he could not be a party to it. He argued that the formation of more Congress ministries would increase the power of the Congress and weaken the position of the British government. The formation of a coalition ministry in Bengal of which the Congress was a part was for Subhas 'practical politics'. The reasons for Gandhi's objections were never clear. He may have been influenced by Sarkar and Birla, both of whom had reasons to fear a radicalized Congress in power in Bengal. Subhas made it clear that if Gandhi did not change his decision, Subhas would 'have to carefully consider my position'.[107]

---

[106] Letter to Bose, 18 December 1938, in Gandhi, *Collected Works*, vol. 68, p. 218.
[107] Letter to Gandhi, 21 December 1938, in *Netaji: Collected Works*, vol. 9, pp. 122–26.

'I shall have to carefully consider my position'—through that declaration to Gandhi a tocsin had been sounded. Jawaharlal, for reasons of emotional and personal attachments, could yield completely to Gandhi even when the latter's views and decisions ran completely counter to Jawaharlal's own. But Subhas could not be pushed beyond a point. He respected Gandhi but not without reservations. In the twilight of Subhas's first presidency, the seeds of discord with Gandhi had been sown. Subhas would assert himself by wanting a second term as president. That desire would have dramatic, if tragic, implications for Subhas's life and his friendship with Jawaharlal. 'The die is cast'—Subhas could say for the second time in his life.

6

The End of the Friendship

When Jawaharlal had asked for a second term as president at the end of 1936, he had told Gandhi that one term was too short a time for him to revitalize the party.[1] Subhas must have harboured similar thoughts when he decided he needed a second term as the leader of the Congress. Yet he was worried about his own popularity within the organization. To his wife, he wrote, '[I]t is doubtful if I shall be re-elected President for the coming year. Many people are jealous of me.'[2] Jealousy may not have been the sole or even the most important reason for the objections that were raised regarding Subhas's candidature for the presidentship the second time round. One person who was seriously unhappy was Vallabhbhai Patel.

The relationship between Subhas and Patel had been somewhat fraught since the will left behind by the latter's brother, Vithalbhai. Vithalbhai had died in Vienna in 1933 and had been devotedly nursed by Subhas during his illness. In his will Vithalbhai had endowed more than three-fourths of his estate to Subhas, to be spent by him 'for the political uplift of India and preferably for publicity work on behalf of India's cause in other countries'. Vallabhbhai refused to accept the will as genuine. In the spirit of bonhomie that prevailed at Haripura, Subhas agreed to Patel's suggestion that the money should go to a special committee of the Congress. But they failed to agree

---

[1] See Rajmohan Gandhi, *Patel*, p. 257.

[2] Letter to Emilie, 6 December 1938, in *Netaji: Collected Works*, vol. 7, p. 203.

on the composition of the committee. The matter was dragged to the
law courts and Subhas lost the case in the Bombay High Court and
subsequently on appeal as well. With the money, Vallabhbhai set up
the Vithalbhai Memorial Trust having first obtained a commitment
from all the legal heirs of his brother that none of them would accept
or claim a penny from the estate.[3]

It is not clear if this cause célèbre influenced Patel's assessment
of Subhas as Congress president but he did write in July 1938 to
Rajendra Prasad who had been taken ill: 'Jawahar has gone abroad
for at least four months. You go out for six months and we have to
deal with a President who does not know his own job.'[4] This harsh
judgement may have had something to do with the fact that while
Subhas undertook whistle-stop tours across the country, he had very
little time to speak to the Working Committee. The official history
of the Congress praised his indomitable energy but noted, 'Subhas
Babu was one of the silent Presidents of the Congress. The occasions
on which he spoke at a meeting of the Working Committee during
a whole year of his first Presidentship could be counted on one's
fingers.'[5]

Gandhi's first choice as president for the next session at Tripuri
was Abul Kalam Azad as Gandhi felt that a Muslim as the head of
the Congress could ease the communal situation. Azad's candidature
was, in fact, announced at a Working Committee meeting held
at Bardoli. Azad had not voiced his objections there but he later
withdrew his name.[6] He did not want to contest against Subhas
because both of them came from Calcutta where Subhas's popularity
was high and growing daily. After Azad's withdrawal, Gandhi wrote
to Nehru, 'Maulana Saheb does not want the crown of thorns. If you
want to try again please do. If you won't or he [Subhas] won't listen,
Pattabhi [Sitaramayya] seems to be the only choice.'[7] Jawaharlal

---

[3] Rajmohan Gandhi, *Patel*, pp. 236–37.

[4] Ibid., p. 277.

[5] Sitaramayya, *History of the Congress*, vol. 2, p. 104.

[6] Ibid., p. 105.

[7] Letter from Gandhi to Nehru, 21 December 1938, in *Together They Fought*, p. 352.

had no desire to be president again and so Sitaramayya became a reluctant contender. According to him, he was not even asked if he wanted to be a candidate.[8]

Subhas's desire to be the president a second time had the support of Tagore who expressed his desire to have a 'modernist' in the post. In his opinion there were only 'two genuine modernists' in the Congress high command—Subhas and Jawaharlal. Since the latter was the chairman of the Planning Committee, Tagore was eager to see Subhas elected again as president.[9] Jawaharlal in his reply to the poet's views did not address the question of Subhas's second term—one reason for this may have been the timing of this correspondence, November–December 1938, when the controversy over Subhas's candidature had not acquired the dimensions that it did—but wrote, 'Gurudeva seems to attach more importance than is warranted to the office of the Congress President. No major policy has been determined by the Congress President for some time past. It was because of this that I felt unhappy as President and I came to the conclusion that I would be far more useful without office. The real problems have to be determined quite apart from the presidentship of the Congress.'[10] Tagore also wrote to Gandhi to say that Subhas should be given a second term. Gandhi responded to Tagore by saying that in his personal opinion Subhas 'needed to be free from the Presidential work, if he was to rid Bengal of corruption'.[11] In January 1939, Tagore wrote to Subhas to inform him that he had been requested to publicly express his support for Subhas as the next president. But since he saw himself as 'a person away from the political arena [he had] no right to do more than express my wishes'. He had done so, the poet said, by writing to both Gandhi and Jawaharlal.[12]

---

[8] Sitaramayya, *History of the Congress*, p. 105.

[9] Letter from Anil Chanda to Nehru, 28 November 1938, in Jawaharlal Nehru, *A Bunch of Old Letters*, p. 308.

[10] Letter to Anil Chanda, 1 December 1938, in Nehru, *Selected Works*, vol. 9, p. 367.

[11] Letter to Nehru, 24 November 1938, in Gandhi, *Collected Works*, vol. 68, p. 144.

[12] Letter from Tagore to Bose, 19 January 1939, in *Netaji: Collected Works*, vol. 9, p. 239.

After the withdrawal of Azad from the race, Subhas issued a statement on 21 January. This produced a counterstatement from the Working Committee against Subhas's candidature. This joint statement, as Patel told Jawaharlal, was issued at Gandhi's insistence.[13] Jawaharlal cabled his inability to sign the joint statement. He admitted that he would have preferred Subhas's not standing but a joint statement raised 'difficulties and questions of principle'.[14] Gandhi expressed to Patel his disappointment at Jawaharlal's refusal to sign and Patel conveyed this to Jawaharlal.[15] The latter decided to issue a public statement on his own on 26 January, the same day he expressed his inability to sign the joint statement.

There was another context to Jawaharlal's statement. This was about the statement that Subhas had given to the press on 21 January. There Subhas said that the issue was not a personal one but one of policies and programmes. According to Subhas, '[T]he progressive sharpening of the anti-imperialist struggle in India has given birth to new ideas, ideologies, problems and programmes. People are consequently veering round to the opinion that as in other free countries the Presidential election in India should be fought on the basis of definite problems and programmes so that the contest may help the clarification of issues.' Subhas felt that under these circumstances, an election contest 'may not be an undesirable thing'.

Although in this statement Subhas did not spell out any policy or programme, he did mention 'the prospective fight over Federation'.[16] In their joint statement, Vallabhbhai Patel and six other members of the Working Committee countered Subhas's claims. The Working Committee members said that all of them shared Subhas's opposition

---

[13] Letter from Patel to Nehru, 8 February 1939, in Nehru Papers, vol. 81.

[14] Telegram to Patel, 26 January 1939, in Nehru, *Selected Works*, vol. 9, p. 480.

[15] Letter from Patel to Nehru, 8 February 1939, in ibid.

[16] The first statement of Subhas Chandra Bose, 21 January 1939: *Netaji: Collected Works*, vol. 9, pp. 67–68. By 'the fight over Federation', Subhas was referring to the British scheme of federation with the princes. He suspected that what he called the 'right wing' within the Congress was willing to compromise with the British on this issue.

to federation and this opposition was a part of Congress policy. They went on to state, '[T]he Congress policy and programmes are not determined by its successive Presidents.' The statement elaborated that the position of the president was akin to that of a chairman, and that the policies and programmes of the Congress, 'when they are not determined by the Congress itself, are determined by the Working Committee'. The office of the president carried great honour because, according to the signatories, 'the President represents and symbolizes as under a constitutional monarchy, the unity and solidarity of the nation'. The statement deeply regretted that Azad had pulled out of the contest and urged Subhas to reconsider his decision and allow Sitaramayya to win uncontested.[17]

Subhas issued a rejoinder on 25 January to this statement of Patel and other members of the Working Committee. He said in his view it was unfair of the members of the Working Committee to take sides when two of their colleagues were contesting the election. More importantly, he pointed out that the candidature of Sitaramayya had not been discussed in the Working Committee. He did not add that his own candidature had not been agreed upon by the Working Committee, since the committee's chosen candidate was Azad. Subhas admitted that he had not wanted to be a candidate but had been compelled to do so by friends and supporters from several provinces. He was willing to withdraw if 'a genuine anti-federationist' like Acharya Narendra Deva was accepted as president.

Subhas's more substantive objections concerned the position of the president. He argued that it was 'altogether wrong to liken the Congress President to a constitutional monarch'. In his view the president was like the prime minister of Britain or the president of the United States of America who nominates his own Cabinet. He also asserted that it was 'widely believed' that the right wing within the Congress was in the process of striking a compromise with the British government on the federal scheme. Such a prospect made it

---

[17] Statement by Patel and six other members of the Working Committee, 24 January 1939, in ibid., vol. 9, pp. 69–70.

imperative to have a president who will be 'an anti-federationist to the core of his heart'.[18]

When Jawaharlal had issued his statement on 26 January from Almora, he had not seen the statement made by the members of the Working Committee and the second statement of Subhas. He had only read the first statement of Subhas dated 21 January. Jawaharlal began by saying that without gainsaying the importance of the presidential election it was actually a 'secondary matter'. For him what was far more important was the policy and the programme of the Congress which, according to him, was laid down by the Congress itself; the policies and programmes were thus independent of presidential elections. He added, 'A President can, however, make a difference in the carrying out of a policy, and a Congress President is not in my opinion merely a speaker.' Jawaharlal declared that he was not against an election contest since that would help to clarify matters relating to policies and programmes. But he asked what the different programmes in conflict were in the elections that were about to take place. Jawaharlal found that reference had only been made to federation and from this he assumed that there was no debate on other issues. But even regarding federation, Jawaharlal said he was not aware of any conflict. On this subject, according to him, 'the Congress attitude is definite and clear'. To Jawaharlal, 'it [seemed] to be monstrous for any Congressmen to think in terms of compromising on Federation'. He admitted that there were many conflicts within the Congress but none of these had anything to do with federation or with the results of the election. He felt because of the international situation, India would soon face a crisis and he wanted greater clarity within the Congress to face that situation. He believed—and he had told Subhas this—that Subhas should not stand for re-election. He added, 'his [Subhas's] and my capacity for effective work would be lessened by holding this office [the presidentship] at this stage'.[19]

---

[18] The second statement of Bose, 25 January 1939, in ibid., pp. 70–73.

[19] 'The Congress Presidential Election': statement to the press, 26 January 1939, in Nehru, *Selected Works*, vol. 9, pp. 477–79.

There were further statements by Patel, Rajendra Prasad and Sitaramayya himself. All these denied the prospect of a compromise with the British government on federation. They reiterated that the Congress was bound by the policies and resolutions it had adopted on this subject. Subhas issued two more statements—making his tally four before the elections—but in none of this could he substantiate the charge that some Congress leaders belonging to what he called the Right were trying to strike a deal with the British on federation. In this atmosphere the presidential election was held on 29 January. The results showed that Subhas had polled 1580 votes to Sitaramayya's 1377. The bulk of Subhas's votes had come from Bengal, Mysore, Punjab, Uttar Pradesh and Madras. He had scored a clear victory.

Gandhi's reaction to Subhas's win was uncharacteristically devoid of grace. In a public statement he said that since he had prevailed upon Sitaramayya not to withdraw from the contest, the latter's defeat 'was more mine than his'. He was glad Subhas had won even though he did not subscribe to Subhas's facts or the arguments in his manifestos. He said that the election had provided Subhas with an opportunity 'to choose a homogeneous Cabinet and enforce his programme without let or hindrance'. In a backhanded compliment, he said, '[A]fter all Subhas Babu is not an enemy of his country. He has suffered for it.' He added that in Subhas's own opinion, Subhas's policy and programme were 'the most forward, the boldest'.[20] Subhas confessed that he was pained to read Gandhi's statement, especially as the latter had taken the defeat personally. Subhas pointed out, very pertinently, that the delegates had not been called upon to vote for or against Gandhi. Regarding his relationship with Gandhi, he admitted that on some occasions he had been constrained to differ with Gandhi on public questions, but he said, he would 'yield to none in my respect for his personality'. Very significantly, he added, 'It will always be my aim and object to try and win his confidence for the simple

---

[20] Statement of Gandhi, 31 January 1939, in *Netaji: Collected Works*, vol. 9, pp. 87–88.

reason that it will be a tragic thing for me if I succeed in winning the confidence of other people but fail to win the confidence of India's greatest man.'[21]

Jawaharlal and Subhas met in Santiniketan in early February and chatted for an hour over recent events. No record of this conversation is available in the papers of either but the contents can be gathered from an exchange of letters that followed between the two. Jawaharlal wrote on 4 February to say that their talk had failed to clear up the situation. He confessed to Subhas that he was uncertain about his future course of action because he felt 'entirely at sea' regarding what Subhas wanted the Congress to be. He said none of the vital questions concerning leftists, rightists, federation and so on had been discussed 'by us' during Subhas's presidentship. (What Jawaharlal meant when he wrote 'by us'—between Subhas and himself or in the Working Committee, or both—is not clear.) He considered Subhas's use of the term leftists and rightists to be 'wholly wrong and confusing'. Subhas's use of these terms seemed to imply that Gandhi and whoever was part of his group belonged to the right, and those who were opposed to Gandhi were of the left. Jawaharlal commented, '[S]trong language and a capacity to criticize and attack the old Congress leadership is not a test of Leftism in politics.' If responses to the question of federation were to be yardsticks of leftism or otherwise, it would have been better if Subhas had discussed the matter fully in the Working Committee and even to bring a resolution on the subject and then to note the reactions, Jawaharlal said. Instead, without even a proper discussion, Subhas had accused his colleagues 'en bloc of back-sliding'.

Jawaharlal raised other issues—the states question, the Hindu–Muslim question, the kisans and the workers, foreign policy—and wanted to know if Subhas held any definite views on these which were at variance with those held by his colleagues. Jawaharlal foresaw that the formation of the Working Committee would be fraught with problems and he thought the best way out of the tangle would be a clarificatory note from Subhas. Such a note could be the

---

[21] Statement of Bose, 4 February 1939, in ibid., 89–90.

basis of discussion and others could decide where they would fit in. He requested Subhas to particularly develop his suggestion about giving an ultimatum to the British government: 'How exactly do you wish to proceed about it and what will you do afterwards?' Jawaharlal admitted that he did not 'appreciate this idea at all'. He ended the letter by saying that any cooperation in public affairs involved faith in colleagues and he appealed for 'perfect frankness' from Subhas, and hoped that 'all of us will be perfectly frank'.[22]

It is evident from Subhas's short letter of acknowledgement that he had taken Jawaharlal's comments personally and felt that the latter had referred to his shortcomings.[23] This was an odd inference because Jawaharlal had made no personal comments but had concerned himself with policies, the future course of action and the steps Subhas could take to resolve the problems that had arisen because of the election. The only personal element in Jawaharlal's letter was his own confusion regarding where Subhas stood and what he wanted to do. Writing to Gandhi, Jawaharlal also emphasized the need to concentrate on policies rather than on individuals. Gandhi had written expressing his desire to resign from the Working Committee, and Jawaharlal wrote back to say: 'It is not for me to advise others but I see no reason whatever why I should resign. Even if Subhas asked me to resign it is not clear to me that I should do so just at this stage. Of course Subhas should have the upper hand in putting forward his policy. Nobody will obstruct him. But surely the questions before us are not personal or individual. They transcend personalities. I think we should forget for the moment Subhas as well as others and consider our problems on these [sic] merits.'[24]

It is obvious from Jawaharlal's letter to Gandhi that immediately in the aftermath of Subhas's victory, Gandhi had mooted the idea of the Working Committee stepping down. On 8 February 1939, Patel had written to Rajendra Prasad that '[I]t was impossible for us to

[22] Letter to Bose, 4 February 1939, in Nehru, *Selected Works*, vol. 9, pp. 480–85.

[23] Letter to Nehru, 10 February 1939, in *Netaji: Collected Works*, vol. 9, pp. 189–90.

[24] Letter from Nehru to Gandhi, 9 February 1939, in *Together They Fought*, pp. 354–55.

work with [Bose] and he also really desires that he should have a free hand.'[25] In spite of Jawaharlal's letter to Gandhi, this is exactly what happened when the Working Committee met at Wardha on 22 February. Subhas was unable to attend because of illness and he had written to Gandhi proposing a postponement. At the behest of Gandhi, Patel and other members of the Working Committee, barring Jawaharlal and Sarat Bose, resigned. Subhas had tried his best to avoid a confrontation. He had travelled to Wardha to meet Gandhi and have a face-to-face discussion. But no solution resulted in the talks held on 15 February. Subhas had been warned about such tactics by M.N. Roy who had written to him immediately after his victory to say that Gandhi's statement on Sitaramayya's defeat was nothing short of a 'declaration of war'. He added that the war would 'be waged in true Gandhian fashion, namely non-cooperation'.[26] He urged Subhas to challenge and overthrow the Gandhian leadership. Subhas evidently had no desire to take any such drastic steps, otherwise he would not have gone to meet Gandhi on 15 February. But it is also true that Subhas's own mind was unclear. He wrote to his wife, far away in Vienna, significantly in German: 'Ich weiss nicht was ich in zukunft tun werde. Bitte sagen Sie was ich machen soll.' Translated, this means, 'I don't know what I should do in the future. Please tell me what I should do.'[27]

Jawaharlal's reaction to the resignation of the Working Committee members was uniquely his own and ambiguous. He could not get himself to side with those who resigned but neither could he see himself in agreement with Subhas. So he did not join the collective resignation but resigned on his own. He thus pleased no one, neither Gandhi and his group nor Subhas. He may not even have pleased himself. His anguish and indecision were expressed in a three-part article he wrote for the *National Herald*. He was aware of the contradictions in his position; he wrote, 'The newspapers say

[25] Rajmohan Gandhi, *Patel*, p. 280.

[26] Letter from Roy to Bose, 1 February 1939, in *Netaji: Collected Works*, vol. 9, p. 280–83.

[27] Letter to Emilie, 11 February 1939, in ibid., vol. 7, p. 208–09.

that I have resigned from the Working Committee. That is not quite correct, and yet it is correct enough. When twelve members had resigned from a Committee of fifteen, there was not much of the Committee left; the rump could hardly function as such. The reasons that impelled me to act as I did differed in many ways from those that moved my colleagues.' He wrote about his own dissatisfaction with the way the Working Committee had acted; he said his decision grew out of 'an overwhelming desire to be out of committees and to function as I wanted to'. He admitted that the gulf between the twelve who had resigned and himself 'had grown and not again would I be a member of a Committee fashioned as the Working Committee had been for three years'. It would appear from this that Jawaharlal was no less unhappy with the prevailing leadership of the Congress than Subhas. Such was the distance between him and the twelve who had resigned that after the Working Committee meeting at Segaon, the twelve took possession of two cars and went off to Wardha, leaving Jawaharlal and Kripalani with no other alternative but to walk the five miles to Wardha.

Jawaharlal believed that after the charges that had been brought against the members of the Working Committee—these attacks, he said, were tantamount to an attack on Gandhi who had been 'the guide and mentor of the Working Committee'—they had no choice before them save resigning. He was critical of the fact that the Working Committee had not been allowed to transact even routine business by Subhas who because of ill health had requested Gandhi to postpone the meeting of the Working Committee. 'And so,' according to Jawaharlal, 'the Committee, having no function to perform, dissolved and faded away.' Subhas's decision to stop the Working Committee from carrying out routine work was interpreted as an act of no confidence in the Working Committee. Personal loyalty to the new president had prevailed over loyalty to the organization.

Jawaharlal saw the deadlock as a result of a 'desire to control the Congress organization'. He noted that a reaction had set in against 'what was considered an authoritarian tendency in the Congress high command' but added, 'curiously enough the new leadership is far more authoritarian than any during the recent history of the Congress'. Jawaharlal had no problems with a radical policy, irrespective of whether he agreed with it or not, but 'radical slogans allied to authoritarianism is a wrong and dangerous trend. It is wrong because it leads people to think that strong language and much shouting are substitutes for action. It is dangerous because radical slogans delude the people and under their cover authoritarianism creeps in and entrenches itself.' Jawaharlal did not leave any doubts in the minds of his readers that he had the rise of fascism in mind, as immediately after the quoted sentences, he referred to 'strange happenings in Europe' and to the fall of 'the proud edifice of democracy . . . before our eyes'.[28]

Jawaharlal's analysis of the situation, especially the point regarding the control of the Congress organization, was acute and valid. Perhaps his views were formed by his personal experience in dealing with the Congress high command. Watching the majority of the Working Committee resign, he must have recalled that many of these men had meted out the same treatment to him when he had been president in 1936 for the Lucknow session. They had resigned because they differed from Jawaharlal's views and programmes. With Subhas, matters were a little more complicated, but the fundamental issue was one of differences in ideology and programme. Jawaharlal must have felt some empathy for Subhas even though his own differences with him were growing. When Subhas inquired if he had resigned from the Working Committee, Jawaharlal's reply was a trifle brusque: 'I do not want to complicate the situation further by formally resigning. Under the existing circumstances the Committee cannot function as it cannot raise even a quorum. Apart from this, under the circumstances I feel I cannot be of much help to you.'[29] It is difficult not to note a dash of exasperation in the last sentence.

Jawaharlal in 1936 had seriously contemplated resigning from the post of president, but he had refrained from doing so as he knew

---

[28] All quotations in the three previous paragraphs are from 'Where Are We?', in Nehru, *Selected Works*, vol. 9, pp. 488–520. The article originally appeared in the *National Herald* in eight parts on 28 February and 1–6 March 1939.

[29] Letter to Bose, 1 March 1939, in Nehru, *Selected Works*, vol. 9, p. 520.

the consequences of such an act would be serious. There was also his bond with Gandhi. As he watched events unfold after Sitaramayya's defeat, he must have wondered about how Subhas would react as he was pushed into a corner. He must have been aware that Subhas shared none of his affinity with Gandhi. He had a sense of foreboding especially as Subhas, 'on whom the burden primarily rests', was lying ill and Gandhi had begun a fast.[30]

Subhas, defying doctors' orders, travelled with a raging fever to Tripuri near the Narmada. Gandhi did not attend the session, held between 10 and 12 March, as he had undertaken a fast in Rajkot.[31] But his men—all those who had resigned from the Working Committee—were present. The showdown occurred when Govind Ballabh Pant moved a resolution which affirmed the Congress's firm adherence to the fundamental policies of Gandhi; it also expressed its confidence in the work of the Working Committee that had functioned for the last one year; and it requested 'the president to nominate the Working Committee in accordance with the wishes of Gandhi'.[32] Subhas failed to secure the total support of the left which he claimed he represented. The largest leftist group within the Congress, the Congress Socialist Party, decided to abstain. Some other leftists offered amendments to the resolution, but these failed to be carried. The supporters of Gandhi naturally spoke very strongly in favour of the resolution. Rajagopalachari, who had actually drafted the Pant resolution, said, 'There are two boats . . . One is an old boat . . . piloted by Mahatma Gandhi. Another man has a new boat . . . Mahatma Gandhi is a tried boatman who can safely transport you. If you go into the other boat, which I know is leaky, all will go down, and the river Narmada is indeed deep. The new boatman says, "If you don't get into my boat, at least tie my boat to yours." This is also impossible. We cannot tie a leaky boat to a

---

[30] 'Where Are We?', in ibid., vol. 9, p. 518.

[31] Gandhi's decision not to attend the session at Tripuri was taken soon after Subhas's victory; Gandhi wrote to Nehru on 3 February 1939: 'After the election and the manner in which it was fought, I feel that I shall serve the country by absenting myself from the Congress at the forthcoming session.' See *Together They Fought*, p. 352.

[32] See Sitaramayya, *History of the Congress*, vol. 2, p. 110.

good boat, exposing ourselves to the perils of going down.'[33]

The Pant resolution was passed. This left Subhas in an unenviable position: he was the elected president who was bound to the wishes of Gandhi, someone who had taken the defeat of Sitaramayya as his personal defeat. Rajagopalachari's words were an indication of the rigid position he and his group had adopted. This was also revealed by the fact that when Sarat Bose told Patel that Subhas and his supporters would support the resolution provided certain changes were introduced, he got no response from Patel. Sarat Bose complained to Gandhi that Patel wanted that 'not a word, not a comma should be changed'.[34] Patel and his group obviously believed that there was only one solution to the impasse: Subhas had to abandon his new boat and come aboard on Gandhi's as a part of the crew. But these signals of intransigence did not deter Subhas from trying to find some kind of middle ground with Gandhi. He embarked on this effort through letters while convalescing in a place near Dhanbad.

While Subhas was trying to sort out his differences with Gandhi, he wrote a long letter—twenty-seven typed pages—to Jawaharlal at the end of March. This missive is crucial for understanding how fast their relationship was deteriorating. In the first paragraph of this letter, Subhas wrote, 'I find that for some time past you have developed tremendous dislike for me. I say this because I find that you take up enthusiastically every possible point against me; what could be said in my favour you ignore.' What followed in the rest of the letter were illustrations of this point. Subhas said that since he had come out of prison in 1937, he had treated Jawaharlal with 'the utmost regard and consideration, in private life and in public'. He had looked upon Jawaharlal as 'politically an elder brother and leader and have often sought your advice'. But Jawaharlal's response to such advice-seeking had been 'vague and non-committal'. The letter went on to become a tirade against Jawaharlal, picking on

---

[33] Rajmohan Gandhi, *Patel*, p. 280; the same page mentions that Rajagopalachari had drafted the resolution.

[34] Ibid.

various recent incidents or statements in the course of which Subhas felt he had been treated badly or misrepresented or ignored by his political elder brother. The tone was distinctly personal and bitter.

To take one example: referring to Jawaharlal's statement of 26 January where he had urged that the discussion be on policies and programmes and not on personalities, Subhas wrote, 'It never struck you that you want us to forget persons, only when certain persons are concerned. When it is a case of Subhas Bose standing for re-election, you run down personalities and lionize principles etc. When it is a case of Maulana Azad standing for re-election, you do not hesitate to write a long panegyric. When it is a case of Subhas Bose versus Sardar Patel and others, then—Subhas Bose must first of all clear up the personal issue. When Sarat Bose complains of certain things at Tripuri (viz. of the attitudes and conduct of those who call themselves orthodox followers of Mahatma Gandhi)—he is according to you, coming down to personal questions, when he should be confining himself to principles and programmes.' Subhas threw his hands up in despair at what he considered to be Jawaharlal's many inconsistencies and his attempts to ride two horses at the same time.

In this letter, Subhas had indeed brought the controversy to the level of personalities—the Bose brothers against the Congress high command and Jawaharlal. Subhas was, however, aware that he had written a very harsh and shrill letter. He concluded by saying, 'If I have used harsh language or hurt your feelings at any place, kindly pardon me. You yourself say that there is nothing like frankness and I have tried to be frank—perhaps brutally frank.'[35] Hemmed in completely within the Congress, Subhas had looked to Jawaharlal for support. When this had not been forthcoming, Subhas chose to lash out. Unable to hit out at his actual opponents, he decided to go for the person who he had once considered close to him and who had now deserted him at a very critical juncture.

With all the compelling reasons that Subhas did have to write in the manner that he wrote to Jawaharlal, there is one passage in the letter that is bound to bewilder readers. Subhas deeply resented

[35] Letter to Nehru, 28 March 1939, in *Netaji: Collected Works*, vol. 9, pp. 193–216.

the statement that Jawaharlal had issued on 22 February after twelve members of the Working Committee had resigned.[36] He said that the statement 'was unworthy of you'. He implied that it was unkind. The members of the Working Committee who had resigned, Subhas wrote, had not said a single unkind word against him. But Jawaharlal's statement had been different and Subhas had no words to describe it without lapsing into strong language.[37] Reading Jawaharlal's statement today it is difficult to gauge why Subhas had been so cut to the quick by it. He may have been angered by Jawaharlal's failure to take a position but there was nothing in Jawaharlal's statement that was particularly unkind.

Jawaharlal's reply to Subhas's volley of words was restrained and subdued. He thanked Subhas for his frankness and added, '[F]rankness hurts often enough, but is almost always desirable, especially between those who have to work together.' This would suggest that in spite of all their differences, Jawaharlal was still eager in April 1939 to have Subhas as a colleague. In the beginning of the letter, he turned to Subhas's indictment of him and his failings. Replying to this, Jawaharlal said, was 'difficult and embarrassing' but so far as his failings were concerned, he pleaded guilty to them and acknowledged that he had the 'misfortune to possess them'. He was deeply appreciative of the regard and consideration that Subhas had shown towards him and wrote that '[P]ersonally I have always had, and still have, regard and affection for you, though sometimes I did not like at all what you did or how you did it.' In the rest of the letter, Jawaharlal proceeded to rebut paragraph by paragraph the points that Subhas had raised in his letter.

In terms of the differences that were increasingly becoming evident between Subhas and Jawaharlal, there are two aspects that the latter touched upon that are worth noting. Jawaharlal wrote, '[T]he association of vague Leftist slogans with no clear Leftist ideology or principles has in recent years been much in evidence in Europe. It has led to Fascist development . . . The possibility of such

---

[36] Nehru's statement can be found in Nehru, *Selected Works*, vol. 9, pp. 485–87.
[37] Letter to Nehru, 28 March 1939, in *Netaji: Collected Works*, vol. 9, p. 194.

a thing happening in India possessed my mind and disturbed me. The fact that in international affairs you held different views from mine and did not wholly approve our condemnation of Nazi Germany or Fascist Italy added to my discomfort, and looking at the picture as a whole, I did not at all fancy the direction in which apparently you wanted us to go.' In a more general context, Jawaharlal commented, 'We are temperamentally different and our approach to life and its problems is not the same.' And as if to elaborate his attitude to life, Jawaharlal, towards the end of his reply, mused thus with more than a hint of self-pity: 'I am an unsatisfactory human being who is dissatisfied with himself and the world, and whom the petty world he lives in does not particularly like.'[38] The two points are important as they throw some light on the two different paths the two men would take.

At the time of this exchange, Subhas was also busy trying to form a Working Committee. To do this, he had to secure Gandhi's cooperation and consent. In the first letter that Subhas wrote to Gandhi to ask what the latter's conception was regarding the composition of the Working Committee, he added that if Gandhi adhered to the view that the committee should be homogeneous, then it was obvious that 'people like myself on the one side and Sardar Patel and others on the other, cannot be on the same committee'. If the committee was not going to be homogenous, then Subhas suggested that he should recommend seven names and Patel the other seven. More fundamentally, he asked Gandhi how the latter wanted him to function as a president: 'Do I count at all?' He reminded Gandhi that in Wardha when the two of them had met on 15 February, Gandhi had told him 'that unless I voluntarily accepted your viewpoint, self-effacement would in reality amount to self-suppression and that you could not approve of self-suppression'. Subhas wrote that he was now faced with two alternatives— 'either to efface myself or to stand up for my honest convictions'. Would Gandhi like him to be a dummy president, he queried.[39] In a subsequent letter, written four

[38] Letter to Bose, 3 April 1939, in Nehru, *Selected Works*, vol. 9, pp. 534–549.

[39] Letter to Gandhi, 25 March 1939, in *Netaji: Collected Works*, vol. 9, pp. 127–30.

days later, Subhas appealed to Gandhi to be 'truly non-partisan' and thus command the confidence of both parties. He told Gandhi that the latter had two alternatives before him—he could accommodate the views of Subhas in the formation of the Working Committee, or he could insist on his own views in their entirety. If he chose the second alternative, Subhas warned Gandhi, 'We may come to the parting of the ways.'[40]

Gandhi in his reply did not address any of the questions directly posed by Subhas. But he did reiterate, as he had done at Wardha in the middle of February, that 'there are differences on fundamentals' and for this reason 'a composite Committee would be harmful'. He advised Subhas to be unfettered in his choice of the committee members, especially since Subhas believed the Pant resolution to be ultra vires. He assured Subhas that 'Gandhiites' (Gandhi used this word and then added, 'to use that wrong expression') would not obstruct him if they are in a minority but '[t]hey may not suppress themselves if they are clearly in a majority'. Subhas's hands should be unfettered if he had to function as a president. 'The situation before the country,' according to Gandhi, 'admits of no middle course.'[41] Gandhi was implicitly challenging Subhas to form his own Working Committee and prove his strength within the Congress.

This interchange set the tone for the subsequent correspondence between the two on the formation of the Working Committee. Gandhi wanted Subhas to name his own committee but the latter refused to do so without Gandhi's advice. But Subhas cautioned that if there was a parting of ways 'a bitter civil war will commence'. He also informed Gandhi about his own programme for the Congress: 'The international situation, as well as our own position at home, convinced me nearly eight months ago that the time had come for us to force the issue of Purna Swaraj.' He was so confident that he declared that if such a movement were to be launched, India would have 'Swaraj inside of eighteen months at the most'. Unfortunately, he said, Gandhi did not share this view. But this did not deter Subhas

---

[40] Letter to Gandhi, 29 March 1939, in ibid., pp. 133–34.

[41] Letter from Gandhi to Bose, 30 March 1939, in ibid., vol. 9, pp. 134–36.

from urging Gandhi to prepare and lead such a struggle. He added, '[I]f you feel that the Congress will be able to fight better with another President, I shall gladly step aside.'[42]

In spite of such pleas and the passing of many letters and telegrams, there was no agreement between the two on the making of a Working Committee. Gandhi advised Subhas in no uncertain terms to form his own Working Committee, to formulate his programme and place both before the AICC. But with Subhas's analysis of the situation, he dissented wholly. He wrote, 'I see no atmosphere of non-violent mass action. An ultimatum without effective sanction is worse than useless . . . I have the firm belief that the Congress as it is today cannot deliver the goods, cannot offer civil disobedience worth the name.' He added, '[T]herefore if your prognosis is right, I am a backnumber and played out as the generalissimo of Satyagraha.'[43] Was there in that last self-deprecating sentence, a veiled challenge to Subhas to defy Gandhi as the leader of the Congress? It is also possible that Gandhi and Subhas meant completely different things when they spoke of mass campaign. Gandhi suggested this when in an interview given in May 1939, he said, 'He [Subhas] does not mean the same thing as satyagraha as I do.'[44]

By the middle of April, Jawaharlal, who was privy to the ongoing Gandhi–Bose correspondence since Gandhi was sending him all the letters, wrote to Gandhi to say that he feared that the exchange of views had reached a deadlock out of which he saw no way out. He confessed that he himself was 'in the unfortunate position of a person who does not agree with either of the viewpoints taken'. For this reason he had remained silent, but the situation could not be allowed to drift as '[T]he issues are too serious and the consequences distressing to contemplate.' Jawaharlal then made a straightforward suggestion to Gandhi: 'It seems to me that there is no way out unless you are prepared to shoulder the responsibility yourself to

[42] Letter to Gandhi, 31 March 1939, in ibid., pp. 137–43.

[43] Letter from Gandhi to Bose, 2 April 1939, in ibid., pp. 144–46.

[44] Answers to questions at Gandhi Seva Sangh meeting, Brindaban, 5 May 1939: Gandhi, *Collected Works*, vol. 69, p. 210.

a very large extent. You have to give the lead and you cannot wait for things just to happen. Subhas has numerous failings but he is susceptible to a friendly approach. I am sure that if you made up your mind to do so you could find a way out.'[45] Jawaharlal seems to be suggesting here, particularly in the last sentence, that Gandhi was not doing enough to resolve the problem. The other point to note is that Subhas's harsh letter to him notwithstanding, Jawaharlal retained a fund of goodwill for Subhas.

It was out of this goodwill that Jawaharlal travelled to see Subhas in Jealgora where the latter was recuperating.[46] He knew that the visit would not lead to anything as he believed he could not help in finding a solution. But he went to see Subhas nevertheless because 'I cannot say no to him'.[47] He conveyed to Subhas the same sentiment.[48] Subhas and Jawaharlal talked for several hours. The latter reported this to Gandhi first by cable: 'Feel your guidance control situation essential. Earnestly hope you will agree.'[49] He followed this up with a letter written on the same day. He informed Gandhi that it was absolutely necessary to resolve the deadlock before the AICC met and that Gandhi was the 'only person who can do it'. Elaborating on how a resolution could be affected, he wrote that it was possible to tone down the difficulties. 'So far as the programme of work is concerned,' Jawaharlal told Gandhi, 'there are obvious differences between what Subhas says and what many others feel. But in actual practice, it is clear that there should be no basic change in our programme and outlook . . . In effect it comes to this that the Working Committee should be formed according to your wishes and the programme should be carried through under your guidance . . . I understood from Subhas that he was agreeable to do this, not in

---

[45] Letter to Gandhi, 17 April 1939, in Nehru, *Selected Works*, vol. 9, pp. 553–55.

[46] Bose wrote to Nehru on 15 April: 'Will it be possible for you to run up here for a few hours? We could then have a talk and I could have your advice as to how to proceed next.' *Netaji: Collected Works*, vol. 9, p. 234.

[47] Letter to Gandhi, 17 April 1939: Nehru, *Selected Works*, vol. 9, pp. 553–55.

[48] Letter to Bose, 17 April 1939, in ibid., p. 557.

[49] Nehru's telegram to Gandhi, 20 April 1939, in *Together They Fought*, p. 365. He also sent a copy of the telegram to Bose. See Nehru, *Selected Works*, vol. 9, p. 559.

any spirit of resentment but because he felt it was the right course now. He acts strangely at times and is fond of issuing statements which create difficulties. I hope, however, that this kind of thing will lessen.'[50] On the same day, he wrote to Azad to say that his 'talk with Subhas [had been] friendly and frank'. Regarding the constitution of the Working Committee, the main problem, Jawaharlal wrote, 'I am quite sure that the only thing to be done now is for Subhas to leave the formation of the Working Committee entirely to Gandhiji and to promise his loyal support to whatever is done . . . Subhas was agreeable to what I suggested but, of course, I do not know what reservations he might have in his mind.'[51]

Jawaharlal's optimism proved to be misplaced. For one thing, Gandhi did not respond to Jawaharlal's report. For another, on the day Subhas and Jawaharlal met, 19 April, Gandhi had sent a telegram to Subhas which said, 'Despite many suggestions contained in your letters, I feel helpless, carry out terms of Pant's resolution in this atmosphere of mutual distrust, suspicions and in face of marked differences of opinion between groups. I still maintain you should boldly form committee. It would be unfair to you with the views you hold.'[52] It is not clear if Jawaharlal knew about this cable when he wrote to Gandhi. The latter clearly had not changed his mind: he wanted Subhas to form his own Working Committee. One reason for this may have been his disapproval of the Pant resolution.[53] On 27 and 28 April, Subhas and Gandhi met in Sodepur, near Calcutta, to try and resolve the deadlock before the AICC was convened on 29 April. Jawaharlal was a part of these conversations. The talks were futile. On 29 April, Gandhi wrote to Subhas: 'You have asked me to give you in terms of Pant's resolution the names for the Working Committee . . . I feel myself utterly incompetent to do so. Much has happened since Tripuri. Knowing your own views, knowing how

[50] Letter to Gandhi, 20 April 1939, in Nehru, *Selected Works*, vol. 9, pp. 559–60.

[51] Letter to Azad, 20 April 1939, in ibid., pp. 561–62.

[52] Gandhi's telegram to Bose, 19 April 1939, in *Netaji: Collected Works*, vol. 9, p. 177.

[53] Gandhi wrote to Bose on 10 April 1939: 'Pandit Pant's resolution I cannot interpret. The more I study it, the more I dislike it.' See ibid., p. 165.

you and most of the members differ in fundamentals, it seems to me that if I gave you names, it would be an imposition on you. I have argued this position at length in my letters to you. Nothing that has happened during the three days of closest conversation between us has altered my view. Such being the case you are free to choose your own committee.'[54]

Thus, when the AICC met, Subhas was in the odd position of being the president of the Congress who had no Working Committee. He realized that this was not a tenable position. Left with no options, Subhas did the honourable thing: he tendered his resignation. The statement he made to the Congress was of necessity short—he had had very little time to prepare it since Gandhi's letter dated 29 April (referred to above) must have reached him just before the AICC met. The statement was dignified and without any recriminations. It merely presented the facts that had led to his failure to form a Working Committee.[55]

There was a coda to Subhas's resignation that is worth noting only because it concerned Jawaharlal. The latter moved a motion in the AICC calling upon Subhas to withdraw his resignation. Jawaharlal believed that it would not be wise 'to change horses mid-stream'. He thus wanted that the previous Working Committee should continue in office and the two vacancies that were coming up because of the ill health and the imprisonment of two members should be filled by Subhas. He appealed to all concerned to do their 'utmost to bury the hatchet. We should look forward and should forget the past.' Contrary to all that had transpired between Subhas and Gandhi, he averred that the 'differences are not over principles but only superficial . . . there is no difference between Mr Subhas Chandra Bose and Mahatma Gandhi on any issue involving principle'.[56] Subhas, however, was unwilling to withdraw his resignation unless

---

[54] Letter from Gandhi to Bose, 29 April 1939, in *Netaji: Collected Works*, p. 181.

[55] Statement on resignation from Congress presidentship, 29 April 1939, in ibid., pp. 107–09.

[56] Appeal to Bose to withdraw resignation, 29 April 1939, in Nehru, *Selected Works*, vol. 9, pp. 562–64.

the AICC showed greater consideration for his views about a composite Working Committee. Jawaharlal then withdrew the motion he had tabled. Subhas's exit from the office as Congress president thus became an accepted fact. He was replaced by Rajendra Prasad. Both Subhas and Jawaharlal refused to serve on the new Working Committee that was formed by Prasad.

In a private letter to his young friend V.K. Krishna Menon, Jawaharlal expressed his utter dissatisfaction with many things that had happened in Calcutta. Subhas, Jawaharlal wrote, 'so far as the Calcutta proceedings were concerned, seemed to me to be very accommodating and desirous of pulling together. But there is so much suspicion and prejudice against him and some of his close associates are considered so undesirable that some people find it difficult to think in terms of close cooperation with him.'[57] Jawaharlal's sympathies were with Subhas. He must have been disappointed with the outcome of the AICC since before he went to see Subhas in the middle of April, he had requested Gandhi to accept Subhas as president: '[T]o try and push him out seems to me to be an exceedingly wrong step.'[58] In the context of what he called his dissatisfaction, it is of some significance that after the AICC session in Calcutta in late April, according to the available evidence, not a single letter passed between Jawaharlal and Gandhi till 27 July.

The hostility to Subhas's re-election, the Pant resolution in Tripuri, Gandhi's obduracy and what happened at the AICC seem to be linked by a common thread. Jawaharlal, probably because he knew from experience how Gandhi and his men thought and acted, had apprehended this when he had written to Gandhi about the error involved in pushing Subhas out of the office of president. Gandhi proceeded to do exactly this, assuming all the time the moral high ground that he wanted Subhas to have a completely free hand in forming the Working Committee. Gandhi could not have been unaware that Subhas was actually tied down by the Pant resolution that had been conceived, drafted and presented by Gandhi's close

---

[57] Letter to Krishna Menon, 4 May 1939, in ibid., pp. 570–71.

[58] Letter to Gandhi, 17 April 1939, in ibid., p. 554.

associates and had then been passed by the Congress. Subhas was, in fact, completely hemmed in and outmanoeuvred by superior ring craft.

Gandhi emerges from this episode at his worst: petty and given to machinations, the archetypal Tammany Hall politician, his moral posturing notwithstanding. At one level, Gandhi seriously differed with Subhas's analysis that conditions in India were ripe for an ultimatum to the British and a mass campaign. At another, there was the question of control over the Congress. Here, Gandhi could not ignore the feelings of the people who were politically close and unquestioningly loyal to him. These men were united in their antipathy to Subhas and his views. They were also acutely aware that Gandhi had less influence on Subhas than he had on Jawaharlal. In 1936, they had depended on Jawaharlal's close emotional ties with Gandhi to tame him. But with Subhas there was no such guarantee: Jawaharlal, in spite of differences, loved Bapu; Subhas respected Gandhi. There was always the danger, from their point of view, of Subhas being his own man. At quite another and somewhat shadowy level, there was the presence of G.D. Birla. It is always difficult to pinpoint the kind of influence Birla exercised over Gandhi and his associates but that they were very close is undeniable as is Birla's disapproval of any left-leaning views. It is telling in this context that when Gandhi decided that Patel should not attend the AICC in Calcutta, it was to Birla that he communicated this decision.[59]

It was open to Subhas to follow the advice of M.N. Roy and defy Gandhi and the Congress leadership. But in April 1939, he felt he was not in a position to do this, though events as they unfolded after the AICC pushed him in that direction. The immediate aftermath of the AICC session was heady for Subhas. He was in Calcutta and Bengal a popular and charismatic leader. Events at Tripuri and the Calcutta AICC took his popularity to a new crest. A large crowd had gathered in Wellington Square in central Calcutta where the AICC was meeting. The crowd turned angry as the news of Subhas's resignation spread. Subhas had to personally escort some of the

[59] Telegram to Birla, 25 April 1939, in Gandhi, *Collected Works*, vol. 69, p. 173.

Congress leaders in order to protect them from the wrath of his supporters.

More satisfying for him was the message of solidarity he received from Tagore. On learning about the resignation, the poet wrote: 'The dignity and forbearance which you have shown in the midst of a most aggravating situation has won my admiration and confidence in your leadership. The same perfect decorum has still to be maintained by Bengal for the sake of her own self-respect and thereby to help to turn your apparent defeat into a permanent victory.'[60] He had in January 1939 hailed Subhas as *deshnayak* (leader of the nation). It was this show of affection and support that made Subhas write to Emilie to say, 'I have not lost anything by resigning. As a matter of fact I have become more popular now.'[61] In his next letter to her, he observed, 'India is a strange land where people are loved not because they have power, but because they give up power. For instance, at Lahore I had a warmer welcome this time than when I went last year as Congress President.'[62]

Within days of his resignation, Subhas, as indeed Jawaharlal had anticipated,[63] began organizing the Forward Bloc—a forum within the Congress where all the radical elements could come together. It would also be a forum that would seek no compromise with the Right in the Congress.[64] But the kind of unity that Subhas was looking for proved elusive as all the various left groups and parties preferred to keep their distinct identities. What all of them agreed to form was a Left Consolidation Committee of which Subhas was made chairman. Subhas's enthusiasm and energy were not diminished by this. He

---

[60] Tagore's message (undated) to Bose on the latter's resignation: *Netaji: Collected Works*, vol. 9, p. 109. Earlier, after the Tripuri session of the Congress, Tagore had written to Gandhi (29 April 1939): 'At the last Congress session some rude hands have deeply hurt Bengal with ungracious persistence. Please apply without delay balm to the wound with your own kind hands and prevent it from festering.' See Gandhi, *Collected Works*, vol. 69, p. 99n1.

[61] Letter to Emilie, 14 May 1939, in *Netaji: Collected Works*, vol. 7, p. 212.

[62] Letter to Emilie, 16 June 1939, in ibid., p. 213.

[63] Letter to Krishna Menon, 4 May 1939, in Nehru, *Selected Works*, vol. 9, pp. 570–71.

[64] 'Why Forward Bloc', 5 August 1939, in *Netaji: Collected Works*, vol. 10: 'The Alternative Leadership', pp. 1–4.

began to tour various parts of the country to whip up support for his cause of an uncompromising anti-British campaign.

In an attempt to take the wind out of Subhas's sails, the AICC passed two resolutions. By one it barred members of the Congress from undertaking satyagraha without prior permission of the party leadership. By the other it freed provincial ministries from taking orders from provincial parties. Subhas and the Left Consolidation Committee saw these two resolutions as steps to curb democracy within the Congress and it announced 9 July as a day of protest against what they interpreted to be impositions on the part of the party's high command. Subhas led the protest meeting in Bombay. The Congress Working Committee hit back by accusing him of breaking party discipline and by banning him from holding any elective office for three years in the Congress. Even under this kind of provocation, Subhas refused to abandon his loyalty to the Congress. In August, he declared, 'I shall cling to the Congress with even greater devotion than before and shall go on serving the Congress and the country as a servant of the nation.' But his loyalty was not free of criticism. In the same statement he said, '[T]his decision is the logical consequence of the process of "Right-consolidation" which has been going on for the last few years . . . The action of the WC has served to expose the real character of the present majority in the Congress.'[65] It was obvious that Subhas's political career within the Congress was nearing its end.

Subhas's forming of the Forward Bloc and his protests against the two resolutions failed to evoke any sympathy in Jawaharlal. On the formation of the Forward Bloc, he said he did not approve of it and did not attach much importance to it. He added, '[I]n any active organization, there would be differences of opinion, but these differences must not be confused with personalities. Such a course would not be in the interests of the country.'[66] In a longer article in the *National Herald*, he analysed the formation of the Forward

---

[65] Statement on Disciplinary Action, 19 August 1939, in ibid., pp. 7–8.

[66] 'On the Formation of the Forward Bloc', 21 May 1939, in Nehru, *Selected Works*, vol. 9, p. 574.

Bloc in greater detail. He wrote that as it stood, the Forward Bloc was no more than 'a negative grouping, an anti-bloc, whose sole binding cement is dislike of, or opposition to, the individuals or groups that control the Congress today. There is no positive policy based on definite principles.' The Forward Bloc had an open-door policy and this according to Jawaharlal had dangers: 'It is quite possible that fascist and communal elements might also enter its folds and seek to exploit it to further their animus against the Congress and its anti-fascist policy. How will Subhas Babu deal with this situation when it arises? We must remember that fascism grew in Europe under cover of radical slogans and popular phrases . . . The recent history of Europe has a lesson for us which we cannot ignore.'[67] Jawaharlal was critical of Subhas's show of protest against the two resolutions; he argued that such protests were disruptive and encouraged factionalism within the party. He did not accept Subhas's view that the resolutions interfered with the basic principles and traditions of democracy. Jawaharlal wrote, '[D]emocracy does not mean license for one to do anything he likes. The Congress is a democratic body with a certain definite creed and objective. It cannot allow its members to carry on an agitation which injures the cause of the furtherance of its creed.'[68]

Jawaharlal's criticisms, especially about the Forward Bloc, upset Subhas who launched an attack on him. Subhas wrote, 'I would ask Panditji in the first place wherein he finds opportunism or fascism in the programme of the Forward Bloc. I would ask him in the second place to tell us who among the members of the Forward Bloc are either opportunists or fascists . . . I should rather label as opportunists those who would run with the hare and hunt with the hound—those who pose as leftists and act as rightists—those who talk in one way when they are inside a room and in quite a different way when they are outside . . . Are those people to be called fascists

---

[67] 'The AICC and After', 27–28 May 1939, in ibid., pp. 575–80.

[68] 'On the Defiance of the AICC Resolution', 13 July 1939, in ibid., 583–5; also see 'A Dangerous Proposal' and 'Demonstrations Against the AICC Decision', in ibid., pp. 582 and 585 respectively.

who are fighting against fascism within the Congress and without or should they be dubbed as fascists who support the present autocratic "high command" either by openly joining the present homogeneous Working Committee or by secretly joining in their deliberations and drafting their resolutions.'⁶⁹

This was clearly a personal attack on Jawaharlal and came close to casting aspersions on the latter's intellectual and moral integrity. Jawaharlal refused to be provoked and responded by pointing out that he had never called the Forward Bloc a fascist or an opportunistic organization. All that he had said, Jawaharlal admitted, was to point out that since the Forward Bloc had no clear policy there was always the danger of it being infiltrated by opportunist and adventurist elements; he had also added that socialist slogans had been used in the past even by fascist organizations in their early stages. 'I strongly deprecate personal criticisms,' Jawaharlal commented in an obvious reference to the general tenor of Subhas's criticisms, 'and I have always tried to avoid them. In public life we must presume the *bona fides* of each other, unless facts and circumstances compel us, in the interests of the public good, to do otherwise . . . I trust that all our criticisms will be based on policy and not on personalities.'⁷⁰

This bitter controversy in the public domain inevitably caused a rift in the personal relationship between Subhas and Jawaharlal. In the course of the brief correspondence they had in July 1939 regarding H.V. Kamath's tenure in the National Planning Committee (referred to in the previous chapter), Jawaharlal concluded his letter with the words: 'I am sorry you find it difficult to understand me. Perhaps it is not worth trying.'⁷¹ With those two sentences, Jawaharlal signalled the beginning of the end of his friendship with Subhas. They never wrote to each other after this. The fact that they stopped writing to each other cannot be explained only by their

---

⁶⁹ Bose wrote this on 25 July 1939 and it is quoted in Nehru, *Selected Works*, vol. 9, p. 595. More or less the same points were made by Subhas, using the same terms, in 'Our Critics', 19 August 1939, in *Netaji: Collected Works*, vol. 10, pp. 10–13.

⁷⁰ 'On the Forward Bloc', 26 July 1939, and 'The Congress is the Only Weapon', 26 July 1939, in ibid., pp. 594–95.

⁷¹ Letter to Bose, 11 July 1939, in Nehru, *Selected Works*, vol. 9, pp. 401–02.

preoccupation with the fast-paced events that overtook India and the world from the middle of 1939, and the way Jawaharlal and Subhas came to be involved in them. Political differences had made personal bonds irrelevant. The end of the friendship had had its period of incubation and cannot be described as entirely unexpected.

In the immediate aftermath of Tripuri and while he was in the midst of his intense exchange of letters and telegrams with Gandhi, Subhas had written to one of his nephews, '[N]obody has done more harm to me personally, and to our cause in this crisis, than Pandit Nehru. If he had been with us, we would have had a majority. Even his neutrality would have probably given us a majority. But he was with the Old Guard at Tripuri. His open propaganda against me also has done me more harm than the activities of the twelve stalwarts.'[72] It is a measure of Subhas's inconsistencies and of his ambiguous feelings towards Jawaharlal that two days before he penned these lines to his nephew, he had on 15 April, as noted earlier, written to Jawaharlal to come and see him in Jealgora, where Subhas was recuperating. Why at a very critical conjuncture Subhas wanted to seek the advice from the very man who had rendered to his cause and him the biggest harm will remain a mystery. Jawaharlal, many years later, looking back on the Tripuri episode, confessed that he had 'let him [Subhas] down' especially as he had 'agreed with' what Subhas had been trying to do.[73]

Subhas's letter to his nephew seems to suggest that the breakdown of his relationship with Jawaharlal was rooted in the latter's failure to break with the 'Old Guard' of the Congress in the course of what happened at Tripuri. This appears to be unfair because Jawaharlal, as he had made clear, did not approve of either the views or actions of his colleagues in the Working Committee. He had made this clear in his public utterances and writings at the time. This is the reason why he did not sign the collective letter of resignation. He left the Working Committee on his own because in his view the committee

---

[72] Letter to Amiya Bose, 17 April 1939, in *Netaji: Collected Works*, vol. 9, pp. 288–89.

[73] Taya Zinkin, *Reporting India* (London, 1962), p. 217: cited in Sugata Bose, *His Majesty's Opponent*, p. 162.

had become defunct as it lacked a quorum after the resignations. But he could not also reconcile himself to Subhas's statements and actions. He had suggested to Subhas that he should first clear up the 'aspersions' that Subhas had cast on the integrity of some members of the Working Committee—this referred to Subhas's allegation that some members of the Working Committee were secretly trying to work out a deal with the British government on the issue of federation. Unless Subhas did that first, Jawaharlal felt he could not help him. In spite of these reservations, the evidence shows that Jawaharlal repeatedly urged Gandhi to take the initiative and the responsibility to find a way out of the impasse. He was certain that only Gandhi could do this and stop Subhas from being turned out from the office of Congress president. He even went to the extent of suggesting to Gandhi that he was not doing enough. Jawaharlal knew of Subhas's suspicions that he was working against Subhas's interests. To Krishna Menon, Jawaharlal had written: 'Subhas has lately come to the conclusion, most unjustifiably, that I am pulling the strings against him from behind the scenes. As a matter of fact, I have done my utmost to stand up for him and to tone down the hostility of the older leaders to him.'[74]

Subhas probably expected that Jawaharlal would come out totally in his favour. Such expectations were belied as Jawaharlal did not see the situation in simple black-and-white terms or, as he repeatedly told Subhas, as a battle between the left and the right within the Congress. It is also possible that Subhas had misread or ignored recent events within the Congress involving Jawaharlal. In 1936 when he was president, Jawaharlal had also won for himself the wrath of what Subhas called the 'Old Guard' who had at Gandhi's behest all resigned from the Working Committee. The treatment meted out to Jawaharlal in 1936 was a near rehearsal of what happened to Subhas with the difference that Jawaharlal had then not raised a flag of defiance but had chosen to work within the Congress system and with the men who ran that system.

This choice was based on two premises which were very important

---

[74] Letter to Krishna Menon, 4 April 1939, in Nehru, *Selected Works*, vol. 9, p. 550.

to Jawaharlal. One was his assessment of and closeness to Gandhi. And second, he did not believe that there was any one else in India other than Gandhi who could lead the people of India. Personally he saw Gandhi, always acknowledging that he had differences with Gandhi, as a kind of father figure, always calling him Bapu. This prevented him from making a break with the Congress and Gandhi. Embedded in this attitude of Jawaharlal's was an admission of his own shortcomings as a mass leader and of his own emotional vulnerability that made it impossible for him to conceive his own life without Gandhi. Jawaharlal was probably aware, as he confessed later, that he was letting Subhas down. But he felt helpless given his mental make-up and his attachments. Subhas was not unaware of Jawaharlal's predicament: he had noted with great prescience in the early 1930s when he was in Vienna that Jawaharlal's head pulled in one direction and his heart in another. The heart pulled towards Gandhi. Subhas had little time for the invasion of such sentimentality into what he saw to be the rational world of politics where one sought to maximize the possible.

Jawaharlal suggested deeper causes for the breakdown. He had written to Subhas in early April 1939 about how different the two of them were in their temperaments and their attitude to life. However, paradoxical this might sound, there were aspects of Subhas's attitude that were more akin to Gandhi's than to Jawaharlal's.[75] With Gandhi he shared the sense of certainty about the path he had chosen. Neither of them had Jawaharlal's persistent self-doubt and proneness to self-scrutiny. Possibly since the time he refused to join the ICS, Subhas had an idea of his own mission and destiny. This was imbricated with his own notions of sacrifice. Gandhi had his own commitment to the quest for truth from which he never separated his political activities. He was always sure of his inner voice.[76] The

---

[75] This point is suggested by S. Gopal in his very penetrating essay, 'Tradition and Dissent: The Paradoxes of Subhas Bose', in S. Gopal, *Imperialists, Nationalists, Democrats: The Collected Essays*, (ed.) Srinath Raghavan (Delhi, 2013), p. 290.

[76] These attitudes of Gandhi were formed and were apparent long before he immersed himself in the national movement in India. See Ramachandra Guha, *Gandhi Before India* (Delhi, 2013).

temperaments of both Gandhi and Subhas were imbued with a sense of religiosity, not in any narrow and sectarian meaning of the term but in a more profound way that pertained to their understanding of what bestowed an inner significance to human lives and human history. This is evident from Subhas's *An Indian Pilgrim* and of course from Gandhi's autobiography and other writings.

Jawaharlal's intellectual trajectories had different orientations. He was not drawn easily, as he himself wrote in his autobiography, towards religion and spirituality. This was one factor in his intellectual distance from both Gandhi and, more agonizingly, from Kamala. He was less sure of his path, troubled as he always was by introspection. These features of his personality invariably made him appear torn and occasionally vacillating. Both Gandhi and Subhas believed that their politics derived a purpose from activism. As the latter reminded Jawaharlal in the harsh letter of 28 March 1939: '[T]he unity that we strive for or maintain must be the unity of action and not the unity of inaction.'[77] Jawaharlal paused before he acted and this often irked those who, like Subhas, made a virtue of their own impatience.

The temperamental differences between Subhas and Jawaharlal was nowhere better revealed, as indicated in Chapter Four, than in the two books they wrote during 1935–36—*The Indian Struggle* and *An Autobiography*. One strident, sure and assertive; the other low-key, understated and perhaps more gracious. Subhas's stridency occasionally appeared to Jawaharlal to be tasteless. Subhas's campaign to get himself re-elected he could not accept from his heart. He informed Subhas of this in the most gracious of terms: 'I felt all along that you were far too keen on re-election. Politically there was nothing wrong in it and you were perfectly entitled to desire re-election and to work for it. But it did distress me for I felt that you had a big enough position to be above this kind of thing.'[78] Jawaharlal perhaps felt that Subhas was spoiling for a fight and needlessly precipitating a confrontation with the established

---

[77] Letter to Nehru, 28 March 1939, in *Netaji: Collected Works*, vol. 9, p. 203.

[78] Letter to Nehru, 28 March 1939, in *Netaji: Collected Works*, vol. 9, p. 203.

Congress leadership. With an international crisis looming because of an impending war in Europe, the Congress could ill afford to get bogged down in an internal feud. He believed that the party and the country needed at that juncture a credible and non-partisan leadership and only Gandhi could provide this. He felt helpless and feared that Subhas was falling prey to provincial forces and aspirations. To Krishna Menon he wrote in early April, '[F]or the moment Subhas has become a kind of symbol of Bengal and it is quite impossible to argue with or about symbols. I feel very helpless.'[79]

Subhas had certainly captured the imagination of the political consciousness of Bengalis, including that of Tagore. There had existed in Bengal since the late nineteenth century an admiration for armed revolutionaries who, individually or in small groups, took on the might of the British government; this current of ideas and actions could not accept the leadership of Gandhi and its espousal of non-violent struggle. Subhas's decision to defy the Gandhian leadership won him many accolades in Bengal as it tapped into the pool of disapproval of Gandhi and his methods. He was perceived as a hero, the man who could wear the mantle of an alternative leader. It could not but have been heady for Subhas who may have even seen it as his destiny.

When he put himself up for re-election, Subhas also expected at the all-India level to receive support from the left groups within the Congress. He did see his battle for the presidency as a fight between the left and the right. But at Tripuri, he failed to win the support of all the left groups. He saw the abstention of the Congress Socialist Party (CSP) to be a real blow to his campaign to win a majority in the debate regarding the Pant resolution.[80] His belief that the support of the CSP would have won him a majority in the open session was perhaps a trifle optimistic—Azad called

---

[79] Letter to Krishna Menon, 4 April 1939, in ibid., vol. 9, p. 550.

[80] Letter to Gandhi, 25 March 1939: 'If the CSP had not remained neutral, then in spite of various handicaps . . . we would have had a majority in the open session.' *Netaji: Collected Works*, vol. 9, p. 128.

it an 'extravagant assertion'.[81] Once it became obvious, after the Pant resolution was introduced, that what was emerging was a challenge to Gandhi, many of Subhas's supporters, like the CSP, reviewed their own positions. Jayaprakash Narayan summed up the situation rather well: 'The whole issue then stood thus—acceptance of Pant's resolution would mean supporting Gandhian leadership and opposition to it would mean an advocacy of alternative leadership. The socialist line was opposed to both.'[82] There was a growing realization within the left group that it was not strong enough to precipitate a clash with the Gandhian leadership. Rammanohar Lohia had written with some insight in March 1939 that the 'Leftists in the Congress should not aspire to set up an alternative leadership to the present leadership of the "Right". They have not the strength to control the destiny of the nation, nor can they hope to attain it in the future. A direct offensive against the Right Congress leaders would result in internal conflict.' Jayaprakash Narayan also held a similar view.[83] Subhas in his unbounded optimism had overestimated his support base. Or, to put it differently, he had failed to read the pulse of the Congress, even of those he saw as his own supporters. He had brought himself perilously close to becoming a hero without a chorus.

Jawaharlal had written to Subhas about his fears about a break with Gandhi and the weakness of the 'Left': 'I was against your standing for election for two major reasons: it meant under the circumstances a break with Gandhiji and I did not want this to take place. (Why this should have necessarily happened I need not go into. I felt that it would happen.) It would also mean a setback for the real left. The left was not strong enough to shoulder the burden by itself and when a real contest came in the Congress, it would lose and then there would be a reaction against it. I thought it probable that you

---

[81] Letter to Nehru, 17 April 1939, in Nehru Papers, vol. 5.

[82] Note dated 17 March 1939: cited in Som, *Differences within Consensus*, p. 250.

[83] Lohia in the *Times of India*, 24 January 1939; Narayan wrote on 19 March: 'We do believe that unless the highest executive of the Congress commands the confidence of Gandhiji, it will not be possible to maintain unity in the Congress.' Both cited in Som, *Differences within Consensus*, p. 250.

would win the election against Pattabhi, but I doubted very much whether you could carry the Congress with you in a clear contest with what is called Gandhism.' Subhas, as is evident from his actions and statements, had no such doubts about his own position within the Congress. Even after his defeat he asserted that it had been caused by CSP's neutrality and some tactical blunders. What is even more revealing of Subhas's attitude is that in his analysis the defeat had resulted in 'a sharpening of political consciousness' and that in the long run 'it will prove a great incentive to progress'.[84] Subhas had an undying faith that his own charisma and sacrifice would enable him to overcome the hurdles and objective conditions surrounding him. The pursuit of leadership prevailed over realism.

Apart from the differences in their temperament, Jawaharlal had also written to Subhas about their divergent understanding of the international situation, especially what was happening in Italy and Germany under fascism and Nazism respectively. Subhas's views on these totalitarian regimes was obvious in his willingness to meet the Nazi official Dr O. Urchs in Bombay on 22 December 1938. He was also of the view that Germany was the only power with the strength to challenge Britain.[85] When and if it did so, he thought, there would be a real opportunity for Indian nationalism to strike against British rule in India. Jawaharlal's condemnation of fascism and Nazism was not tempered by any considerations of realpolitik. It was forthright and ideological. His views on India's position in the event of a war between Germany and Britain was more considered, calibrated and different from Subhas's. He wrote, 'The fascist powers would very much like India to be a thorn in the side of England when war comes, so that they might profit by the situation we create. There is nothing that we would dislike so much as to play into the hands of the fascist powers, just as we dislike being exploited by imperialist Britain. Our anti-war policy must therefore be based on freedom and democracy and opposition to fascism and imperialism. And yet

---

[84] Letter to Amiya Bose, 17 April 1939, in *Netaji: Collected Works*, vol. 9, pp. 288–89.
[85] Gordon, *Brothers Against the Raj*, p. 370.

with a little twist it might well be turned into a pro-fascist policy.'[86]

Thus it was not just the Tripuri crisis that made Jawaharlal and Subhas drift apart personally and politically. There was a deeper context to the breakdown. The presidential election and its sequel was the proverbial last straw. More important was their differing understanding of politics and their very different personalities. Their lives had come to a fork: Subhas chose the road less travelled. He had once written to Jawaharlal, as if to sum up the spirit that drove him, that 'life was one big adventure'.[87] Little did he know then that he was poised to embark on the real great adventure of his life—an adventure that would take him further and further away from his once close friend.

[86] 'The AICC and After', 24 May 1939, in Nehru, *Selected Works*, vol. 9, p. 578.
[87] Letter to Nehru, 28 March 1939: *Netaji: Collected Works*, vol. 9, p. 218.

7

Friendship Regained?

In September 1939, the movement of German tanks into Poland had an impact on history in faraway India. Political leaders in India, especially Jawaharlal and Subhas, had been apprehensive from the beginning of the year that Europe would soon be plunged into war. Subhas heard about the war in Europe while he was addressing a huge public rally in Madras on 3 September. His immediate reaction was how to seize this opportunity—Britain's declaration of war on Germany—to the advantage of India's freedom movement. The issues involved in the war were of no concern to him. He thought this was 'India's golden opportunity'.[1] When the war broke out, Jawaharlal was in China. He returned to India on 9 September to learn that Gandhi, in his private capacity, had met the viceroy, Lord Linlithgow. He had informed the viceroy that his sympathies were with France and England. He had also deplored the fact that Hitler knew 'no God but brute force'.[2]

Jawaharlal had been intellectually prepared for a major armed conflict in Europe; he did not react in the manner that Gandhi did. His response was analytical rather than emotional, and it was Jawaharlal, according to his biographer S. Gopal, who formulated

---

[1] Subhas Chandra Bose, *The Indian Struggle*, p. 379.

[2] Statement to the Press, 9 September 1939, in Gandhi, *Collected Works*, vol. 70, pp. 161–62.

the Congress's response to the war crisis.[3] Jawaharlal had been a strong critic of Chamberlain's appeasement policy. In his view, fascism and imperialism were interlinked; he was opposed to both and he wanted the Congress to adopt a similar position. 'What has been perpetrated by fascism in Europe,' he wrote, 'is being done by British imperialism in India . . . in the event of war we will not help imperialism. Nor is it our desire that Germany or Italy should gain power.'[4] He argued that the Indian people had the right to decide their own attitude to the war and that they were determined to resist any imposed decision on them.[5] After the war broke out, he said in a speech, 'Only a free India can decide whether we can participate in the war or not. We want a declaration whether the principles of democracy, liberty and self-determination for which the war is claimed to be fought will be applicable to India also . . . A slave India cannot help Britain. We want to assume control of our government and when we are free we can help the democracies.'[6]

The context of such statements was the unilateral decision of Linlithgow to make India a part of the war effort. He consulted no one—not a single important Indian leader nor any of the provincial ministries. The Working Committee of the Congress met, under the shadow of a war into which India had been forcibly drawn, in Wardha from 9 September for three days. Subhas joined the deliberations as a special invitee. This was possibly the last time that Subhas and Jawaharlal saw each other.

Subhas's position was clear. The war presented an opportune moment to launch a mass civil disobedience movement for India to win independence. The Congress leadership was not quite ready to do this. The resolution of the Working Committee reflected the views of Jawaharlal who drafted the resolution. He had prepared two drafts only slightly different from each other, and a merged version

---

[3] Gopal, *Jawaharlal Nehru*, vol. 1, p. 250.

[4] 'Socialism, Fascism and Imperialism', 13 April 1939, in Nehru, *Selected Works*, vol. 9, pp. 283–85.

[5] 'The Congress and War', 22 April 1939, in ibid., p. 294.

[6] 'A Slave Cannot Help Britain', 11 October 1939, in Nehru, *Selected Works*, vol. 10, p. 184–85.

was accepted at the meeting. The resolution invited the British government to clarify its war aims with regard to democracy and imperialism and till such time this was forthcoming, the Congress postponed a final decision. But the committee emphasized that time was of the essence.

This was obviously unacceptable to Subhas who described the resolution as 'long-winded', amounting to nothing more than mere words—'in the midst of verbiage, the kernel was missing'.[7] The viceroy took the resolution a little more seriously in spite of taking no cognizance of the Congress's position and demands. He saw the Congress's attitude to the war as being directed by 'a doctrinaire like Nehru with his amateur knowledge of foreign politics and of the international stage'.[8] He found the Congress's demands to be of no relevance in his efforts to ensure that India became an integral part of the Allied war effort. With his detestation for fascism and Nazism, Jawaharlal was very eager to secure some concession from the British government that would enable India and the Congress to fight the menace that Mussolini and Hitler represented. To secure this end, at the suggestion of Gandhi, he wrote to Linlithgow in October 1939: 'This letter, written on the train to Wardha, has grown long. But I want to add a few words to it and to tell you how much I desire that the long conflict of India and England should be ended and that they should cooperate together. I have felt that this war, with all its horrors, has brought this opportunity to our respective countries and it would be sad and tragic if we are unable to take advantage of it.'[9]

Even though he was unaware of this letter of Jawaharlal to the viceroy, Subhas had no time for the sentiments expressed in the letter and the Congress's resolution. He was convinced that the Congress was seeking some form of compromise with the British government,

---

[7] 'Whither High Command', 18 November 1939, in *Netaji: Collected Works*, vol. 10, p. 36.

[8] Letter from Lord Linlithgow to Zetland, 18 September 1939: quoted in Gopal, *Jawaharlal Nehru*, vol. 1, p. 253.

[9] Letter to Lord Linlithgow, 6 October 1939, in Nehru, *Selected Works*, vol. 10, pp. 170–73.

and attacked the Congress policy in the strongest language possible. He wrote that if the resolution and the attitude of the Working Committee were to be paraphrased, it would read as 'We shall continue to lick the feet of the British government even though we have been kicked by them . . . resolutions of the Working Committee are mere verbosity, calculated to hoodwink and bluff the innocent people of this country . . . for the Rightists, British imperialism is a lesser enemy than Indian Leftism.'[10] Throughout the second half of 1939 and early 1940, he continued his attack on the Congress in this vein. Subhas's outbursts angered Jawaharlal. In public he issued no statements to condemn what Subhas was saying, but in private he did not restrain himself. To Krishna Menon, he wrote, 'Subhas Bose is going to pieces and has definitely ranged himself against the Congress. This is very unfortunate, but there it is . . . He now talks the most arrant nonsense about rival Congress and the like . . . Subhas Bose does not seem to have an idea in his head, and except for going on talking about leftists and rightists he says little that is intelligible.'[11] Jawaharlal was not prone to using this kind of language about anybody. These words can only be taken as signs of his growing anger at, and his political and personal distance from Subhas.

Jawaharlal's own temporizing position, however, became untenable in the face of Linlithgow's firm refusal to revise any aspect of the British policy. The Working Committee now had no alternative but to direct its Congress ministries to resign. The Congress decided to approach the Muslim League which was also committed to the idea of independence that Linlithgow had so firmly turned down. The day after the latter's statement, Jawaharlal wrote to Jinnah: 'I entirely agree with you that it is a tragedy that the Hindu–Muslim problem has not so far been settled in a friendly way. I feel terribly distressed about it and ashamed of myself, insofar as I have not been able to contribute anything substantial towards its solution. I must

[10] 'Whom They Fight?', 25 November 1939, in *Netaji: Collected Works*, vol. 10, pp. 39–42.

[11] Letter to Krishna Menon, 2 March 1940, in Nehru, *Selected Works*, vol. 10, 343–46.

confess to you that in this matter I have lost confidence in myself, though I am not usually given that way. But the last two or three years have had a powerful effect on me. My own mind moves on a different plane and most of my interests lie in other directions. And so, though I have given much thought to the problem and understand most of its implications, I feel as if I was an outsider and alien in spirit. Hence my hesitation. But this does not come in the way of my trying my utmost to help to find a solution and I shall certainly do so. With your goodwill and commanding position in the Muslim League that should not be so difficult as people imagine. I can assure you with all earnestness that all the members of the Working Committee are keenly desirous of finding a solution.'[12]

As a follow-up to this letter, Jawaharlal, Gandhi and Rajendra Prasad met Jinnah in Delhi. But nothing came out of this meeting even though Jawaharlal felt that Jinnah was satisfied. He wrote very optimistically, '[T]he whole fabric of communal disunion as a bar to India's progress . . . fades away and vanishes at the touch of reason and reality. The only reality that counts today is Britain's carrying on a war, which becomes more and more imperialistic, and her refusal to declare her war aims explicitly.'[13] A month later, Jinnah in a letter to Jawaharlal referred to the Delhi meeting and explicitly stated that no understanding between the Congress and the Muslim League was possible 'so long as the Congress is not prepared to treat the Muslim League as the authoritative and representative organization of the Mussalmans of India'.[14] Jawaharlal in reply said, '[I]f your desire is that we should consider the League as the sole organization representing the Muslims to the exclusion of all others, we are wholly unable to accede to it.'[15]

Two major doors of negotiations—with the British government and the Muslim League—were thus shut. The Congress ministries

---

[12] Letter to Jinnah, 18 October 1939, in ibid., pp. 359–60.

[13] 'The Right and the Wrong of It', 6 November 1939, in Nehru, *Selected Works*, vol. 10, pp. 368–71.

[14] Letter from Jinnah to Nehru, 13 December 1939, in Jawaharlal Nehru, *A Bunch of Old Letters*, p. 414.

[15] Letter to Jinnah, 14 December 1939, in ibid., pp. 414–15.

had resigned but the future steps were uncertain. Gandhi maintained that the Congress should not cooperate with the British but neither should it embarrass the British government when it was fighting a war. The Working Committee toed this line and in two resolutions on 23 November and 22 December it reiterated the Congress's commitment to non-violence, the constructive programme and to seeking an honourable settlement.

Jawaharlal, once again, felt totally out of tune with what was going on around him. He agreed with Gandhi that their views and approach to life's problems differed in many fundamental respects. He added, 'I have grown into my present views after many internal struggles and I cannot say that even now the process of change or growth has stopped. If I have to do anything worthwhile in life I must be true to myself insofar as I can. I have tried very hard to adapt myself to others, notably to you, but with little success, I fear. As for the Working Committee you know how badly I fit into it . . . It is my misfortune that I can find no place elsewhere where I can fit in. I function individually, lonely and weary at heart, disliking much that happens, including myself. I suppose that I must play that role since there is no other for me. But I cannot shed responsibility for what is happening, nor can I retire when every fibre in my being calls for action.'[16] On Christmas Day 1939, Jawaharlal in a mood of supreme intellectual detachment wrote, 'for the present all of us have to go through the valley of the shadow'.[17]

The Congress's resolutions exasperated Subhas. In a thinly veiled attack on Jawaharlal, he wrote at the end of 1939: 'It would be more honest to follow the clear lead of Mahatma Gandhi, however erroneous it may be. Lengthy resolutions, high-sounding phraseology savouring of Leftism, frothy speeches, periodic doses of bellicose utterances, frequent references to a new world order that need not be

---

[16] Gandhi had written to Nehru on 26 October 1939 to say, 'I could see that though your affection and regard for me remain undiminished, differences in outlook between us are becoming more marked.' *Together They Fought*, p. 376. Nehru's reply is dated 31 October 1939: ibid., 378–79.

[17] Letter to Madame Chiang Kai-shek, 25 December 1939, in Nehru, *Selected Works*, vol. 10, pp. 553–55.

fought for, but will fall from the skies—Imperialism crashing under its own weight without any onslaught from outside—all these fit in with what we know as Kerensky-tactics and ill-accord with the demands of Real-Politik.' Ridiculing the resolutions of the Working Committee, he added, 'Under the order of the Congress Working Committee we have to spin yarns and also spin our way to Swaraj.'[18] At the end of his tether, Subhas decided to strike out on his own.

The directions he wanted to take were indicated in the speeches he made around this time. Addressing the All India Students' Conference in January 1940, Subhas gave the clarion call for action: 'I . . . appeal to you to gird up your loins and prepare for the impending struggle. The struggle is coming . . . "Freedom comes . . . to those who dare and act." The time has come for all of us to dare and act and let not any of us flinch at this critical juncture. I am also reminded of the inspiring words addressed by a famous Italian general to his innumerable followers while the Revolution was still in progress. "I shall give you hunger, thirst, privation, forced marches and death," said he, "if you will follow me." Let these words ring in our ears now and inspire us to march forward and to dare and act. Only then shall we win victory and Swaraj.'[19]

Subhas was already setting out some of the themes of his future speeches—sacrifice, daring, action and heroism. The choice of a general to quote from was also not without significance. Subhas was seeking an alternative leadership to the Gandhian one, a radically different source of inspiration. The progress of the war in Europe at this time seemed to provide him with one fount of excitement. He wrote in March 1940, 'It seems that in modern warfare speed and mobility are exceedingly important factors. There is an old saying—"Well begun is half done". One should in these days modify it and say—"Quick begun is half done". Germany has been practicing this teaching with scrupulousness and precision. Whether in the military occupation of the Rhineland, or in the annexation of

---

[18] 'Leaders Misleading', 30 December 1939, in *Netaji: Collected Works*, vol. 10, pp. 56–7.

[19] 'An Address to Students of India', January 1940, in ibid., pp. 58–64.

Czechoslovakia or in the invasion of Poland or in the latest inroad into Scandinavia, she has always acted with lightning rapidity . . . Such swooping tactics presuppose careful planning over a long period and adequate preparation in accordance with it. Nazi Germany has been a past-master in this art of detailed planning and careful preparation . . . Germany may be a fascist or an imperialist, ruthless or cruel, but one cannot help admiring these qualities of hers—how she plans in advance, prepares accordingly, works according to a timetable and strikes with lightning speed. Could not these qualities be utilized for promoting a nobler cause?'[20] There were aspects of the Nazi project, in Subhas's scheme of things, that were worth admiring and emulating.

When the Congress held its session in Ramgarh in March 1940, Subhas organized the All India Anti-Compromise Conference in the same place. He spoke in this conference as its president and urged his audience to 'take time by the forelock' and to act 'while it is not too late'. He presented the examples of Lenin and Mussolini as leaders who seized the moment in history and provided decisive leadership to their countries. He ended his speech with 'Inquilab Zindabad'—a sign-off that would soon become his trademark.

His rhetoric notwithstanding, Subhas had not given up on Gandhi. In June, he travelled to Wardha to meet Gandhi—this was the last time that Gandhi and Subhas met. But the meeting was fruitless. This was not unexpected: Gandhi's views on Subhas had hardened. In January 1940, he wrote, 'The love of my conception, if it is as soft as a rose petal, can also be harder than flint. My wife has had to experience the hard variety. My eldest son is experiencing it even now. I had thought I had gained Subhas Babu for all time as a son. I have fallen from grace.'[21] The last sentence was a characteristic Gandhian reversal: it was Subhas who had suffered the fall. When Tagore had sent a telegram to Gandhi in December 1939 requesting that the ban on Subhas be lifted, Gandhi had replied that Tagore

[20] 'A Word about Germany', 13 March 1940, in ibid., vol. 10, pp. 81–82.
[21] 'The Charkha', 9 January 1940, in Gandhi, *Collected Works*, vol. 71, p. 94.

should advise Subhas to submit to discipline.[22] In January, Gandhi followed this up in a letter to C.F. Andrews; referring to Tagore's telegram, Gandhi wrote, 'I feel that Subhas is behaving like a spoilt child of the family. The only way to make up with him is to open his eyes. And then his politics show sharp differences. They seem to be unbridgeable. I am quite clear the matter is too complicated for Gurudev to handle.'[23]

Having spoken about action, Subhas chose to act in the summer of 1940 by launching a movement for the removal of Holwell's monument from Dalhousie Square.[24] Significantly, he announced this movement in Dacca. He was looking for new allies and had come to a seat-sharing arrangement with the Muslim League in the Calcutta Corporation. Holwell's monument, which sought to commemorate the infamous Black Hole incident from Siraj-ud-daulah's time, appeared to Subhas to be an issue that could bring Hindus and Muslims together in one movement. He announced on 3 July, the day the movement would begin, as Siraj-ud-daulah Day. He described the monument as 'an unwarranted stain on the memory of the Nawab'.[25] The day before the protest was to begin, Subhas was arrested under the Defence of India rules and incarcerated in Presidency Jail without charges. This was Subhas's last imprisonment and the beginning of the most extraordinary and critical phase of his life.

Even as a prisoner, Subhas refused to let the dominance of the British go unchallenged. Towards the end of November 1940, he began a hunger strike: 'Release me, or I shall refuse to live.' A few days before he began this fast unto death—ironically a mode of protest associated with Gandhi—he had written out what he called his 'political testament'. This was in the form of a handwritten letter addressed to the governor and the chief minister of Bengal and it ran to thirteen pages. The letter began by pointing out the illegality

---

[22] Telegram to Tagore, 22 December 1939, in ibid., p. 50 and Note 2.

[23] Letter to C.F. Andrews, 15 January 1940, in Gandhi, *Collected Works*, vol. 71, pp. 113–14.

[24] For a history of the Holwell's monument, see Partha Chatterjee, *The Black Hole of Empire: History of a Global Practice of Power* (Delhi, 2012).

[25] 'Holwell Monument', 29 June 1940, in *Netaji: Collected Works*, vol. 10, pp. 128–29.

and the injustice of his detention but moved on to themes relating to conscience and the purpose of life. Subhas wrote that there could be no greater solace than the feeling that he had lived and died for a principle and that future generations would be inspired by his example. 'What higher consummation can life attain,' he asked, 'than peaceful self-immolation at the altar of one's cause?' He added that '[T]he individual must die, so that the nation may live. Today I must die, so that India may live and may win freedom and glory.'[26] Subhas thus returned again to the twin themes of sacrifice and freedom, which were to receive a new salience in his life and activities in the near future.

The Government of Bengal was aware of the inflammatory repercussions of Subhas dying in prison: it released Subhas a week after he began his fast. Subhas was sent home in an ambulance with the prospect of rearrest once his health had recovered looming over him. It was made clear that Subhas was 'neither in custody nor on bail'—the government had only temporarily suspended his order of detention.[27] For all practical purposes, Subhas remained interned in his father's house on Elgin Road and was under constant police surveillance.

It was from this house, defying the ring of security, that Subhas made, on the night of 16–17 January 1941, his escape which has become the stuff of legend. That adventure can only be briefly recounted here. At the dead of night, Subhas, disguised as a Pathan, left in a car driven by his nephew Sisir, and arrived at Bararee, near Dhanbad, where another nephew Asoke lived. From here travelling under the alias Muhammad Ziauddin, Subhas boarded the Delhi–Kalka Mail at Gomoh station. From Delhi, he changed to the Frontier Mail to arrive in Peshawar from where with the help of comrades he proceeded to Kabul.[28]

---

[26] 'My Political Testament', 26 November 1940, in ibid., pp. 192–98.

[27] Letter from Herbert (Governor of Bengal) to Linlithgow, 11 December 1940: cited in Sugata Bose, *His Majesty's Opponent*, p. 183.

[28] The most detailed account of this escape is in Sugata Bose, *His Majesty's Opponent*, pp. 184–92.

The escape was as incredible as it was intriguing. How had Subhas and his nephew managed to fool and get past the police surveillance that surrounded the house on Elgin Road? The government in Bengal woke up to Subhas's disappearance only after it was reported in *Ananda Bazar Patrika* and *Hindustan Standard*. The police and the information branch had obviously been very incompetent. Or was it that the government had let him escape on the basis of the argument that Subhas would be less trouble outside India than within? Even after so many decades, there are many mysterious aspects to his escape which have burnished the legends about him.

By the end of January 1941, Subhas was in Kabul and beyond the tentacles of the British Indian police. Once he was in Kabul, Subhas was outside the jurisdiction of the British government—but was he beyond the radar of British Intelligence? This question is worth asking. It is clear now from documentary evidence that Bhagat Ram Talwar, who under the alias of Rahmat Khan had played a pivotal role in transporting Subhas from Peshawar to Kabul and then onwards to Berlin, was actually an agent of the British Intelligence services and was codenamed Silver.[29] What the documentation does not make explicit is precisely when Talwar became a British agent. That he was passing on information to the British after Hitler's invasion of the Soviet Union in June 1941 cannot be doubted. One implication of this is that whatever information he received from Subhas after June 1941 was known to both the British government and the Soviet authorities. Was Talwar performing a similar role before that date when he was actually with Subhas in Kabul? If he was, then one of Subhas's close comrades had actually compromised his movements. It is significant that in March 1941, Britain's Special Operations Executive (SOE) was aware that Subhas was planning to travel from Afghanistan to Germany. The SOE mistakenly thought that he would travel through Iran, Iraq and Turkey but they were right about Subhas's eventual destination.[30]

---

[29] See Calder Walton, *Empire of Secrets: British Intelligence, the Cold War and the Twilight of Empire* (London, 2013), pp. 51–53.

[30] Sugata Bose, *His Majesty's Opponent*, p. 197.

Berlin was not Subhas's first choice. On Subhas's arrival in Kabul, Talwar, who was with him, made attempts to contact the Soviet ambassador but failed. It was then that Subhas gatecrashed into the German embassy.[31] He had a better reception there. He was received by the minister Hans Pilger, to whom Subhas explained his plans to promote the Indian freedom movement from Berlin; Subhas requested him to arrange for his transit there via the Soviet Union. Pilger reacted with alacrity and sent off a telegram to Berlin; he also informed his counterparts in the Italian embassy and alerted Subhas that he was in danger and that he should keep in touch with the German embassy through the local representative of Siemens. Berlin did not sit on Pilger's cable. The secretary of state, Ernst von Weizsäcker, ordered a short biography to be produced. This was ready by 2 February and proved to be remarkably accurate. It was also well informed about Subhas's attitude towards Germany: 'Bose has always expected Germany to proclaim a clear political viewpoint with regard to India and has openly shown his disappointment that this has not happened.' The writer of the note did not hesitate to put down his reservations about Subhas: 'Bose is a very vain and pushy character. He engages in opposition for opposition's sake.'[32] Pilger's reaction to Subhas was also not very favourable. He warned that 'certain happenings' might suggest that Subhas did work with the British. He added that an Indian had come to him as Subhas's negotiator, and Pilger had the distinct impression that this man had links with the British embassy.[33] If the negotiator on Subhas's behalf had been Talwar—an extremely likely possibility—then Pilger was extraordinarily prescient; and this seems to strengthen the suspicions voiced in the previous paragraph.

Weizsäcker informed the Kabul legation that Subhas could travel to Germany provided the Soviet Union gave him a transit

---

[31] Ibid., p. 195.

[32] Unsigned memorandum, 2 February 1941, *Auswärtiges Amt* (German Foreign Office): cited in Jan Kuhlmann, *Netaji in Europe* (Delhi, 2012), p. 33.

[33] Pilger to AA (German Foreign Office), telegram No. 46, 12 February 1941: cited in ibid., pp. 33–34.

visa. The Nazi–Soviet pact made possible the request for such a travel document. This decision to get Subhas across to Berlin was probably related to the German Foreign Office's attempts during this period to increase its India-specific propaganda.[34] After what for Subhas was an agonizing wait, he left Kabul on 18 March 1941 for Moscow en route to Berlin. He arrived in Moscow on 31 March and left for Berlin the same day. Three days later he wrote to Emilie from Berlin—his first letter to her after the one he wrote on 4–6 July 1939.[35]

Where Subhas found himself—in the heart of Nazi Germany and seeking its support—was the farthest from Jawaharlal's mental and ideological location in the early 1940s. He had always been severely critical of fascism and Nazism, and this antipathy increased as the Nazi military machine swept through Western Europe. He watched these developments with apprehension and was dismayed by the Nazi–Soviet pact and by the invasion of Finland by Soviet Russia. His biographer S. Gopal comments that the failure of Russia, a country that Jawaharlal admired, to 'keep her means above reproach' alerted him to the importance of ethical action and thus brought him even closer to Gandhi. This is the context of Jawaharlal's acceptance of the Gandhian constructive programme as the next step after the resignation of the Congress ministries. In fact, Jawaharlal himself took up spinning in 1940 after a break of four years.[36]

Where Jawaharlal found himself torn was in the conflict between his commitment to India's independence and his sympathy for Britain as it battled to save democracy and liberty against the onslaught of Nazism. He had expressed this dilemma in a letter to Rajendra Prasad in 1940: 'To say that Nazism is worse than the present form of British imperialism is true in some respects, though I doubt if there is fundamentally much difference. But to say that because Nazism is worse therefore we must prefer the domination of the British is surely [a] dangerous doctrine. It means that we are helpless

---

[34] Ibid.

[35] Letter to Emilie, 3 April 1941, in *Netaji: Collected Works*, vol. 7, pp. 216–17.

[36] Gopal, *Jawaharlal Nehru*, vol. 1, p. 261.

people who must have a master and the little choice we have is to choose masters. To say this is to put an end to all our pretensions and to admit the fundamental basis of British rule . . . We stand for independence and we shall resist any and every foreign authority which seeks to dominate over us.'[37] As he watched the early years of the Second World War—a part of it from prison where he was from the end of October 1940 for thirteen months—Jawaharlal never retreated from this understanding. It is important to flag this point since it would colour his assessment of Subhas's activities during the Second World War. In a speech immediately after his release from prison and delivered the day after the Japanese attack on Pearl Harbour, Jawaharlal expressed his apprehension that '[T]he war might even spread to India.'[38] This fear was possibly based on the Thai government's decision to allow Japanese troops to pass through its territories. This cleared the ground for the Japanese invasion of Southeast Asia—Malaya and Singapore (and eventually Burma)—thus bringing the war to India's eastern borders.

The physical proximity of the war brought about changes in the Congress's position. It was no longer a question of waiting for changes in British policy. The more urgent issue was what the Congress would do if the Japanese actually entered Indian territory or bombed parts of it. Over Christmas 1941, the Congress Working Committee met at Bardoli. Here, with Rajagopalachari providing the lead, the committee recognized the new world situation and accepted the impossibility of defending India non-violently against a Japanese invasion. The Congress offered to cooperate in the war effort provided India's independence was declared. The Bardoli resolution created divisions within the Working Committee. Jawaharlal, Azad and Rajagopalachari were ready to offer conditional support to the British but Patel and Rajendra Prasad insisted on no participation because it entailed association with violence. Patel and Prasad were following Gandhi who provided the most important dissent. At the end of the year he wrote to Azad, the Congress president, to relieve

---

[37] Letter to Rajendra Prasad, 16 May 1940, in Nehru, *Selected Works*, vol. 11, p. 31.
[38] 'On War', 8 December 1941, in Nehru, *Selected Works*, vol. 12, p. 2.

him of leading the Congress in individual satyagraha as he was against the Bardoli resolution. The Working Committee accepted his withdrawal.

Jawaharlal, once again at odds with Gandhi, rushed to clarify his own position: 'In the last twenty-two years of India's struggle, I have fully accepted the principle of non-violence . . . [but] what is in store for the world appears very difficult for a politician to spell out. Therefore if necessary I may even give up the principle of non-violence . . . India cannot become timid because of non-violence for in our eyes nothing is worse than cowardice. Mahatmaji once said that people should fight for their rights through non-violence, but if they failed and lost strength, they should do so with the sword.' Jawaharlal sought in his speeches to emphasize that Gandhi and the Congress had not parted ways.[39] To reiterate the fact that his own bond with Jawaharlal remained as strong as always, Gandhi announced on 15 January 1942 that Jawaharlal was his chosen heir. At the AICC session in Wardha on 15 January, Gandhi announced, 'Somebody suggested that Pandit Jawaharlal and I were estranged. It will require much more than differences of opinion to estrange us. We have had differences from the moment we became co-workers, yet I have said for some years and say it now that not Rajaji, nor Sardar Vallabhbhai, but Jawaharlal will be my successor. You cannot divide water by repeatedly striking it with a stick. It is just as difficult to divide us . . . When I am gone, he will speak my language.'[40]

Jawaharlal's life, in spite of the turmoil in the world, was proceeding on expected tracks. Subhas's life in Germany reflected the tumult. There was, however, one oasis of peace. He and Emilie were together as she had come over to Berlin and the two of them lived together. But Subhas's political project hit many obstacles. Hitler in April 1941 was at the apogee of his power in Europe which his military machine dominated, apart from Britain and the Soviet Union. In early April, the Wehrmacht had invaded Greece and Yugoslavia, the last two pro-British outposts in Europe. In North

---

[39] 'Congress Unity', 2 January 1942, in ibid., vol. 12, pp. 61–72.

[40] Gandhi, *Collected Works*, vol. 75, p. 224.

Africa, General Erwin Rommel had begun his offensive and forced British troops to withdraw across the Libyan desert. Subhas thus met a representative of a very confident Germany in the person of Ernst Woermann, the under-secretary of state. Subhas suggested that a free Indian government be established in Berlin, and much to the surprise of Woermann spoke about sending 100,000 German troops to invade and free India.[41] It became evident to Woermann that Subhas's aims and Germany's priorities were incompatible. Subhas believed that Germany wanted to destroy the British Empire. He was possibly unaware that Hitler's priorities did not include the British Empire at this point of time. He was occupied full time with the planning of Operation Barbarossa—the invasion of the Soviet Union. A quick victory in Russia, Hitler believed, would force Britain out of the war. This was his limited aim in early 1941. A significant section of the Nazi leadership that may have even included Hitler, was not averse to a peace agreement with Britain around 1940–41. Witness, Rudolf Hess's flight to Scotland with an offer of peace.[42]

These circumstances notwithstanding, when Hitler learnt of Subhas's proposal to set up an Indian government in exile, he responded positively. Privately, the Fuhrer told Joseph Goebbels on 2 May that he was seriously contemplating such a move.[43] Subhas may not have been privy to what was known only to Hitler's closest circle. What he experienced first-hand was aloofness on the part of German foreign office officials. In the course of Subhas's meeting with the German foreign minister, Ribbentrop, there was no discussion of an Indian government in exile and the training of Indian prisoners of war—two subjects vital for Subhas's plans to

---

[41] Hayes, *Bose in Nazi Germany*, p. 29; also see Kuhlmann, *Netaji in Europe*, p. 37.

[42] For Hitler's preoccupation with the invasion of Soviet Russia, see Ian Kershaw, *Hitler, 1936–45: Nemesis* (London, 2000), chapter 8; Peter Padfield, *Hess, Hitler & Churchill: The Real Turning Point of the Second World War—A Secret History* (London, 2013) makes a very persuasive case that Hess could not have flown to Scotland without Hitler's knowledge and that British secret services, especially Stewart Menzies, head of MI6 during the war, not only knew of Hess's flight but may even have encouraged him.

[43] Hayes, *Bose in Nazi Germany*, p. 38.

free India. What may also have dismayed Subhas somewhat was Ribbentrop's references to Gandhi. In the memorandum Subhas had written—'Plan for Co-operation between the Axis Powers and India' and an 'Explanatory Note'—he had not mentioned Gandhi and, in the course of his conversation with the German foreign minister, had dismissed Gandhi as a 'man of compromise' who did not want to 'shut the door in the face of the English'. But Ribbentrop was not fooled by this rhetoric; he insisted that Gandhi be 'always' taken into consideration and his passive resistance should not be so easily dismissed.[44]

In early May, Subhas prepared a detailed note for the German Foreign Office emphasizing the need for an immediate declaration on Indian independence. In this note he asserted that even though there existed a 'large measure of pro-Soviet feeling' in India, it was accepted that it was 'the Axis Powers alone (and not the Soviet)' which could help to bring about India's freedom.[45] This note was obviously well received since Subhas was requested to draft the declaration on India. What Subhas wrote was very straightforward: 'Germany . . . recognizes the inalienable right of the Indian people to have full and complete independence . . . She assures the Indian people that the New Order which she is out to establish in the world will mean for them a free and independent India . . . It will, of course, be for the Indian people to decide what form of government they should have . . . Germany conveys its sincerest good wishes to the Indian people in their struggle for freedom and declares that she is prepared to render them such assistance as lies in her power, so that the goal of liberty may be reached without delay.'[46] The Foreign Office accepted the draft without suggesting any changes, and Hitler on 10 May approved of Subhas's request for a declaration on Indian independence. In May 1941, Subhas was high on optimism and he sent a message to Talwar in which he said, '[B]ig events will happen soon in the sphere of international politics which will help

---

[44] Ibid., p. 43.

[45] Quoted in ibid., p. 45.

[46] Quoted in ibid., p. 48.

the overthrow of British imperialism . . . I am expecting from the Axis powers within a fortnight an open declaration regarding Indian independence.'[47]

Disappointment was soon to follow since the declaration that Subhas so ardently wanted was postponed not once but twice—first on 24 May and again on 6 September. As if to humour Subhas, on 10 September, Ribbentrop instructed Woermann to assure Subhas about Germany's commitment to the declaration. As late as 25 May 1942—one year after Subhas had presented his draft—Ribbentrop was writing to Hitler urging him to issue the declaration.[48] These postponements were only one source of Subhas's disappointment. In June 1941, while he was on a visit to Italy, Subhas learnt that Germany had invaded Soviet Russia on the 22nd. Subhas was quick to grasp how adversely this affected his plans. He knew opinion in India would inevitably veer in favour of the Soviet Union. To Woermann, he wrote on 5 July from Italy, '[T]he prospect for the realization of my plans looked gloomy in the altered circumstances and I was thinking that an early return to Berlin would not be of much use . . . The public reaction in my country to the new situation in the east is unfavourable towards your government.' Back in Berlin, he told Woermann in the middle of the month that Germany was now seen by Indians as the 'aggressor' and as another 'imperialist power'; the approach of German troops towards India would be seen by Indians as a project to substitute British rule with German rule.[49]

Subhas received another blow when in the middle of August 1941, the US president, Franklin Roosevelt, and the British prime minister, Winston Churchill, issued a joint declaration that said, *inter alia*, that both countries 'respect the right of all peoples to choose the form of government under which they will live; and they wish to see sovereign rights and self-government restored to those who

---

[47] Ibid., p. 49.

[48] The dates for the postponement of the declaration are easily available in the chronology presented at the beginning of Hayes, *Bose in Nazi Germany*.

[49] Ibid., pp. 56–57; and Kuhlmann, *Netaji in Europe*, p. 59.

have been forcibly deprived of them.'[50] For Subhas, this made the absence of a declaration from Germany even more stark. He could see that the Churchill–Roosevelt joint declaration would be welcomed in India. The idea was perhaps beginning to dawn on Subhas that his presence in Nazi Germany was proving to be a handicap to his political aims and ambitions, especially as from around November 1941, it became officially known that he was based in Berlin. But it was not easy for him to extricate himself from the situation he found himself in.

He was quite comfortably ensconced in Berlin. The Foreign Office provided him a rather luxurious residence along with a butler, cook, gardener and a SS-chauffeured car with special petrol rations. He was also fully involved in the work of the Free India Centre which worked with the help of Indians in Germany to promote the cause of India's freedom. But these activities did not match up to the grandiose plans that Subhas had for the liberation of his country. For him personally, the high point of his stay in Germany was his meeting with Hitler—the only one he had. The meeting took place at the end of May 1942, by which time the entire dimensions of the war had changed with the Japanese bombing of Pearl Harbour, the entry of the USA into the war and the dogged Russian resistance to the brutal invasion of their country by Nazi Germany.

Subhas addressed Hitler as an 'old revolutionary' and added that he would always remember this occasion. Hitler told Subhas that Germany and India were both fighting the same 'merciless opponents' and these included Soviet Russia. Regarding the declaration on India, Hitler said he was fighting the war as a soldier and not as a politician and was unwilling to make 'false prophecies' and guarantee anything 'beyond the range of his own effectiveness'. His advice to Subhas was to 'bank on the Japanese' and to get as close to India as possible. Only an internal rebellion combined with external pressure would ensure India's liberation. He described 'Japan's astonishingly rapid advance' as a major 'historical event' and impressed upon Subhas

---

[50] The text of the declaration is available in Winston Churchill, *The Second World War*, vol. 3 (London, 1950), pp. 346–47.

the importance of quickly reaching an agreement with the Japanese. He also insisted that Subhas travel to Japan not by air but in the Japanese submarine that was scheduled to reach German-occupied France in the summer.[51]

Preparations were thus afoot for another of Subhas's grand adventures—an underwater trip from Europe to Japan with a change of submarines in the choppy waters of the Indian Ocean.[52] Subhas left Germany in February 1943 and he left empty-handed. His 'pact with the devil'[53] had proved to be a fruitless one. It had fetched Subhas nothing save the taint that he had been a 'collaborator' with the Axis powers and had cozied up to the Nazis. Subhas was aware of the incongruity inherent in his attempts to seek the help of the Nazi regime. When asked about this by one of his co-workers in Berlin, Girija K. Mookerjee, Subhas answered that it was a tactical alliance: he had not befriended the Nazis. He went on to say that if Britain could make an alliance with the Soviet Union overcoming their ideological hostility, Indian nationalists could also seek help from governments with a dubious track record. He added, '[W]e have nothing in common with the Nazis, it is true. But why should that prevent us from taking some help from them, provided they did not try to interfere with our work or influence us ideologically . . . We won't say anything either in favour of or against the Germans for what they do in Europe does not strictly concern us.'[54]

The comparison of his own position with the Anglo-Soviet alliance was self-evidently naïve. Both Stalin and Churchill, during the course of the war, enjoyed advantages from the alliance they had forged. There was an element of reciprocity that benefited both parties. This cannot be said for the tactical friendship that Subhas had struck with Nazi Germany. Neither party gained from it because in Hitler's overall war strategy what Subhas wanted was

[51] An account of the Bose–Hitler meeting is available in Hayes, *Bose in Nazi Germany*, pp. 114–16.

[52] This trip is described in Sugata Bose, *His Majesty's Opponent*, pp. 234–36. Subhas travelled first in a German submarine and then changed to a Japanese one.

[53] The phrase is from ibid., p. 203.

[54] Hayes, *Bose in Nazi Germany*, p. 80.

of little or no consequence. Thus, Subhas could not even secure a German declaration supporting India's independence. It was an alliance sans consequences. There were some personal gains that Subhas made. Thanks to the rather lavish hospitality the Nazi government bestowed on him, Emilie and he enjoyed a brief period of domestic bliss.

In terms of the treatment that Subhas received in the hands of the Nazis, a number of aspects need to be underlined. The regime was known for its laws against inter-racial marriages but the Nazis did not interfere with the relationship between Emilie and Subhas. It is difficult to believe that the Nazi government was unaware of their marriage or that they were living as husband and wife. The Nazis were also not known for their toleration of dissent, but Subhas in his discussions with German officials, including Ribbentrop, did not hesitate to voice his disappointments and his disapprovals. He was not victimized for this. In every meeting that Subhas was officially asked to attend, he was treated with dignity and made to sit on the German side if Italians and Japanese were present. It is possible that these exhibitions of hospitality made Subhas remain silent on the Nazi atrocities about which he could not have been ignorant.[55] The protection of Emilie was justifiably paramount in his mind.

There is another factor to be considered and this is suggested by what Subhas told Girija Mookerjee: 'What they [the Germans] do in Europe does not strictly concern us'. Subhas self-consciously cultivated a tunnel vision. Through that tunnel he could only see India's freedom, nothing more and nothing less. It was a vision that was both noble and myopic at the same time. It also made the man who had written in his philosophical testament that love was what drove his life seek an alliance with one of the most oppressive regimes in human history. It made him seek his country's freedom

---

[55] Subhas lived in the Charlottenburg neighbourhood of Berlin and it is inconceivable that he was ignorant of the Nazi policy to make Berlin *judenfrei* (free of Jews)—a policy whose implementation began with vehemence from the night of 16 October 1941. See Alexendra Richie, *Faust's Metropolis: A History of Berlin* (London, 1998), pp. 515–17. A few days after the Nazis began the process of making Berlin free of Jews, Subhas inaugurated the Free India Centre in Berlin.

with the help of a regime that suppressed liberties across Europe.

Subhas's departure from Europe this time was even more heart-wrenching than his previous ones. He was not only leaving behind his wife but also a daughter who was only two months old. He may even have had an inkling that he might not see them again. Before he embarked on his journey to Asia—a journey fraught with uncertainty and danger—he wrote to his elder brother Sarat: 'Today once again I am embarking on the path to danger . . . I may not see the end of the road. If I meet with any such danger, I will not be able to send you any further news in this life. That is why today I am leaving my news here—it will reach you in due time. I have married here and I have a daughter. In my absence please show my wife and daughter the love you have given me throughout your life.'[56] He had surrendered all to seek his destiny.

While Subhas was away in his fruitless quest in Germany, Jawaharlal become involved in an unproductive enterprise initiated by the British government. This was what historians call the Cripps Mission. Before Stafford Cripps arrived in India with a portfolio of proposals in March 1942, the government and the Congress were deadlocked. From the point of view of the Congress and Jawaharlal, satyagraha had been called off so that the British government was not embarrassed, but this did not mean a softening of attitude. Jawaharlal wrote to a correspondent: 'The war is our war. But you don't understand; in this war *Britain is on the other side*.'[57] The Congress had extended its cooperation to be part of the war effort if the British promised freedom and the British had scoffed at it. Jawaharlal appealed to his countrymen not to surrender to a foreign army. And in a thinly veiled reference to Subhas's efforts to seek external help to achieve independence, he said in a speech in Calcutta, 'You must not look to any outsider for help. You must rely absolutely on your own inherent strength to achieve your

[56] Letter from Bose to Sarat Bose, 8 February 1943: quoted in Sugata Bose, *His Majesty's Opponent*, p. 231.

[57] Letter from Nehru to Eve Curie, 22 March 1942: quoted in Gopal, *Jawaharlal Nehru*, vol. 1, p. 276. (The emphasis is Jawaharlal's.)

independence. The pages of Indian history bear testimony to the fact how the lure of outside help has brought about India's slavery. The story of the imperialist venture of Japan and Germany is not unknown to you . . . But whatever happens, India will not bow down her head before any invader.'[58]

As the Japanese forces swept across Southeast Asia and an invasion of India seemed imminent, the British government woke up to the possibility of changing its policy towards India and to retrieve a modicum of goodwill so that India could be defended. Attlee mooted the idea of sending out to India 'some person of high standing with wide powers to negotiate a settlement in India'.[59] Even Churchill was not averse to this idea. The person entrusted with the responsibility was Cripps, who had been appointed Lord Privy Seal and had become an influential member of the War Cabinet. The proposal that Cripps brought for negotiations with Indian leaders consisted of 'steps . . . [that] shall be taken for the earliest possible realization of self-government in India'. India would be treated as a Dominion and this would lead to independence, which would be preceded by a post-war constituent assembly, subject only to the right of any province not to accede. For the immediate handling of the war effort, the proposal said that while the responsibility rested with the British government, principal sections of the Indian population would be brought into participate 'in the counsels of their nation'.[60] Churchill's rueful comment on this proposal was rather apt. He said, '[W]e have resigned ourselves to fighting our utmost to defend India in order, if successful, to be turned out.'[61]

But behind these proposals and the choice of Cripps to go to India were more covert motives of which Cripps himself was not aware. Amery, the secretary of state for India, wrote to Linlithgow,

---

[58] 'No Compromise with the British', 21 February 1942, in Nehru, *Selected Works*, vol. 12, pp. 138–40.

[59] 'The Indian Political Situation': Memo by the Lord Privy Seal [Attlee], 2 February 1942, War Cabinet Paper, W.P. (42); (ed.) Nicholas Mansergh, *The Transfer of Power, 1942–47* (London, 1970), vol. 1, pp. 110–12.

[60] 'Draft Declaration', 28 February 1942, in ibid., pp. 266–67.

[61] Letter from Churchill to Mackenzie King, 18 March 1942, in ibid., pp. 440–41.

the viceroy, about ten days before Cripps's departure that the scheme that had been worked out 'was entirely unsuitable to figure as a public declaration' and would 'have had an adverse reaction in all sorts of quarters, and be damned from the outset'. He thus felt that 'the only way out, and incidentally a way of gaining a little time, was to send someone to discuss and negotiate in order to find out how far Indians, when really brought up against the logic of the situation, would accept its conclusions'. The Congress hoped, according to Amery, that the British government would 'take some step which prejudged the situation in their favour and against the Muslims and the Princes'. The Congress needed to be 'definitely told in so many words, and by someone whom they regard as not unsympathetic, that their game is up and that they must either find ways and means of compromising with the minority elements, or face the disadvantages of a divided India.' He added, '[T]here is much to be said for sending out someone who has always been an extreme Left Winger and in close touch with Nehru and the Congress . . . the result in the end should be both to increase the chances of success, slight as they are, and to mitigate any blame thrown upon the government as a whole for failure.'[62] Cripps thus arrived in India oblivious that he was hamstrung since both Amery and Churchill hoped that he would fail.[63]

The Cripps Mission began on the wrong foot. Gandhi dismissed the offer as 'a post-dated cheque'.[64] He wrote to Jawaharlal on 27 March 1942 after meeting Cripps: 'I am clearly of the view that we cannot accept the "offer".' The importance he gave to the offer is indicated by the fact that he wrote this letter on the back

[62] Letter from Amery to Linlithgow, 10 March 1942, in *The Transfer of Power*, vol. 1, pp. 401–04.

[63] 'If it is rejected by the Indian parties . . . our sincerity will be proved to the world': Churchill's letter to Linlithgow, 10 March 1942, in *The Transfer of Power*, vol. 1, pp. 394–95.

[64] It is commonly believed that Gandhi described the offer as 'a post-dated cheque on a crashing bank' but he never used the phrase 'on a crashing bank'. It was the addition of an innovative journalist. See Gopal, *Jawaharlal Nehru*, vol. 1, p. 279n4.

of a bill at two in the morning while he was having a massage.[65] In the letter, Gandhi advised Jawaharlal to discuss the matter with Rajagopalachari who was in favour of accepting the Cripps offer. To Cripps, he was more forthright. He told Cripps: 'Why did you come if this is what you have to offer? If this is your entire proposal to India, I would advise you to take the next plane home.'[66] Both Azad and Jawaharlal were more concerned about the extent to which the declaration would enable Indians to collaborate in the defence of India. But there was no agreement on this since both Linlithgow and Wavell, the commander-in-chief, were not willing to concede ground on allowing Indians to have a critical say on matters pertaining to defence. The Cripps offer thus became a dead letter. Jawaharlal, in his rebuttal to Cripps's parting statement that Congress wanted all or nothing, said, '[O]ur price is going to be blood and tears, not of a few only but of vast numbers of people. Already we have had a foretaste of it in Malaya and Burma. But our time in itself is coming and it was because of this that we went to the uttermost limits of concession in our talks with Sir Stafford Cripps. For, we were anxious to face this peril with the organized power of the state and our masses functioning together. That is not to be now and we function separately. From our side, there are going to be no approaches to the British Government, for we know now that whoever comes from them speaks in the same accent as of old and treats us in the same way.'[67]

From Berlin, Subhas echoed these sentiments: he condemned Cripps for acting at the behest of imperialists and appealed to the Indian people and leaders to reject the offer that Cripps had brought.[68] Disillusioned in Germany, Subhas was encouraged by the Japanese premier's assurance regarding 'India for the Indians'.[69]

---

[65] Letter from Gandhi to Nehru, 27 March 1942, in *Together They Fought*, p. 433, and Notes 837 and 838.

[66] Quoted in Clarke, *The Cripps Version*, p. 301.

[67] 'Freedom First', 15 April 1942, in Nehru, *Selected Works*, vol. 12, pp. 233–34.

[68] Sugata Bose, *His Majesty's Opponent*, p. 217.

[69] Ibid.

After his long and perilous submarine voyage, Subhas surfaced in Sabang off the north coast of Sumatra and from there flew to Tokyo where he lodged at the Imperial Hotel. By July 1943, he was in Singapore with plans to mobilize the two million Indians who were in Southeast Asia.

From the time he had escaped from India to his arrival in Singapore, the course of the war had undergone a dramatic transformation. In early 1941, the Nazi war machine was triumphant in Europe but in 1943, at least in Soviet Russia, it was meeting serious resistance and suffering reverses; in the Pacific theatre of the war, the United States was gaining ascendancy over Japan. It was only in Southeast Asia that the Japanese forces held sway. Subhas chose this as his area of operation from which to lead an army of liberation into India. He revived the Indian National Army that had first been formed in February 1942, a few days after the British forces surrendered to Japan in Singapore. In a small handwritten calendar that he kept with himself to record the important events of his life, Subhas wrote, 'Began work' against the date July 1943. He had begun the most important phase of his life.

The situation in India was crying out for a saviour. The fiasco of the Cripps Mission had left the Congress with no other alternative but to confront the British government. The Quit India Movement was begun as the final onslaught in 1942. The immediate outcome was the arrest of all the major Congress leaders. For most of them, like Jawaharlal, this meant the last long spell in a British prison. In the medium term, India witnessed the suppression of the most serious outburst of popular anger and violence against the British since the revolt of 1857. When Subhas began his Azad Hind (Free India) movement in Southeast Asia, nationalist forces within India were in disarray and temporarily defeated. Bengal, from where Subhas hailed, was soon to be devastated by a man-made famine. Indians needed a morale booster. Subhas provided this initially by his broadcasts: 'This is Subhas Chandra Bose speaking' became the inspiration and an anchor in the hearts of countless Indians, even among those who were not completely in sympathy with all that Subhas stood for. It was the voice of a hero—and India, the unhappy land, then needed a hero.

The perception of Subhas as a hero was reinforced as Subhas saw as his mission the liberation of India. In one of his first speeches in Singapore, Subhas announced: 'Indians outside India, particularly Indians in East Asia, are going to organize a fighting force which will be powerful enough to attack the British army of occupation in India. When we do so, a revolution will break out, not only among the civilian population at home, but also among the Indian Army, which is now standing under the British flag. When the British government is thus attacked from both sides—from inside India and from outside—it will collapse, and the Indian people will then regain their liberty.'[70] Subhas's plan hinged on the promise of unconditional support he had received from the Japanese prime minister, Hideki Tojo, who on 16 June 1943 had declared in the Imperial Diet that Japan would do 'everything possible' to support the cause of India's freedom. Included in the 'possible' was a military move into India from Burma, of which Subhas's force would be a part.[71]

From July 1943, Subhas's life was caught up in a whirl of activity—recruiting, training, raising funds, planning, and whistle-stop tours across Southeast Asia.[72] His popularity was at its peak; he led by his personality and example; and he galvanized thousands through his outstanding oratory. He was in his element. Denied the role of a leader within the Congress, he demonstrated in 1943–44 what he was capable of. From his adolescence, he had harboured a fascination for things military and now he lived the life of a military leader in full uniform.

There are some aspects of Subhas's mobilization that need to be underlined. One is the unqualified loyalty he commanded from all who came under his spell. Without exception, all who joined his force spoke of his charisma and the warmth of his personality. For them Subhas epitomized greatness. Looking back on his experiences,

[70] 'Why I left Home and Homeland', 9 July 1943, in *Netaji: Collected Works*, vol. 12, pp. 51–54.

[71] Sugata Bose, *His Majesty's Opponent*, p. 243.

[72] Ibid. Chapter 8 vividly and in great detail recounts this phase of Subhas's life.

one officer, when asked what he had got in return for his suffering, said without hesitation, 'Netaji embraced me.'[73] There could be no better testimony to the reverence and loyalty Subhas received from the men and women he brought into his fold.

The second point is already indicated by the deliberate use of the word 'women' in the previous sentence. Subhas raised a regiment composed entirely of women and named it after the Rani of Jhansi. This not only marked a departure in military terms but also revealed Subhas's attitude towards the equality of the sexes. Even in retreat, his first and foremost concern was the safety and security of the members of the Rani of Jhansi regiment. He put the safety of his women comrades before his own personal safety.

The names he chose for his other regiments were Gandhi, Nehru and Azad. Whatever had happened in the past, Subhas was not willing to slough off his Congress lineage. Obviously, he still saw the Congress as a principal vehicle of Indian nationalism and wanted to retain for himself and his movement the talisman of the Congress. At the moment of his apparent triumph, during the battle for Imphal, on 6 July 1944, Subhas spoke directly to Gandhi over the radio. Addressing him as 'Father of our Nation', he concluded with the words: 'In this holy war for India's liberation we ask for your blessings and good wishes.'[74] The squabbles of Tripuri were forgotten in the common quest of India's freedom. Subhas could not have been unaware of the political and strategic importance of seeking Gandhi's goodwill and support. Once the INA entered Indian soil, it would need the support of the Congress and the millions of Congress followers. The invasion from outside would have to be backed by an uprising within. Also, after August 1942, with Gandhi in prison, Subhas could no longer insist that Gandhi wanted to placate the British.

Within the force that he created he eradicated all religious and caste divisions. Everyone was a freedom fighter and therefore equal.

---

[73] Ibid., p. 282.

[74] 'Father of our Nation', 6 July 1944, in *Netaji: Collected Works*, vol. 12, pp. 212–222.

On one remarkable occasion, Subhas declined the invitation of the priests of the main Chettiar temple in Singapore because of their discriminatory practices. He agreed to go only when the occasion was made open to all castes and communities, and he attended the function flanked by two of his Muslim comrades.[75] He retained his own deep religious faith but never allowed his own religious beliefs to influence his public activities.

Finally, the vision he had for India when she was free: he declared in the proclamation of the Provisional Government of Azad Hind, 'It [the provisional government] guarantees religious liberty, as well as equal rights and equal opportunities to its citizens. It declares its firm resolve to pursue the happiness and prosperity of the whole nation equally and transcending all the differences cunningly fostered by an alien government in the past.'[76]

Having revived the Indian National Army and begun the process of raising its strength to around 50,000, Subhas, in October 1943, announced the formation of the Provisional Government of Azad Hind in Singapore. And a little after midnight on 23–24 October, the Provisional Government of Azad Hind declared war on Britain and the United States. The government received the recognition of nine Axis or pro-Axis states. In Malaya alone, 30,000 Indians took written oaths of allegiance. By the end of November, plans were well under way for the march towards India.

On 7 January 1944, in preparation for the thrust into India, Subhas moved the headquarters of the Provisional Government from Singapore to Rangoon. The Japanese government had by January approved of the plan to attack India. The aims of the Japanese and the INA were, however, different. The Japanese wanted to prevent the British reconquest of Burma while the INA aimed at inciting a civil uprising within India. Subhas emphasized this and said on 8 January that 'action within the country must synchronize with the

---

[75] Sugata Bose, *His Majesty's Opponent*, p. 256.

[76] 'Proclamation of the Provisional Government of Azad Hind', 21 October 1943, in *Netaji: Collected Works*, vol. 12, pp. 108–120.

action from without'.[77] For the INA the main theatre of military
operations was Imphal where the offensive began on 8 March. By
April the news of events in the Imphal sector encouraged Subhas to
move his headquarters northwards from Rangoon to a village near
Mandalay. He also prepared plans and assigned responsibility for the
administration of Indian territories, which he hoped would soon be
liberated by the INA and placed under the Provisional Government.

This optimism was based on the assumption, not unjustified in
April 1944, that the INA and the Japanese army would soon capture
Imphal and Kohima. In fact, the INA forces led by Shaukat Ali Malik
actually unfurled the Indian flag in Moirang, a few miles south-east
of Imphal. But the British army—numerically superior (and with
superior air power)—with their retreat from Imphal cut off by the
Japanese commander Mutaguchi (who acted contrary to Subhas's
advice), fought back under General William Slim. The onset of an
early monsoon in May reduced the encounter to skirmishes as the
terrain became slushy. The INA offensive was thus stalled despite
instances of great bravery. Subhas had to temper his overwhelming
optimism when the Japanese informed him on 10 July 1944 that
their position in Imphal was untenable and they would have to order
a retreat. This meant the retreat of the INA, too. Subhas announced
the failure of the Imphal offensive in a radio address from Rangoon
on 21 August 1944.[78]

During the course of the battle and while retreating, soldiers of
the INA endured incredible suffering, and this profoundly affected
Subhas. His noble human qualities were articulated in the way he
involved himself with the suffering of his comrades, always ensuring
that their safety and treatment came first. He marched with them
sharing their ordeals. The conditions of the retreat were aggravated
by changes in the outcome of the war. By May 1945, Germany had
surrendered, and the Japanese capitulation followed in August.
Subhas was left without allies but his spirit was indomitable. The
reality of defeat threatened Subhas's own future and safety as the

---

[77] Quoted in Sugata Bose, *His Majesty's Opponent*, p. 266.

[78] Ibid. All facts in this paragraph and the next one are taken from chapter 8.

Allied troops began their operations in Southeast Asia. It was to escape from Southeast Asia that Subhas took a flight in the middle of August 1945 from Bangkok to Saigon and then onwards to Tokyo via Taipei. Taking off from Taipei, the plane crashed and Subhas died from the severe burns he had received while trying to get off the burning aircraft.[79]

The most exciting period of Subhas's life was in sharp contrast with one of the more dull periods in Jawaharlal's. The principal reason for this was the fact that from 9 August 1942 to 15 June 1945 he was in prison—his longest term, 1040 days. Before this period of internment, his anti-fascist views had hardened as had his views against British rule in India. He came round to the view that India's survival depended on a swift end to British rule. If the Congress continued its policy of doing nothing to embarrass the British, the morale of the people would be shattered and this would adversely affect India's ability to combat Japanese aggression. The converse was also true: resistance to the British would prepare Indians to resist the Japanese. Speaking to the UP Congress committee Jawaharlal said, 'Personally, I am so sick of slavery that I am even prepared to take the risk of anarchy.'[80] After much vacillation and discussion, Gandhi and the Congress decided to move against a British government that refused to withdraw from India in spite of all pleadings. The Quit India Movement was announced on 8 August 1942 and all the Congress leaders were imprisoned on the morning of 9 August. Jawaharlal thus watched the greatest popular uprising against the British since 1857 from behind bars. He emerged from prison a bitter and disillusioned man. One observer who saw him in the summer of 1945 left behind the following description: 'I felt he was gnawing some sorrow inside him. He seemed to me a seeking soul, happy to follow a track if he

---

[79] Subhas's biographers, Leonard Gordon and Sugata Bose, both accept this account of his death based on the available documentation and interviews. These leave little doubt that Subhas did die in the air crash, but in fairness it should be recorded that there is a body of opinion that does not accept the above account of Subhas's death to be beyond all reasonable doubt.

[80] Gopal, *Jawaharlal Nehru*, vol. 1, p. 292.

could conscientiously do so; and now by fate, or our unamiability perhaps, is made to oppose so that our unpleasantness and all must make it worse.'[81]

It was when Jawaharlal was in this kind of mood, immersed in some deep and ineffable sorrow, that he received the news of Subhas's death. According to one report, when he received the news Jawaharlal was 'moved to tears' and said that Subhas had now 'escaped all the pending troubles which brave soldiers, who do such things, might have to face'. He reiterated that though he did not agree with Subhas, there was no doubt about his sincerity in his struggle for Indian independence.[82] Jawaharlal wept at the passing of a colleague and a friend with whom he had once shared the struggle to make India free. Later differences could not diminish the sense of loss nor eradicate the memories of comradeship. Just as Subhas could not help but name a regiment after Jawaharlal, the latter could not forget Subhas. They had shared too much together.

Jawaharlal showed his remembrance of Subhas when he decided to defend the INA prisoners who the British charged as being guilty of treason. In spite of his known disapproval of the means adopted by the INA, Jawaharlal had no doubt in his mind about the idealism and patriotism of these men. They had fought for their country's freedom and it was morally wrong to accuse them of treason. Jawaharlal organized relief for the INA men, women and their dependents; he campaigned to raise awareness about the plight of these men and established the INA Defence Committee of lawyers. And when in an ill-advised move, the British government in India decided to stage a public trial at the Red Fort, Jawaharlal, after well over a quarter of a century, donned his barrister-at-law's gown to defend the accused.[83] During the war, censorship had prevented any news about Subhas and the INA from entering and circulating in India. The end of the war and the onset of the INA trial made it possible for the news of Subhas's march to become widely known.

---

[81] Ibid., p. 303; the observation was made by Freya Stark.

[82] Nehru Papers, File No. 184 (Part 5).

[83] Gopal, *Jawaharlal Nehru*, vol. 1, pp. 307–08.

This made Subhas and the INA heroes in the eyes of Indian public opinion. For Jawaharlal, it made good political sense to be at the forefront of this popular sentiment. There can be little doubt that from the Valhalla of heroes Subhas would have smiled at the irony of Jawaharlal defending the INA, but he would also have admired the actions of his erstwhile friend.

*

In the lore that surrounds the Indian national movement and its cast of characters, it is common, especially in Bengal, to pit Subhas and Jawaharlal against each other. Their relationship is seen as the great rivalry in which Jawaharlal emerged triumphant only because an accidental death removed Subhas. A more extreme view is that Subhas, had he been alive, would have been a contender for the prime ministership of independent India and would have fashioned India along different lines than what actually happened under Jawaharlal. The account of this great divide between the two leaders hinges, in terms of hard evidence, on the statement that Subhas made to his nephew immediately after Tripuri (cited in the previous chapter) that no one had done greater harm to his cause than Jawaharlal. The previous chapter noted that at the same time as Subhas was expressing his grouse against Jawaharlal to his nephew, he was inviting Jawaharlal to visit him to discuss the situation. The latter's response was that he could not say no to Subhas. Jawaharlal consistently interceded with Gandhi to settle the issue with Subhas. This does not give the impression of a relationship laced by bitterness and hostility.

The other piece of evidence that is cited to show their rivalry pertains to something that Jawaharlal said in 1942. In April 1942, he said: 'Hitler and Japan must go to hell. I shall fight them to the end and this is my policy. I shall also fight Mr Subhas Bose and his party along with Japan if he comes to India. Mr Bose acted very wrongly though in good faith. Hitler and Japan represent the reactionary forces and their victory means the victory of

244	*Nehru & Bose: Parallel Lives*

the reactionary forces in the world.'[84] What is evident from this statement is that it does not contain a *personal* attack on Subhas. Jawaharlal was taking an *ideological* and *political* position against Subhas's decision to seek the help of the Axis powers. He did not doubt Subhas's 'good faith'. This statement of Jawaharlal's must be read in conjunction with another statement he made around the same time: 'I do not . . . doubt the bona fides of Mr Bose. I think he has come to a certain conclusion which I think is wrong, but nevertheless a conclusion which he thinks is for the good of India. We parted company with him many years ago. Since then we have drifted further apart and today we are very far from each other. It is not good enough for me, because of my past friendship and because I do not challenge his motives, to say anything against him. But I do realize that the way he has chosen is utterly wrong, a way which I not only cannot accept but must oppose, if it takes shape. Because any force that may come from outside will really come as a dummy force under Japanese control. It is a bad thing psychologically for the Indian masses to think in terms of being liberated by an outside agency.'[85]

Jawaharlal makes two things very clear here. One is that given the nature of his past relationship with Subhas, he is not willing to say anything personal against him. And second, he has no doubts in his mind about Subhas's motives and intentions. His differences with Subhas are political and it is at the political plane that he proposed to oppose Subhas if the occasion so arose. Jawaharlal saw both Germany and Japan to be aggressively imperialistic powers and sincerely believed that India's freedom could not be achieved with the assistance of these powers.

What is often overlooked is that what Jawaharlal said in 1942 regarding Subhas's political views and movement was by no means his final assessment. Speaking on Subhas's birthday in 1946, Jawaharlal clarified his views: 'Subhas Bose and I were co-workers

[84] Interview to the press, 24 April 1942, in Nehru, *Selected Works*, vol. 12, pp. 262–63.
[85] 'The Congress and the Cripps Offer', interview to the press, 12 April 1942, in Nehru, *Selected Works*, vol. 12, pp. 225–26.

in the struggle for freedom for twenty-five years . . . Our relations with each other were marked by great affection. I used to treat him as my younger brother. It is an open secret that at times there were differences between us on political questions. But I never for a moment doubted that he was a brave soldier in the struggle for freedom.' He admitted that he had waited to get the full picture regarding the INA before he formed an opinion about it and said, 'I do not know even today what I would have myself done at a time of crisis like that . . . The manner in which Netaji faced the crisis inspires admiration. Perhaps I might have done the same thing if I were in his position.' He paid tribute to Subhas for the way he had 'stoutly resisted Japanese attempts at overlordship and maintained an independent status' and complimented the INA for maintaining 'complete communal unity and harmony in its ranks'. Having said all this, Jawaharlal maintained his reservations about seeking the help of another country for gaining freedom.[86] Even when Gandhi, for a brief period in early 1942, believed that the Axis powers would win the war and that a victorious Japan would make no demands on India, Jawaharlal had made his opposition to Gandhi's ideas known.[87]

The political differences between Jawaharlal and Subhas revolved around their radically different attitudes to fascism, represented in the early 1940s by the Axis powers. Jawaharlal was opposed to fascism (and of course to its most virulent form, Nazism) since its inception in Europe. He read the fascist movement—it so happened, rightly—as the greatest threat to hard-won democratic liberties. He made no secret of this opposition—his writings of the 1930s are replete with his condemnation of fascism as are his letters on history that he wrote to his young daughter. Subhas did not share this antipathy. He saw Mussolini as a great man who represented the aspirations of the age. He met him a number of times and sought his advice. His admiration for Mussolini ran so

---

[86] 'The Achievements of Subhas Bose', 23 January 1946, in Nehru, *Selected Works*, vol. 14, p. 373.

[87] Gopal, *Jawaharlal Nehru*, vol. 1, p. 289.

high that he thought that the highest compliment he could pay to Gandhi's Salt March was by comparing it to Mussolini's march on Rome: a march in which Mussolini was not even present. Subhas saw fascism as a movement that represented discipline and efficiency; he argued that the future of India would have to be fashioned through a mixture of fascism and communism. Subhas had from his youth a fascination for things military, and this may have been one factor that attracted him to militaristic regimes. There is no record of Subhas ever criticizing the atrocities committed by the Black Shirts in Italy, the Nazi regime in Germany and other parts of Europe, and the Japanese army in Southeast Asia. He had studied philosophy and in his personal life was a deeply religious man, but he saw no ethical problems in trying to achieve his noble vision through an alliance with regimes that stood for all that was ignoble in humanity.

These two diametrically opposed views of contemporary history as articulated by Jawaharlal and Subhas were inevitably to clash even if the Tripuri crisis had not occurred and Subhas had stayed within the Congress. As it turned out, Subhas's hand was forced and given his ideological predilections he had little or no option save seeking the help of the Axis powers. As Subhas's options closed, he had to change his views. At Haripura, he had stated categorically that 'I do not want for a moment nor do I expect any outside country to help us.'[88] Tipped out of the Congress after a failed rebellion against the Gandhian leadership, he sought external help. This gave to his views on fascism a greater salience and thus underlined Jawaharlal's ideological opposition to him.

Between the relationship of Jawaharlal and Subhas fell the shadow of Gandhi. The attitude of the two men towards Gandhi was respectful but they differed in the way they showed their respect to the man who both acknowledged to be the undisputed leader of the Indian national movement. Subhas did not see Gandhi's authority as something that could not be challenged. He believed that by the middle of the 1930s, the Gandhian phase of the national

---

[88] Bose at Haripura, 22 February 1938, in AICC Papers, File No. G 27.

movement was over. New forms of struggle and younger and more dynamic leaders less prone to making compromises with the British had become the need of the hour. He believed that he and Jawaharlal were capable of providing this leadership if only the latter could rid himself of the spell that Gandhi had put on him. From the day the two of them first met, Subhas's attitude to Gandhi was tempered by scepticism. He did not allow his own political views and ideology to be completely submerged by those of Gandhi even though he did not, in his writings, clarify where exactly he disagreed with Gandhi except in the latter's complete rejection of all forms of violent struggle. Without disregarding the achievements of Gandhi's non-violent struggle, Subhas believed that some form of violence would be required to finally push the British out of India.

However, Subhas's admiration for Gandhi reached a different level when he was in Southeast Asia waging his own heroic struggle to expel the British from India. He addressed Gandhi as the Father of the Nation, sought his blessings and wanted to share the triumph of expelling the British with Gandhi and the Indian people. Gandhi, in his turn, thought of Subhas as a son he had unfortunately lost,[89] as an individual who had chosen to sail on a different boat,[90] and on Subhas's fiftieth birthday in January 1947 paid a handsome and an apposite tribute.[91] Thus Subhas's relationship with Gandhi was not bereft of love, respect and admiration. It was not, however, a relationship of mentor and protégé. Subhas refused to offer unquestioning obeisance to the man the entire nation revered as the Mahatma. There was a rebel in Subhas that was evident even in his youth: witness his rejection of the ICS against all parental and societal expectations. This spirit also informed his attitude and dealings with Gandhi.

Jawaharlal's relationship with Gandhi was at one level very forthright and at another more nuanced. No other leader from

---

[89] Gandhi, 13 January 1940, in Gandhi, *Collected Works*, vol. 71, p. 94.

[90] Letter from Gandhi to Bose, 29 December 1940, in *Netaji: Collected Works*, vol. 10, p. 155. This is probably the last letter Gandhi wrote to Subhas.

[91] For the tribute, see Sugata Bose, *His Majesty's Opponent*, p. 322.

within the Congress voiced his differences with Gandhi as explicitly as Jawaharlal did; and no other leader had the bond of trust with Gandhi that Jawaharlal enjoyed. In his autobiography, Jawaharlal had written critically about Gandhi's views as put forward in *Hind Swaraj*. These seemed to him to be 'utterly wrong and harmful doctrine, and impossible of achievement'.[92] Differences between the two over this issue persisted right till Independence.[93] There were many other occasions when the two of them argued and differed. Yet Jawaharlal knew that there was no one in India like Gandhi, no one who was closer to the people of the country and no one who felt their pulse better. In 1930 from prison, Jawaharlal had written to Gandhi: 'May I congratulate you on the new India that you have created by your magic touch? What the future will bring I know not, but the past has made life worth living and our prosaic existence has developed something of epic greatness in it.'[94]

Jawaharlal had no reason later to withdraw this assessment. In *The Discovery of India*, he wrote with more than a hint of purple prose: 'Then came Gandhi. He was like a powerful current of fresh air that made us stretch ourselves and take deep breaths, like a beam of light that pierced the darkness and removed the scales from our eyes, like a whirlwind that upset many things but most of all the working of people's minds. He did not descend from the top; he seemed to emerge from the millions of India, speaking their language and incessantly drawing attention to their condition . . . against an all-pervading fear Gandhi's quiet and determined voice was raised: be not afraid.'[95] He knew that neither he nor any other leader possessed the magic touch that made Gandhi unique. Only he could give to people's lives an epic dimension.

Apart from this political assessment, there was a profoundly personal aspect to the relationship. Gandhi was Jawaharlal's

---

[92] *An Autobiography*, p. 510.

[93] See, for example, letter from Gandhi to Nehru, 5 October 1945, and Nehru to Gandhi, 9 October 1945, in *Together They Fought*, pp. 449–56.

[94] Letter from Nehru to Gandhi, 28 July 1930, in ibid., pp. 122–24.

[95] Nehru, *The Discovery of India* (Calcutta, 1946), p. 427.

emotional anchor, a father figure to whom he could turn to in joy and in sorrow. This dependence was enhanced after Motilal's death. There was something in Jawaharlal's personality that needed Gandhi's sheltering and loving presence. Gandhi was aware of this; he wrote to Jawaharlal at the end of 1946, 'I claim to be like a wise father to you, having no less love towards you than Motilalji.' In the same letter he described Jawaharlal's affection for him to be 'extraordinary and so natural!'[96] Jawaharlal was not exactly a Gandhi acolyte but he knew his life was incomplete without Gandhi. Learning of Gandhi's fast unto death in 1932, he had cried,[97] and seeing Gandhi's lifeless body on 30 January 1948, he sobbed like a child.[98] Gandhi reciprocated these feelings. He named Jawaharlal his heir, and according to Patel, he loved Jawaharlal more than anyone else.[99]

It was Jawaharlal's personal devotion to Gandhi that Subhas did not understand or did not appreciate. Subhas did not allow any sentiment or personal feelings to come between him and his aspiration to make his country free. Even the news of his mother's death did not make him stop his work when he was preparing for battle in Southeast Asia.[100] He did not hesitate to leave behind his wife and his daughter in Europe knowing that he may not see them ever again. The personal was secondary to him: the political was paramount.[101] Thus, it was exasperating for Subhas to see again and again Jawaharlal differing with Gandhi but pulling back at the last moment from an open break. This made him lash out at Jawaharlal on occasion. Subhas believed that he and Jawaharlal could make history together. But Jawaharlal could not see his destiny without Gandhi. This was the limiting point of their relationship. One

---

[96] Letter from Gandhi to Nehru, 30 December 1946, in *Together They Fought*, p. 471.

[97] Prison Diary, 22 September 1932, in Nehru, *Selected Works*, vol. 5, p. 408.

[98] Gopal, *Jawaharlal Nehru*, vol. 2, p. 25.

[99] Letter from Patel to Nehru, 3 July 1939, in Nehru Papers, vol. 81. Patel wrote: 'I don't think that he loves anybody more than he loves you and when he finds that any action of his has made you unhappy he broods over it and feels miserable.'

[100] Sugata Bose, *His Majesty's Opponent*, p. 266.

[101] 'Whatever he did was for the independence of India.' 'Tribute to Subhas Chandra Bose', 24 August 1945, in Nehru, *Selected Works*, vol. 14, p. 336.

man who was certain that nothing mattered to him more than the freedom of India; and another individual who also cherished his country's freedom but tried valiantly to link it to his other and often conflicting loyalties. In the crevasse of this rivalry of aims fell the tension-fraught and passing friendship of Subhas and Jawaharlal. Their lives could have no tryst.

Bibliography

UNPUBLISHED PAPERS

Nehru Museum and Library, New Delh
Jawaharlal Nehru Papers
AICC Papers
Purushottamdas Thakurdas Papers

India Office Records, British Library, London
Papers of Lord Linlithgow
'Activities of Subhas Chandra Bose since his release from jail on
   5.12.40.' (R/3/2/16 and 17)

PRINTED SOURCES

Collected Works of Mahatma Gandhi
Selected Works of Jawaharlal Nehru (edited by S. Gopal)
Netaji: Collected Works (edited by Sisir and Sugata Bose)
The Transfer of Power, 1942–47 (edited by Nicholas Mansergh)

BOOKS

Bose, Sugata. *His Majesty's Opponent: Subhas Chandra Bose and
   India's Struggle Against Empire.* New Delhi: Harvard University
   Press, 2011.

Bipan Chandra. 'Jawaharlal Nehru and the Indian Capitalist Class, 1936'. In Bipan Chandra, *Nationalism and Colonialism in Modern India*. New Delhi: Orient Blackswan, 1979.

Chatterjee, Partha. *Bengal, 1920–1947: The Land Question*. Calcutta: South Asia Books, 1984.

———. *Nationalist Thought and the Colonial World: A Derivative Discourse*. New Delhi: Zed Books, 1986.

———. *The Black Hole of Empire: History of a Global Practice of Power*. Princeton: Princeton University Press, 2012.

Chaudhuri, Nirad C. *The Continent of Circe*. London: Chatto & Windus, 1965.

———. *Thy Hand, Great Anarch!: India: 1921–1952*. London: Chatto & Windus, 1987.

Churchill, Winston. *The Second World War*. London: Houghton Mifflin, 1950.

Clarke, Peter. *The Cripps Version: The Life of Sir Stafford Cripps, 1889–1952*. London: Allen Lane, 2002.

de Waal, Edmund. *The Hare with Amber Eyes: A Hidden Inheritance*. London: Vintage, 2010.

Gallagher, J. 'Congress in Decline: Bengal, 1930 to 1939'. In *The Decline, Revival and Fall of the British Empire*. Cambridge: Cambridge University Press, 1982, 2004.

Gandhi, Rajmohan. *Patel: A Life*. Ahmedabad: Navajivan Publishing House, 1991.

Gopal, S. *Jawaharlal Nehru: A Biography*. 3 vols. London and Delhi: Harvard University Press, 1975, 1979, 1984.

———. *The Viceroyalty of Lord Irwin, 1926–1931*. London: Oxford, 1956.

———. '"Drinking Tea with Treason": Halifax in India'. In *Imperialists, Nationalists, Democrats: The Collected Essays*. Edited by Srinath Raghavan. New Delhi: Orient Blackswan, 2013.

———. 'Tradition and Dissent: The Paradoxes of Subhas Bose'. In *Imperialists, Nationalists, Democrats: The Collected Essays*. Edited by Srinath Raghavan. New Delhi: Orient Blackswan, 2013.

Gordon, Leonard A. *Brothers Against the Raj: A Biography of Indian Nationalists Sarat and Subhas Chandra Bose*. New Delhi: Rupa, 1997.

Guha, Ramachandra. *Gandhi before India*. New Delhi: Penguin, 2013.

Guha, Ranajit. 'Nationalism and the Trials of Becoming'. In *The Small Voice of History: Collected Essays*. Edited by Partha Chatterjee. New Delhi: Permanent Black, 2009.

———. *Elementary Aspects of Peasant Insurgency in Colonial India*. New Delhi: Oxford University Press, 1983.

———. 'Discipline and Mobilize'. In *Subaltern Studies VII: Writings on South Asian History and Society*. Edited by Partha Chatterjee and Gyanendra Pandey. New Delhi: Oxford University Press, 1992.

Hayes, Romain. *Bose in Nazi Germany*. New Delhi: Random House, 2011.

Iyengar, Uma and Zackariah, Lalitha. (ed.). *Together They Fought: Gandhi–Nehru Correspondence 1921–1948*. New Delhi: Oxford University Press, 2011.

Kershaw, Ian. *Hitler, 1889–1936: Hubris*. London: Penguin, 1998.

———. *Hitler, 1936–1945: Nemesis*. London: Penguin, 2000.

Kuhlmann, Jan. *Netaji in Europe*. New Delhi: RainLight, 2012.

Low, D.A. *Britain and Indian Nationalism: The Imprint of Ambiguity, 1929–1942*. London: Cambridge, 1999.

Lynn, Jonathan and Jay, Antony. (ed.). *The Complete Yes Minister: The Diaries of a Cabinet Minister by the Right Hon. James Hacker MP*. London: BBC Books, 1984.

Metcalf, T.R. *The Aftermath of Revolt: India, 1857–1870*. Princeton: Princeton University Press, 1964.

———. *Land, Landlords and the British Raj: Northern India in the Nineteenth Century*. California: University of California Press, 1979.

Moore, R.J. *Escape from Empire: The Attlee Government and the Indian Problem*. London: Oxford University Press, 1983.

Mukherjee, R. *A Century of Trust: The Story of Tata Steel*. New Delhi: Penguin, 2008.

Musgrave, P.J. 'Landlords and Lords of the Land: Estate Management and Social Control in UP, 1860–1920' *Modern Asian Studies*. Vol. 6, No. 3, July 1972.

Nehru, Jawaharlal. *An Autobiography*. London: Bodley Press, 1936, 1939.

———. *Glimpses of World History*. Allahabad, 1934–35; repr. Delhi, 2004.

———. *A Bunch of Old Letters*. Bombay: Asia Publishing House, 1958, 1960.

———. *The Discovery of India*. Calcutta: Signet Press, 1946.

Padfield, Peter. *Hess, Hitler & Churchill: The Real Turning Point of the Second World War—A Secret History*. London: Icon, 2013.

Pandey, Gyanendra. 'Peasant Revolt and Indian Nationalism: The Peasant Movement in Awadh, 1919–1922'. In *Subaltern Studies I: Writings on South Asian History and Society*. Edited by Ranajit Guha. New Delhi: Oxford University Press, 1982.

Ray, Rajat. *Urban Roots of Indian Nationalism: Pressure Groups and Conflict of Interests in Calcutta City Politics, 1875–1939*. New Delhi: Vikas, 1979.

Richie, Alexandra. *Faust's Metropolis: A History of Berlin*. London: HarperCollins, 1998.

Roberts, Andrew. 'The Holy Fox': The Life of Lord Halifax*. London: Phoenix, 1991, 2004.

Rushdie, Salman. *East, West*. London: Vintage, 1994.

Sarkar, Sumit. *Modern India, 1858–1947*. New Delhi: Macmillan, 1983.

Sarkar, Tanika. *Bengal, 1928–1934: The Politics of Protest*. New Delhi: Pan Macmillan, 1987.

Siddiqi, M.H. *Agrarian Unrest in North India: The United Provinces, 1918–1922*. New Delhi: Vikas, 1978.

Sitaramayya, B. Pattabhi. *The History of the Indian National Congress*. 2 vols. Bombay: Padma Publications, 1935, 1946.

Som, Reba. *Differences within Consensus: The Left–Right Divide in the Congress, 1929–39*. New Delhi: Sangam, 1995.

Tendulkar, D.G. *Mahatma*. Bombay: Ministry of Information and Broadcasting, Government of India, 1951.

Walton, Calder. *Empire of Secrets: British Intelligence, the Cold War and the Twilight of Empire*. London: Overlook, 2013.

Acknowledgements

I had initially thought of exploring the friendship between Jawaharlal Nehru and Subhas Chandra Bose in the form of a long essay. Ramachandra Guha and Aveek Sarkar convinced me that I should think in terms of a book. I am grateful to both of them for making me think more ambitiously than I had originally intended. There are two other persons without whom this book could not have been written, even though neither was aware that I was writing this book. One is the late Sarvepalli Gopal, the biographer of Nehru and the first editor of Nehru's *Selected Works*; the other is Sugata Bose, the biographer of Bose, and the co-editor of Bose's *Collected Works*. This book, even where it differs in emphasis and interpretation from those put forward by these two scholars, stands on the work that they have done. I acknowledge my debt to them.

The best friends of scholars across the world are librarians and the dedicated men and women who work in libraries. Saktidas Roy, the librarian of the ABP library, has been ceaseless in his efforts to keep me supplied with books and articles that I needed. I cannot thank him enough. The library of the Centre for Studies in Social Sciences, Calcutta, has also been cooperative and helpful. I am grateful to the staff of the Nehru Memorial Museum, New Delhi, especially those in the manuscript section, for their efficiency and their warmth. It was a pleasure to go back and work in the India Office Library and Records, now a part of the British Library. I want to also thank the staff of the library in the India International Centre in New Delhi.

Asok Sen, Geoffrey Ward, Mechthild Guha, Partha Chatterjee, Ram Guha and Ranajit Guha read through the chapters as they were written and offered their comments and suggestions. They are in no way implicated in the errors and the interpretation. There is another anonymous reader who read, commented on and corrected the manuscript. Following the injunction of T.S. Eliot I will refrain from addressing private words in public.

Index